Extinct Lands,

Temporal Geographies

A BOOK IN THE SERIES

Latin America Otherwise: Languages, Empires, Nations

Series editors: Walter D. Mignolo, Duke University; Irene Silverblatt,

Duke University; Sonia Saldívar–Hull, University of California

at Los Angeles

EXTINCT LANDS,

TEMPORAL GEOGRAPHIES

Chicana

Literature

and the

Urgency of

Space

MARY PAT BRADY

Duke University Press   Durham & London

2002

© 2002 Duke University Press

All rights reserved

Printed in the United States of America

on acid-free paper ∞

Designed by C. H. Westmoreland

Typeset by Tseng Information Systems, Inc.

Library of Congress
Cataloging-in-Publication Data
Brady, Mary Pat.
Extinct lands, temporal geographies :
Chicana literature and the urgency of space /
Mary Pat Brady.
p. cm. — (Latin America otherwise)
Includes bibliographical references and index.
ISBN 0-8223-3005-9 (cloth : alk. paper) —
ISBN 0-8223-2974-3 (pbk. : alk. paper)
1. American literature—Mexican American
authors—History and criticism.   2. American
literature—Southwestern States—History and
criticism.   3. American literature—Women
authors—History and criticism.   4. Mexican
American women—Intellectual life.
5. Southwestern States—In literature.
6. Mexican Americans in literature.   7. Space
and time in literature.   8. Personal space in
literature.   9. Narration (Rhetoric).   I. Title.
II. Series.
PS153.M4 .B69   2002
810.9′9287′0896872—dc21   2002006333

Frontispiece art:
Delilah Montoya's "Tijerina Tantrum."
Courtesy of the artist.

Latin America Otherwise: Languages, Empires, Nations is a critical series. It aims to explore the emergence and consequences of concepts used to define "Latin America" while at the same time exploring the broad interplay of political, economic, and cultural practices that have shaped Latin American worlds. Latin America, at the crossroads of competing imperial designs and local responses, has been construed as a geocultural and geopolitical entity since the nineteenth century. This series provides a starting point to redefine Latin America as a configuration of political, linguistic, cultural, and economic intersections that demands a continuous reappraisal of the role of the Americas in history, and of the ongoing process of globalization and the relocation of people and cultures that have characterized Latin America's experience. *Latin America Otherwise: Languages, Empires, Nations* is a forum that confronts established geocultural constructions, that rethinks area studies and the disciplinary boundaries, that assesses convictions of the academy and of public policy, and that, correspondingly, demands that the practices through which we produce knowledge and understanding about and from Latin America be subject to rigorous and critical scrutiny.

A train station on the border of Mexico and the United States becomes a police station; areas once held sacred by Apaches and Mexicanos become residences or places of commerce; freeway construction hollows out a community and changes the Southwest landscape where the Western frontier and the Southern border once were. These histories of the transformation of space and memories are haunted by the ghost of Spanish colonialism, national conflicts between Mexico and the United States, and U.S. imperial expansion toward the South. The construction of space, whose theorization we owe to Henry Lefebvre and followers such as David Harvey and Edward Soja, acquires here a new dimension and in a sense a new theoretical beginning. That theoretical beginning is located in the female body of Chicana literature.

Mary Pat Brady makes an important move in inverting here the relation between text and theories by locating theory in the literary texts themselves. This is not an antitheoretical book. It is a book that changes the ways theories have been commonly understood. Literary texts become theoretical conceptualizations of space. Her close textual reading provides a foundation for theorizing space, memories, and history in the borderlands. In this reconceptualization she shows that theories of space and the body that evade the materiality of writing remain inscribed in the presupposition of white, masculine, and heterosexual epistemic principles. She offers all the necessary elements to conclude that theoretical constructions and human understanding cannot be detached from the material inscription of the understanding subject. When they are detached from this inscription, they become tools for epistemic violence and domination. *Extinct Lands, Temporal Geographies* alerts us to the theoretical and political dangers of the past and shows us the way toward theoretical and political opportunities in the future.

For Carmelita Spence
Whose stories of gardens, borders, and
boxcars provided my first contrapuntal
cartography lessons

For Antonia Ochoa
Whose own untold story prompted me to dig
deeply into the archives despite my fears

For Mama and Papa
Whose love never seems to stop

And especially for Kate and Ana Luisa
Whose love makes everything new

Contents

Acknowledgments

This book emerges, in part, from my experience growing up as a Chicana, twelve blocks from the U.S.-Mexico border in an Arizona smelter town called Douglas. Like many other company towns, Douglas included neighborhoods defined by race and corporate affiliation whose seemingly benign borders invoked the nearby international border designated by ditches, chain wire, and, occasionally, army troops. Changes in the global economy transformed these social and spatial relations because the city ceased functioning as a major producer of copper anodes and became instead a major artery for the movement of narcotics and migrants. Laid-off miners and smelter workers got jobs as prison and border guards. While still bearing traces of earlier corporate and state planning, the city now reflects these new economic and social relations. What has remained the same, however, is that social power continues to solidify itself through the surveillance and manipulation of space.

Extinct Lands, Temporal Geographies grew out of my attempts to understand the transformation of my hometown, having seen too many people, including familia, go to jail, die working in the narcotics economy, and lose their jobs and homes. While it took me a while to figure out that I had questions to ask, once I got to the University of California, Los Angeles (UCLA), I was fortunate enough to find many who were willing to guide me. There, under the direction of Sonia Saldívar-Hull and Valerie Smith, I developed the root chapters for this project. I cannot begin to thank Sonia enough for her assistance, critical insight, brilliant lectures, gentle mentorship, and continual encouragement. I am also extremely grateful to Valerie Smith who has been deeply generous with her time, friendship, and critical acumen. Edward Soja read the dissertation and gave me some of the keenest advice. I also owe a debt of gratitude to someone I never had the chance to meet, Daniel Calder. As chair of the English department, out of a commitment to affirmative action, he admitted me to graduate school and found

me funding. I hope that he would have found this a fitting, if small, trib-
ute to his efforts to transform the discipline. I received generous funding
while at UCLA, including a Project 88 award for minority scholars and two
travel awards granted by an anonymous donor. A Dissertation Fellowship
from the Women's Studies Program at the University of California, Santa
Barbara allowed me to complete the dissertation version. A UC President's
Postdoctoral Fellowship at the University of California, Berkeley gave me
the opportunity to begin revising this project. While at Berkeley, I was very
fortunate to work with José David Saldívar (whose paper on Arturo Islas
at a 1993 conference sent me to space in the first place); he offered boundless help, encouragement, and advice. I am very grateful to Helena María
Viramontes for her friendship. The members of the Third World and Minority Caucus in particular and the Cornell English department in general
have similarly provided a rigorous and exciting environment in which to
work. I am also grateful to the Woodrow Wilson Foundation for adminis-
tering a Mellon Foundation Postdoctoral Fellowship. Their grant for junior
scholars has given me the time to complete this project and see it toward
publication.

I am very fortunate to work in a field where scholars actively assist each
other. I have benefited from the kindness and critical insight of a number of Chicana/o feminists, and I would very much like to acknowledge
their help: Laura Pérez, Norma Alarcón, Norma Cantú, Angie Chabram-
Dernersesian, Terri de la Peña, Theresa Delgadillo, Michelle Habell-Pallan,
Yvonne Yarbro-Bejarano, Susana Gallardo, and Graciela Hernandez. Rafael
Pérez-Torres deserves special thanks not only for giving this manuscript
a thorough reading and providing the kind of helpful criticism one only
dreams about, but for also listening patiently to my endless natterings about
the needed changes. Rosa Linda Fregoso asked some of the hardest questions
and pushed my thinking much further than it otherwise might have gone.

Along the way, a number of people have been particularly kind. I want
to especially thank Tracy Curtis for her friendship, love, and intellectual
acumen, and Sonnet Retman for her insight and dog walks. I also want
to thank Brenda Kwon, Joni Jones, Alycee Lane, Carla Cain, Susan Koshy,
Martha Garcia, Sallie Marston, Ranu Samantrai, Theresa Tensuan, Susan
Savishinsky, Stacy Snyder, Laura Arnold, King-Kok Cheung, Ali Behdad,
and Katherine Hayles.

At Duke University Press I want to thank Reynolds Smith and Sharon

Parks Torian who have been unflagging in their patience with my plodding pace. I want to thank Tricia Mickelberry for her wonderful copyediting and Leigh Anne Couch for seeing the book through the production process. My thanks also to Delilah Montoya for allowing the reproduction of "Tijerina Tantrum." I would also like to thank the staffs at the Arizona Historical Society, the Bancroft Library, and the Cochise County Historical Society.

Now that I work and live so far from my birth family, I realize the extent to which their love has shaped my opportunities. My parents provided an amazingly intellectual atmosphere in which to grow. They taught me that intellectual life does not begin with wealth and that among the first questions to ask are, who does the work and for whom? My mother's brilliance and curiosity provided the first model of scholarship for me. My father's wit, intuition, dichos, and stories have contoured my approach to all questions. Their continued love, sometimes despite the costs, has been extraordinary. My madrina, Barbara Pon, showed me that someone from the working classes could go to graduate school. My brothers and sisters have also provided help, money when needed, encouragement and love always. I especially want to thank Linda and Steve who gave me many wonderful meals, lifted my anxieties, and got me into the mountains for renewal more times than I can say. Sadly, Cleofilas, to whom I owe a great debt of gratitude, could not see the end of a project whose beginnings she witnessed, and whose progress she encouraged while she slept patiently at my feet.

Kate McCullough has become my lifeline, my greatest love, and the best of friends. She has transformed my life and my heart, and taken the time to read every word of this book more than once. Her style, joy, and creativity, her critical incisiveness and generosity go unmatched. As I was nearing the end of this project, Ana Luisa Brady McCullough entered our family. She has immeasurably improved the texture of daily life, enriching it and filling it with laughter and love.

Introduction

In need of a new depot for the El Paso and Southwestern Railroad, Phelps Dodge Copper Company executives sat down in 1912 to plan a grand new building. They had more than enough money—more than $75,000 in cash reserves available for a project they hoped would signal the increasing importance of their company town, Douglas. Located on the U.S.-Mexico border, more than two hundred miles from the capital of the Territory of Arizona, Douglas had been in existence for fewer than a dozen years as the site for Phelps Dodge's copper-smelting operation but was already significant to the copper company's transnational empire. The building itself would symbolize the company's reach across both sides of the line.

As they began to imagine a new railroad depot, Phelps Dodge executives debated what architectural style might fit their vision for the city and company. Mission revival, a typical choice for train depots, was rejected because it seemed too regional, not serious enough. They turned instead to the neo-classical beaux arts style, popularized not long before in the United States at the World's Columbian Exposition in Chicago; executives apparently relished the style because it more effectively symbolized a "sense of strength" and connected the little town to what they saw as the "prevailing national imagery."[1] Given the depot's context—its construction occurred during the Mexican Revolution when the entire frontera, including Douglas, was engulfed in the battle over democracy, land reform, and the role of U.S. corporate capital in Mexico—it is hardly surprising that the copper company avoided the mission revival style, a style that might have invoked a nostalgia for Mexico's own claims to the region. Having decided that beaux arts, with its monumental scale, its references to Renaissance architecture, and its stark formality made the appropriate statement, Phelps Dodge lavished money on the building by including such details as a Tiffany glass cupola. As a finishing touch they hired a famous landscape architect to design lush gardens and fountains to grace the grounds surrounding the depot and to contrast not only with its desert context but with the growing hills of smelter refuse and the puffing smokestacks of the Copper Queen Smelter a short distance away.

For the next thirty years the depot was used for both passenger and freight service as one node in a network transporting people across Mexico and the United States. After World War II, when passenger rail travel slowed, the depot continued to serve as a junction for freight engines moving ore and equipment throughout Sonora and the U.S. southwest. In the mid-1980s, however, faced with falling demand for copper, a recession, and aging, environmentally unsound facilities, Phelps Dodge began liquidating its assets in the region. It moved its headquarters to Phoenix. It battled a crippling strike at the smelter and broke the union, only to shut the smelter down three years later. And it sold the depot to the city of Douglas for $65,000.

The acquisition of the depot pleased a number of city residents who remembered its more glorious days and who longed to restore the building and elaborate gardens. They debated what to do with the depot: they formed commissions; they wrote grants; they solicited advice. They considered turning it into a youth center, a shopping center, a job training center, a motel. But with the copper smelter shut down and its formal economy in a shambles, the city could not fund any of these dream projects. The depot remained empty. Until 1996. Having made national news for helping to locate a well-engineered tunnel under the border, the Douglas police triumphantly combined their REICO allotment (cash forfeited by alleged narcotics smugglers) and the essentially free labor of the inmates from the nearby Papago Prison to renovate the depot. At a cost of more than $1.5 million, the abandoned railroad depot became the Douglas police headquarters.[2]

At the very least, the building's transformation from railroad depot to police station indicates the broader regional and national transformations under way. If at one time the depot evinced a thriving industrial and ranching economy in which private enterprise, heavily girded by the state, employed the vast majority of workers and deployed international labor and natural resources at its bidding, the depot cum police station signals the growing importance of policing to an increasingly globalized economy. With the demise of the smelter and mines in Douglas and throughout the area, the burdens of employment shifted to the state and federal governments, as well as to an informal narcotics economy. Anticipating growing unemployment in 1982, for example, the state of Arizona built a medium-security prison outside of Douglas at the site of the first international airport in the United States (dedicated by Eleanor Roosevelt in 1928).[3] Laid-off smelter workers found lower-paying jobs as prison guards. Federal subsidies also flowed to the region: the border patrol grew by more than 400 percent—the fifty officers that had patrolled the border near Douglas in the mid-1980s were supplanted by a force nearing five hundred by the turn into the twenty-first century. These forces were augmented by additional Drug Enforcement Agency (DEA) and Immigration and Naturalization Service (INS) agents, as well as by new city police officers funded by federal grants.

Alongside this state-managed economy, the informal narcotics and immigration economies blossomed in the vacuum created by the departed copper industry.[4] Merchants began to rely on the marijuana harvests and later the cocaine traffic. The proliferation of narcotics-related businesses even earned Douglas the ignoble accolade of one of the "ten most corrupt cities in America."[5] Needless to say, policing and imprisonment rates increased dramatically as local dependence on the informal economy grew. This economic transformation led to a homegrown aphorism: people jokingly referred to their friends or relatives as being "with the government"—whether that meant as a prisoner or as a guard. Like the aphorism, the new police station suggested the centrality of the state in the local community's life, just as it indicated its transformed economy.

The railroad depot that became a police station. Why did the city spend more than twenty times its original cost to transform the building? Indeed, why spend so much money on a railroad depot in a tiny town far from centers of power in the first place? The depot's 1912 construction symbolized the successful capitalization of the border; the border's abstraction was visibly memorialized by the building's daunting columns and Tiffany glass. With all its plaster trimmings, the depot acted as a capstone to the transformation of the region, to the fundamental shift in perceptions of space that the region's capitalization and abstraction engendered. The frontera's abstraction meant that as a space it could be understood as isotropic and conceptualized as the same everywhere; it was emptied of meaning except when understood through some formal, seemingly scientific exterior schema, such as a map or grid.[6] Such abstraction indicated the triumph of capital investment less than thirty years after brutal military campaigns decimated the Apaches and represented the culmination of sixty years of discriminatory, harsh policies that had forced Mexican laborers into a perilous position vis-à-vis the whims of the mining companies.

This abstraction in the service of capital flows entailed a shift from the differentiated spaces conceptualized by Apaches, Yaquis, and Mexicanos to the conquered and closed frontier—a shift from the lived and sacred to the measured and homogenized. This shift evacuated space, challenging spaces as differentially weighted (where an area could be designated, for example, as more sacred than another). This shift also resulted in space's abstraction into geometric homogeneities, its reconceptualization as quantitative, its immersion in exchange relations, and the vitalization of the visual as a primary epistemological method.[7] According to Henri Lefebvre, the process of abstraction was also necessarily ocularcentric, for it required the neglect, and even repression, of other sensual knowledges of space, including those derived from auditory, tactile, and olfactory capacities. Given the important role the visual plays in the abstraction of space, it is hardly surprising that Phelps Dodge wished to build a highly visible symbol of its power to regulate and produce space in 1912.[8] And by the early 1990s, although capitalism had shifted from one phase to another in the borderlands, the significance of spatial symbologies had not declined. The money spent to make the railroad depot a police headquarters merely indicated the ongoing capacity of the visual to localize and instantiate power through the manipulation of space.

Furthermore, the depot's construction on the recently solidified national border also bookends the late-nineteenth-century rush to produce space (railroads, canals) in order to overcome space—to push market reaches farther, faster. More important, perhaps, the depot was built shortly after the consolidation of a capitalist system configured around the scale of the nation-state. The border location of the depot, however, also signaled the mining company's claim to power over the entire region, including Sonora. At the end of the twentieth century, the depot's transformation into a police headquarters indicates the transformed role of the nation-state within global capitalism. The nation-state does not disappear under globalization, but its focus shifts, since capital accumulation is no longer intensely tied to the national scale but is reterritorialized, so to speak, at both sub- and supranational scales.[9] The police headquarters suggests the redirection of governmental energies at multiple levels as the United States moves from the managed planning of a Keynesian economy to what Ruth Wilson Gilmore calls "post-Keynesian militarism" in which state resources flow toward policing at all levels, toward the carceral management of people deemed surplus.[10] Looking back on seventy years of industrialization and de-industrialization, that is, on the period marked by the construction and transformation of the depot/police station, one Chicana, Livia Leon Montiel, responded with an acerbic and stunning analysis. While telling Patricia Preciado Martin about her family's presence in Arizona, a presence she traces to at least the 1820s, Montiel discussed this spatial transformation and, with some bitterness, described the loss of her family's rancho to retirement communities and maquilas: "I'd like to leave this piece of land just as a gathering place for all of them [her daughters and sons]. . . . Land is becoming extinct, and all this will be developed. If it would only be possible for them to hold on to this little piece of land for all of them to reunite from time to time. This is my hope and my legacy. Pero no me quiero morir poniendo voluntades [But I don't want to die making demands]."[11]

It would be more than misguided to characterize Montiel's notion of land "becoming extinct" as a malapropism. Rather, her phrase insightfully describes the stakes of the transformation under way, suggesting as it does the turn from lived, embodied space to the abstract space of capitalism. More specifically, her comment indicates the sociality of this spatial change, a change that registers space as performative, shifting the grammar of land from passive noun (as object) to active verb (as doing); space is processual, it changes, goes extinct. Here Montiel underscores what Edward Soja also argues, which is that the "organization, use, and meaning of space is a product of social translation, transformation and experience."[12] Development changes not simply the look of the land but social relationships as well. Montiel's urgency is encumbered by pending loss and the (im)possibility of future gains.

Montiel's insight that "land is becoming extinct" simultaneously captures the imbrication of the temporal within the spatial and illustrates that, despite the seemingly successful abstraction of space, alternative conceptions of space continue to thrive alongside, if not dominate, the flow of capital. Furthermore, as Montiel's recognition that familial relations are intimately linked to the rancho illustrates, such alternative conceptions help to organize social relations differently. Not only is Montiel keenly aware of the process of homogenization that accompanies spatial abstraction, but her sense that the rancho's disappearance corresponds to the severing of close bonds among her children also signals the shift in spatiality that the newly renovated police headquarters loudly proclaims.[13] Montiel's brutally spatial assessment of the changes exemplified by both the police station and the railroad depot, her understanding that the transformation she has witnessed is akin to death, and her sense that space is far from the passive setting for social change that its abstraction would imply offer brilliant spatial insight. Far more than material object, a "real" largely distinct from the discursive, space for Montiel is an intimate participant in sociality. Land, like the social and cultural, can disappear, go extinct, become only a memory.

The railroad depot/police headquarters scaffolds the spatial-historical terrains that *Extinct Lands, Temporal Geographies* traverses. This study begins with the process of capitalizing and abstracting la frontera (the borderlands of Arizona and Sonora) and concludes with the transformation of space brought about by globalized narcotics wars. This spatial-temporal framework illuminates Chicana literature and its deeply spatial insights. For like Livia Leon Montiel, Chicana authors of poetry, prose, and drama have critiqued the production of space, have assessed its effects, have ungrounded its status as inert and transparent.[14] Chicana literature offers an important theoretics of space, one that, like many critical space studies, implicates the production of space in the everyday, in the social, but that unlike many space theories suggests the relevance of aesthetics, of "the literary mode of knowing" for understanding the intermeshing of the spatial and the social. And Chicana literature argues for and examines the relevance of race, gender, and sexuality—as well as class—to the making of space.

Extinct Lands, Temporal Geographies attends to space in order to grasp the nuances of a rich literature. Yet if this is an experiment in reading texts through the lens of space, it is also a study of how Chicana literature has, from its inception, contested the terms of capitalist spatial formation, including the attempts to regulate the meanings and uses of spaces, especially the use of space to naturalize violent racial, gender, sexual, and class ideologies. Chicana literature has consistently offered alternative methods of conceptualizing space not only by noting how social change must be spatialized but also by seeing and feeling space as performative and participatory, that is, by refusing a too-rigid binary between the material and the discursive. In a surprisingly consistent manner, the literature discussed herein offers not just alternative cartographies (or countercartographies—spatial narratives challenging those that have gained a normative or taken-for-granted status) but entirely different conceptualizations of spatiality altogether. These radical concepts emerge through a theoretics of space attentive to its formative power and particularly to the manner in which the nauralization of spatial production hides its power. Thus, for example, Chicana writers are quick to twist realism as a representational strategy that too easily solidifies oppressive spatial alignments by hiding the processual quality of space. Out of such twisting frequently emerge whole new conceptualizations of spatiality and sociality that are revolutionary in their implications.

"Space," Doreen Massey writes, "depends crucially on the notion of articulation."[15] As such, it is never outside of the cultural, the social milieu that is language. If one thinks of space, as Massey suggests, "in terms of the articulation of social relations which necessarily have a spatial form in their interactions with one another," then the understanding of spatial processes, as Chicana literature suggests, might be very much enlarged by attention to narrative, narrative techniques, and the role of narrative in the production of space, as well as to the various grammars that structure spatial articulations.[16] Such attention does not jettison the materiality of space in favor of a metaphorical turn by shifting focus to representation alone, nor does it merely appropriate spatial concepts to revitalize metaphorical analysis.[17] Rather, the concept of spatial articulation highlights the sociality of space and the spatiality of language. For this reason alone, a literary critique of space and a spatial reading of literature may prove useful.

Before discussing Chicana literature's sense of spatial urgency, I should mention that in referring to "the production of space" I am following both the spatial insights of Chicana and Chicano authors such as María Amparo Ruiz de Burton, Américo Paredes, Tey Diana Rebolledo, and José Saldívar, as well as the work of Doreen Massey, Edward Soja, and Henri Lefebvre. Claiming that space is "produced," of course, upends the assumption that space is simply the grand manifestation of the natural terrain. Viewing space as produced, productive, and producing means viewing it as interanimating and dependent in part on narrative for its productive effects—as "active and generative," in Kristin Ross's words—rather than as inert and transparent.

Thus, the production of space involves not simply buildings, transportation, and communications networks, as well as social and cultural groups and institutions (including their regulation and management—what some refer to as "second nature"), but it also involves the processes that shape how these places are understood, envisioned, defined, and variously experienced.[18] The processes of producing space, however quotidian or grand, hidden or visible, have an enormous effect on subject formation—on the choices people can make and how they conceptualize themselves, each other, and the world. Interactions with space are not merely schematic but also highly affective; places are felt and experienced, and the processes producing space therefore also shape feelings and experiences. Yet even as space shapes sociality in powerful ways, spatial processes attempt to keep that shaping power largely hidden, so that space is seen as a background, a setting, rich and interesting, but not in any sense interactive or formative. The concept of space as setting also renders places static, obscuring their temporality. Finally, such a concept ignores the significant role of narrative in the production of place. Narrative, of course, entails forms of conceptualization and the traditions, myths, and meanings ascribed to space, including how places are discussed or named and the grammatical structures that regulate their production.

Literature thrives on the intersections between the shaping powers of language and the productive powers of space. Literature attends to affect and environment; it uses space and spatial processes metaphorically to suggest emotions, insights, concepts, characters. It also shapes the way spaces are perceived, understood, and ultimately produced. Thus literature illustrates and enlarges the shaping force of narrative in the production of space, highlighting the discursiveness of space, its dependence on cultural mediation.

Crucial to this understanding of the production of space is its bodily instantiation. If the production of space is a highly social process, then it is a process that has an effect on the formation of subjectivity, identity, sociality, and physicality in myriad ways. Taking the performativity of space seriously also means understanding that categories such as gender, race, and sexuality are not only discursively constructed but spatially enacted and created as well. That is, while these categories are often considered mobile, spatially independent, or even merely discursive, they emerge in part through the production and sedimentation of space. And they, in turn, further solidify spatial processes in very nuanced ways. If these categories, and subjectivities more generally, are created in part through the formation of space, they are also naturalized by the same kinds of processes that hide space as productive in the first place. Precisely at this conjunction, at what we might call the spatialization of bodies, Chicana/o literature asserts a profound spatial critique. Chicana (and, to some extent, Chicano) literature has been particularly attuned to the complex ways race, gender, sexuality, and class emerge simultaneously, if unevenly, through both the discursive and the spatial, and in this conjunction become something almost hyperreal, or the naturally natural.

Chicanas write with a sense of urgency about the power of space, about its (in)clement capacity to direct and contort opportunities, hopes, lives. They write also with a sense of urgency about the need to contest such power, to counter it with alternative spatial configurations, ontologies, and geneologies. These writers also explore the spatialization of subjectivities in process, the efforts to fix or to make subjects through their spatialization, as well as how such efforts get deterred.

Chicanas' attention to the production of space may seem surprising. Space, any number of writers have argued, has been largely ignored by Euro-American social theorists. History, or change over time, has been the focus of their attention. In contrast, Chicana/os have been considering space, taking it seriously, not simply as something to produce, but as something to understand, since, as it were, our inception. The turn by Chicanas to space can be traced to any number of causes beyond individual writers' critical acumen and skills of observation. As Norma Alarcón reminds us, "displacement and dislocation are at the core of the invention of the Americas."[19] The production of the "Americas" coincided with the solidification of the Cartesian subject as subject of the state, as holder of property, as "cogito ergo sum" and its unspoken corollary, "I conquer." The emergence of the Cartesian subject resulted in a process that "de-spaced" peoples, depriving them of access to their means of subsistence, repressing the Cartesian subject's topophilia (the centrality of property to subjectivity); at the same time, it turned some people into subjects or citizens and other people into slaves, juridically nonexistent.[20] In this sense, the colonization process, an obviously spatial process, has had ongoing ramifications, and Chicano/as have felt and observed them to this day.

Preoccupation with the effect of space is certainly evident, for example, in the nineteenth-century testimonios of Californio/as, former hacendados and their families deprived of their land after the Treaty of Guadalupe Hidalgo was signed. Rosaura Sánchez explains this turn to space succinctly: "Having lost their 'homeland' and the political and economic power to regain their former social status, the narrators turn to representational spaces, wherein the past, the land, and political power can be discursively reasserted."[21] For the Californios, space was necessarily central to their analyses, because its production, its devolution as Mexican, had an immediate effect on their lives. Similarly, even a cursory reading of María Amparo Ruiz de Burton's two novels—the first known to have been published by a Mexican American—*Who Would Have Thought It?* and *The Squatter and the Don,* reveals a deeply spatial stance in her work.[22] In both novels, although especially in *Squatter,* she demonstrates how spatial formation depends on racial ideologies and how gender is in turn utilized to maintain spatial dominance. Her critique of California railroad magnates and the collusions between agribusiness, politicians, and railroad fiefdoms anticipates by more than twenty years the naturalist fiction of Frank Norris and others who would offer, ultimately, far more apologetic narratives of capital's dependence on uneven development.[23] One might go so far as to say that Ruiz de Burton's critique of the development of capital—its spatial voraciousness, its contradictions—anticipates many aspects of the neo-Marxist critique of capital's spatial appetite.

If Chicana/os are at the forefront of spatial change, they are also often the laborers of that change. For if change over time has also meant change across space, it has too frequently been at the expense of Chicana/o communities. Chicanas have not simply witnessed the onslaught of urban change, whether that be freeway constructions that hollow out communities or the revamping of the rural that deprives communities of grazing pastures and water rights; Chicanas have also been deeply attentive to the struggles for civil rights, a struggle that must be understood at least in part as a struggle over the use of space to maintain or disrupt social, political, and financial power. Chicana feminists have further attended to the critique of the public-private binary and its power to structure space, just as they have traced the nuances of spatial formation through other technologies, such as gentrification and segregation. And finally, the insights of Chicano/as about the productive effects of space, the literary insights into how power seems to coagulate around the emergence of various spaces and their control, can be seen as what Rafael Pérez-Torres calls "the critique of the Enlightenment project implicit to Chicano culture."[24]

Chicana writers have deployed an acute spatial analysis as part of the repertoire of what Chela Sandoval calls technologies for "decolonizing the social imagination," not simply because they have found themselves situated in the interstices of dominant narratives of subjectivity.[25] Working from "lives on the border," Chicanas, as Sonia Saldívar-Hull puts it, navigate "between Mexican and American, between rich and poor, between the U.S. and Mexico."[26] Many have therefore refined cognitive skills that not only map the terrains of power but also analyze, critique, and attempt to undermine them. In other words, the "epistemes of mestizaje and diaspora" demand an accounting of space in order to shift the terms by which subjectivity, opportunities, creativity can be produced.[27]

Such a longstanding engagement with space—more than 130 years—has led to an overwhelming sense of its significance. In chapter 1, I examine spatial urgency, its centrality to Chicana letters, as revealed early in Chicana/o literary formation, when newspaper essayists and fiction writers contested Anglo characterizations of Northern Sonora (or the Gadsden Purchase region) that were highly detrimental to Mexican Americans. If in the 1880s Mexicana/o authors deployed sophisticated allegories to critique the organization of U.S. colonies (or territories, as they were then termed), they also deployed concepts such as Aztlán, anticipating by nearly one hundred years the Chicano Movimiento's use of that alternative spatial narrative.

The folding of northern Sonora into U.S. territory and the ensuing subjection of its Chicana/o population were not unrelated to the 150-year effort of the U.S. government to solidify its southern border in both material and discursive terms. That is, the processes used to produce Arizona were fired up again to produce a militarized border. Chapter 2 discusses the border as both abjection machine and state-sponsored aesthetic project, examining how a number of astute authors—Gina Valdés, Norma Cantú, Montserrat Fontes, and Arturo Islas—take up border crossing as a means to perform a sort of autopsy on the border and to push past its uses as boundary-subject making construct.

The three subsequent chapters zoom in on the work of Gloria Anzaldúa, Terri de la Peña, Sandra Cisneros, and Cherríe Moraga to draw into focus not simply the seemingly macrospatial praxis that near monumental spaces like the border entail, but also the more readily hidden microspatial practices that weave together to form the norms of gender and sexuality for women of color. Each of these women-of-color, feminist authors offer literary unmaskings of space, showing how categories such as race, gender, and sexuality can be made to discipline and appear natural and unyielding through their spatialization. If Anzaldúa and de la Peña turn to the spatial work of categories in order to challenge the power dynamics contained therein, Cisneros moves from the management of identities through space to the management of places, revealing that places are processes, not static locales. Cherríe Moraga pushes this critique a step farther in her effort to redefine entirely the concepts of body and land, as well as the micropractices, the little tactics of patriarchy and homophobia, that ensure these systems' longevity, their control of the landscape, and their attendant angles of vision.

The final chapter brings this discussion nearly full circle. Returning to the police station and the narcospatiality it symbolizes, chapter 6 focuses on short stories by Mary Helen Ponce and Alberto Ríos. Both authors offer spatial critiques of the war on drugs and both explore how scale has become a crucial tool in the management of both the formal and informal narcotics economy. Given the prevalence of the spatial in Chicana literature—its thematic privileging, as it were—attention to the spatial broadens understanding of this literature by indicating its layers of aesthetic complexity and theoretical insight.

Extinct Lands, Temporal Geographies can be situated within a growing array of literary studies that take space seriously. Such studies are increasing in literary criticism in general and within Chicano/a literary studies in particular. That such expansion may be viewed as a relatively recent trend is exemplified by J. Hillis Miller's 1995 comment: "The notion that landscape provides grounding for novels has hardly given rise to a distinct mode of the criticism of fiction, as has the criticism of character or of interpersonal relations, or of narrators and narrative sequence."[28] While I would contest Miller's sharp distinction between novel and ground, it is fair to say that until recently the pace of space in literary studies has seemed slow despite Joseph Frank's much celebrated 1945 essay on the role of space in Modernism.[29] Over the course of the last twenty years, however, a number of exemplary studies have been published.[30] *Extinct Lands, Temporal Geographies* will, I hope, add to and extend this field of study, particularly because its focus on gender, race, and sexuality shifts the axis of analysis. I also hope that this work will take literature, especially Chicana literature, into new arenas not yet cognizant of its spatial critique. Chicana literature suggests, in different terms than those that currently dominate space studies, the myriad ways in which narrative techniques, stylistic conventions, plot dilemmas, and resolutions, as well as poetic and dramatic crafting, interrogate how space and social relations (re)constitute each other. Finally, it is my hope that the critical framework presented herein offers a nuanced way to not only engage with these extraordinary texts but also to derive pleasure from them.

I

Razing Arizona

In the warm and sun-filled days
I remember in the haze
The happy sounds of children laughing,
The rustle of the cottonwoods.
Now all is old and cold and dark
Underneath Presidio Park.
—Patricia Preciado Martin,
"The Journey"

Arizona began as a mistake. The United States government used a mistake on a map to take what is now called southern Arizona from Sonora, Mexico—to abscond with it. This far-from-innocent (mis)taking emerged out of contradictions and shifting interpretations; the mistake showcases the seeming aporia structuring the distinctions between the metaphorical and the material, the real and the mapped. Consideration of this particular (mis)take also exposes the politicality of space, revealing a battle over how to characterize space and how to produce places that then almost magically become background or setting, and thereby hide space as a formative, intimate participant in the pleasures and work of sociality and subject formation. Unpacking that mistake, resignifying a dubious nineteenth-century error, requires beginning with contrasting accounts, not of the mistake exactly, but of the spatial work that evolved from it.

Patricia Preciado Martin's short story "The Journey" (1980) offers a layered excavation of spatial memories that functions as testimonio, narrative monument, critique, and reportage of the production of Arizona and the lengthy struggle to remember Mexicano culture and life that such production seemed to pave over.[1] The story begins with the poem quoted above, which invokes memories of a community and place that through the "haze" of dust, smog, memory, and years now lies "old and cold and dark / Underneath Presidio Park." The six-line poem works almost as a chant, conjuring the "disappeared" community and, with the reference to Presidio Park, locating it in Tucson, Arizona—a bit northwest of the originary site of the "mistake" but very much germane to the ultimate (mis)taking.

"The Journey" continues as the narrator first looks at subsidized housing, then reads a building's dedication plaque, moving us immediately into the politics of urban redevelopment in Tucson. "The Journey" takes its readers alongside the narrator and her Tía, Doña Juanita Mendoza, as they accomplish their Saturday errands. The two travel "past" and "slowly," moving the reader through Tucson by remembering significant people, entering important places such as the cathedral, and catching snatches of conversation. With each iteration of place, the narrative returns us to the complexity of development.

> We walk out once more into the brightness. Past an elegant old home that is now a funeral parlor. Down South Meyer and west on Cushing Street. Past a sign that says Barrio Histórico. THIS AREA HAS BEEN OFFICIALLY DESIGNATED AS AN HISTORICAL LANDMARK AND IS OFFICIALLY REGISTERED WITH THE NATIONAL REGISTER OF HISTORICAL PLACES. In Bronze. Most of the houses in the Barrio Histórico are owned by Mr. Kelly Rollings, a local automobile dealer and millionaire and amateur anthropologist. He owns the old Robles House. It is now the Cushing Street Bar. "EAT, DRINK AND BE MERRY IN AN AUTHENTIC RESTORED OLD ADOBE."[2]

The tone suggests a mere documenting of signs and scenes. Only the quiet comment "In Bronze" alerts readers to the story's stringent spatial critique and prepares them for the irony of an old home, a remnant of Tucson's three hundred year Mexican history, advertised as a bar whose authenticity is located in the building material, not its cultural context. The sight of the Robles House inspires Doña Mendoza to remember happy events at their home. The contrast between the preservation of the buildings and the vibrant memories of an elderly woman highlights the work of a historic preservation project that maintains buildings but evacuates them of their complex significance, thereby lending a nostalgic authenticity to the city without threatening alignments of capital by acknowledging its dependency on racial narratives.

As the two continue to walk, Doña Mendoza recalls the gardens in the

barrio that were possible before water tables were drained and rivers di-
verted to build fountains, golf courses, and subdivisions, impoverishing
Chicana/o farmers and families. The politics of water management elliptically dovetails with the geography of race in her account: "The Freeways
had cut the river from the people. The Freeway blocks the sunshine. The
drone of traffic buzzes like a giant unsleeping bee."³ As in so many urban
areas, interstate highway construction in Tucson cut through a Chicana/o
neighborhood. The freeway functions now, the narrator acidly suggests, as
a different type of river—rather than giving life, it separates, impedes, and
engulfs the community's development.

The two pass by additional historic buildings and more urban renewal
projects, moving toward what appears to be their destination.

> The pace of Tía quickens now. I follow her, carrying the straw bag
> laden with groceries. We walk past the Concert Hall to the vast parking
> lot of the Community Center Complex. A billboard reads: CONCERT
> TONIGHT. ALICE COOPER SOLD OUT. We stop in the middle of the park-
> ing lot. The winter sun is warm. The heat rises from the black asphalt.
> The roar of the Freeway is even more distinct. It is the end of the jour-
> ney. I know what Tía will say. "Aquí estaba mi casita. It was my father's
> house. And his father's house before that. They built it with their own
> hands with adobes made from the mud of the river. All their children
> were born here. I was born here. It was a good house, a strong house.
> When it rained, the adobes smelled like the good clean earth."⁴

Their journey might be more accurately characterized as a pilgrimage—but
instead of arriving at a publicly acknowledged shrine, they arrive at a spot
of hot asphalt. Doña Mendoza must conjure her long-gone home, chanting
memories and exclamations, transforming civic projects designed to attract
tourist dollars into something else, revealing the layers of history hidden
and razed.

"The Journey" works as more than a contrary gesture of reclamation. Beyond a critique of waste and excess (dried rivers and dead gardens, but teem-
ing water fountains), the story asserts the presence of Mexicanos long before
the arrival of Anglo colonialists. By asserting such a presence and pointing out the signs of the production of Arizona—the infrastructure projects,
their detritus, and the structural projects, all designed to make Arizona appealing to "winter visitors"—the story destabilizes the dominant narrative

of Arizona history as a wild cowboy frontier by pointing out its costs and by asserting a contrasting historical trajectory. "The Journey" also serves as a monument to or celebration of the strength of Chicana culture and Doña Mendoza's will to remember, despite the onslaught of devastation cum urban renewal.

One hundred years prior to the publication of "The Journey," Brevet Major General E. Carr offered a very different spatial story of Tucson. Speaking in July of 1880 at a celebration marking the arrival of the railroad, Carr gestured toward Tucson and proclaimed: "Tucson, the mud town on the banks of the Santa Cruz, will be magnificent. . . . The rude and unattractive mud front will give place to the stately mansion with pedestal and column, frieze and architecture. . . .Taste and capital and energy are mighty powers in the building of cities."[5] The reference to mud—that is, to adobe— functions as an implicitly racialized counterpoint, intended to exalt the architectural style most characteristic of imaginary Southern plantations; this reference, with its claim to Anglo superiority, would not have been lost on Carr's Anglo audiences, many of whom emigrated from the Southern United States after the Civil War. Carr is baldly clear in his tropes: architecture is a sign of race; narratives of place become shorthand references for racial narratives. Architectural aesthetics merge with bourgeois notions of propriety to become signs of an imaginary Anglo superiority, and the South rises again "on the banks of the Santa Cruz."

Carr further underscores his racial-spatial story through the invocation of temporality: "Seated beside the Santa Cruz she slept a century away, little dreaming of her brilliant life to come. But to-day she awakens, and, conscious to the touch of the magic wand of science and civilization, rises erect, and with elastic step wheels into line with the advancing column." If the metaphors seem a bit mixed, they are nonetheless abundantly clear. Anglos bring science and civilization to a sleeping people, to a community now, as if by magic, incorporated into the (militarized) movement of Manifest Destiny. Carr attributes a Rip Van Winkle-esque quality to Mexicanos in an effort to emphasize the vigor, progress, and superiority of Anglos and to further disarticulate Mexicano contributions to the production of the region. Carr's language also sexualizes space in an effort to emasculate Mexicanos.

Far more than one hundred years lie between Preciado Martin's and Carr's accounts.[6] Reading Carr's narrative alongside Martin's, one must consider that the adobes Carr so arrogantly dismisses are the very buildings preserved with plaques "In Bronze." What Carr sees as a landscape to be destroyed becomes a century later the landscape that authenticates the region for tourists seeking signs of the "Old West" and that signals legacies of survival and imperialism for the descendants of the buildings' first inhabitants. What is at stake, as these two accounts indicate, is not simply a contest over how to imagine the Arizona landscape. Rather, figured through landscape is a battle over both the imaginary of the future as well as of the past. By landscape, I mean not a simplistic depiction of scenery but rather the conscious construction of a perspective, a way of seeing the region that, in concert with policies, laws, and institutions, physically *makes* the land, produces the landscape materially, and sustains it ideologically.[7]

Brevet Major General Carr's envisioned landscape doesn't just entail the dissolution of a Mexican community; he also imagines erasure of that community from history itself, through a seemingly aesthetic if openly racialized hierarchy. In this manner the General worked within a tradition, then nearly forty years old, of depicting Arizona in a manner that would produce an Anglo Arizona landscape at the expense of the colonized Mexicanos, Apaches, Tohono O'odhams, Pimas, and others. Preciado Martin's story points to the smug and contradictory signs of this effort. Yet her story also offers signs that the Anglo Arizona landscape did not fully eliminate Mexicanos or Mexican culture. Indeed, "The Journey" is yet another reminder of the intensive contest waged against the making of such landscapes and their consolidation in historical memory.

The contest over Arizona emerged from a mistake that then became a glorious opportunity; the emergence of the Gadsden Purchase became an *emergency* for Mexicanos who had lived and worked in the region for several hundred years prior to this critical case of (mis)taken identity. Not surprisingly, Mexicanos both recognized the emergency and understood the need to offer a repertoire of responses to the deformation of the area then known as Northern Sonora. Although largely unknown today, Mexicanos' political geographies at the time countered the Arizona fantasized and being developed by Anglo miners, politicians, travel writers, border surveyors, and ethnographers. Producing the Anglo Arizona landscape entailed more than the manipulation of public policy, the establishment of boundaries, and the development of the region's resources; its producers first narratively razed Arizona, demolishing the signs that marked it as a Mexican region with Mexican communities, mines, ranches, and legal and political networks, emptying it of its Mexican inhabitants in order to create an Arizona available for Anglo capital and development. Then, at a less symbolic level, Anglos encouraged and supported the Apache wars with Mexican settlers; they forcefully took over Mexican mining operations; they raided and burned ranches; they then used the legal and political structures to produce an "English-only Arizona" that created a dual wage structure, segregated schools, limited opportunities, and violently promoted Anglo hegemony.[8] Mexicanos responded and contested those productions in numerous forms, including theater, fiction, essay, and testimonio, as well as strikes, mutual aid alliances, and the development of counter-public arenas. Fights over producing the landscape, as "The Journey" makes clear, were not simply fights over metaphorical interpretation but contests whose implications and outcomes would haunt, trouble, nourish, and inspire Chicana authors for the subsequent 150 years.

Felicitous Mistakes

Southern Arizona was not part of the land ceded by Mexico in the Treaty of Guadalupe Hidalgo.[9] Instead, it was purchased in a separate agreement worked out years later. What happened? While the boundary survey commissioners were working to establish the post-1848 border near El Paso del Norte, they discovered a problem: the Disturnell Map used during treaty negotiations incorrectly located both El Paso del Norte and the Rio Bravo. The difference between the "material" and the "metaphorical" was not insignificant. Depending on how that "difference" was resolved and the border produced, the two countries would either gain or lose valuable mineral resources. Not surprisingly, the region subject to dispute possessed rich copper and silver reserves, encompassed lucrative cattle grazing land, and promised a potent agricultural future.

In initial attempts to settle the dispute, Mexico's boundary commissioner, General Pedro Garcia Condé, noted that the map had been "drawn upon false statements—that is to say, things appearing on it which exist not on the ground"; hence, the first serious result of the discrepancy "would be to destroy the boundary system of New Mexico adopted in the treaty."[10] Garcia Condé's sense that the mistake threatened the boundary system was more than a prescient observation: he clearly worried that if Mexico did not cede additional territory, the United States would wage a new war against the nation and take all of Sonora. The boundary system—the settled sense of what the United States had acquired in its most recent war—was in danger because, as Garcia Condé recognized, the crisis over a "mistake" opened the distinct possibility that the United States would again mis-recognize Mexican sovereignty and renew their aggressive acquisition of land. Garcia Condé's anxiety that negotiations toward a compromise would demolish the integrity of the border system before the border had even been established further suggests that built into the production of the border was the anxiety over its demise. The border's destruction had to be imagined and narrated, nostalgically figured in advance, before the border itself could emerge as coherent and intelligible. The result, just as Garcia Condé feared, kept the "Southwest" unsettled, marking it not through a permanent border but with an intermittent or temporary boundary while the United States continued to swallow larger and larger chunks of territory. Indeed, over the next thirty years, the United States tacitly sanctioned filibustering raids on Northern Mexico and, when these failed, pressed Mexico's central government to grant U.S. capital unrestricted access to its mines and agricultural resources.[11]

Almost immediately the initial dispute over the gap between the real and the discursive was incorporated into the debates consuming the United States in the 1850s. These debates included whether or not to extend slavery into the newly acquired territories, whether or not to ensure the South's economic growth by building a transcontinental railroad linking the southern United States directly to California, and whether or not to extend U.S. territory farther south by acquiring the valuable mines, agricultural fields, and shorelines of Sonora. For nearly two years the debate over the compromise increasingly activated tensions between Mexico and the United States until President Pierce, at the urging of Jefferson Davis, sent James Gadsden to negotiate a new treaty and purchase the disputed territory. After repeated U.S. threats of renewed war, alongside outrageous demands for huge swaths of Mexican territory, Mexico agreed to the sale of land.[12] Three years after Garcia Condé had predicted the widespread ramifications of "things appearing" on a map that "exist not on the ground," the United States purchased the only portion of what is now Arizona that was then settled and developed by Mexicanos.[13]

Despite the seemingly ravenous U.S. desire for territory, the proposed

Gadsden Purchase provoked controversy. Figuring into the debates over the Gadsden Purchase was the "value" of a region that one Congressman described as "destitute of wood and of water, and the soil as either a sterile sand or composed of disintegrated flint rocks, that lie open, and without dirt or soil between the fragments. . . . I suppose the land given us by and within the new boundaries to be substantially worthless."[14] Many other Eastern Anglos also greeted the Gadsden Purchase and the repeatedly proposed acquisition of Sonora with ambivalence, perceiving it, as Hubert Howe Bancroft put it, as both a "Southern scheme" and a "barren and worthless waste of sandy deserts and rocky mountains, probably rich in minerals, but of no agricultural value whatever."[15] Kit Carson's characterization of the new colony as "so desolate, desert, and God-forsaken, a wolf could not make a living on it" would also circulate widely.[16] Thirty years later the value of the purchase would continue to be questioned by writers such as Charles Lummis, who reported to the *Los Angeles Times* in 1886 that southern Arizona was "crippled by topographical cussedness" and "utterly bare of anything upon which a white man could exist."[17]

Choreographing a Colony

To counter this conceptualization of the landscape as worthless and forbidding, a host of government surveyors, ethnographers, journalists, mining engineers, cavalrymen, and others wrote long treatises proclaiming the wonders and dangers of southern Arizona and effectively waging a contest over how *to see* the new borderlands.[18] Their maps and descriptions made practical the process of Anglo colonization, while their ethnographic accounts also made it imaginable. Drawing on an already highly evolved imperialist repertoire necessary for the production and management of the newly captured territories, and making use of ethnography, mapmaking, and the discourses of Anglo superiority and Mexican and Indian otherness, they first razed the region produced by nearly three hundred years of Spanish and Mexican colonial projects and then buried the rubble (of bodies and discourses), only to build a new colonial structure and edifice.[19]

In producing these landscapes, these writers initiated capitalism's work of rationalizing (normalizing and abstracting) space, making it available for measuring, assessing, selling. Their landscapes disciplined and systematized perceptions of the region that their audiences would subsequently encounter by assimilating them into the already well-defined vocabulary and grammar of U.S. expansionism. The various accounts energetically described Arizona as available to Anglos precisely because its foreignness, its status as a Mexican region, rendered it vulnerable and weak. The paintings and drawings that accompany these accounts emphasize the vastness of the terrain, the smallness and scarcity of inhabitants, the abandoned and ruinous status of ranchos and towns, and the extraordinary and strange natural formations. By emptying the territory in this manner, writers and artists underscored its availability for Anglo conquest. Drawing on Helena Viramontes' memorable phrase, these writers and artists produced Arizona as "full of empty."[20]

The "exploration" and narration of Arizona by journalists, mining engineers, soldiers, and government surveyors was central to the imperial project of creating that state. The resulting texts described the region as available, indeed begging for Anglo colonization, because Mexicanos had "abandoned" the region, leaving behind undeveloped but bountiful mines and ranches. The writers ascribed the cause of abandonment to the Apaches and to Mexican failure of character and will. Thus, they produced a set of highly contradictory texts that catalogued, reported, and archived the region in the mode of the colonial models before them, including those of Walter Prescott Web and Alexander Baron Von Humboldt (whom these writers frequently cited). Through charts of mineral deposits; illustrations of the peoples encountered in their "traditional garb," which almost never depict those people as working or in any way threatening the colonial enterprise; ethnographic narratives of the communities encountered; long descriptions of the terrain traversed; and ongoing assessments of the value of the region, its future for capital, and the possibilities of developing a pool of laborers, these writers created Arizona. In these accounts, the Mexicanos who mapped the region and developed the roads, mines, and ranches are rendered intellectually impotent, hopeless failures beset by an inept central government, a faulty gene pool, and a hostile, superior set of Apache warriors. Mexicano failure was rhetorically overemphasized not simply to highlight the ferocity of the Apaches and thereby to justify Anglo demands that the region be militarized prior to its colonization, but also in order to render Mexicanos unthreatening to Anglo colonists — although nevertheless capable of providing the cheap labor necessary to the colonial project.

Such ethnographic work began as early as the 1840s, when the U.S. Congress assigned to William Emory the task of assessing what Mexican territory should be considered for colonization by the United States.[21] Subsequently, John Russell Bartlett, later a founder of the American Ethnology Society, would write a two-volume narrative of the region as part of his work as the U.S. Mexican Boundary Commissioner.[22] Emory published a second such narrative after he succeeded Bartlett as boundary commissioner.[23] A host of travel writers would further narrate Arizona, celebrating its exotic potential as "the marvellous country."[24]

While writers such as J. Ross Browne, Emory, and Bartlett narrated Arizona throughout the 1850s and 1860s in a manner that aimed at attracting capital to the area in order to produce a landscape in more than narrative terms, near the end of the century John Gregory Bourke would publish his war memoir cum travelogue cum ethnography, *On the Border with Crook* (1891), from the perspective of successful capitalization and transformation of Arizona. The landscape envisioned by the writers of the 1860s had indeed emerged by 1891. As one of the first soldiers sent to Arizona in 1870 to battle Apaches and make the territory "safe" for large-scale mining operations, Bourke was very much part of Arizona's early production. Perhaps due to his detailed descriptions, *On the Border with Crook* has become an important source for Arizona historians. In a sense, he continues to help produce Arizona.[25]

Given its significance, the opening sentences of *On the Border with Crook* bear quoting.

> Dante Alighieri, it has always seemed to me, made the mistake of his life in dying when he did in the picturesque capital of the Exarchate five hundred and fifty years ago. Had he held on to this mortal coil until after Uncle Sam had perfected the "Gadsden Purchase," he would have found full scope for his genius in the description of a region in which not only purgatory and hell, but heaven likewise, had combined to produce a bewildering kaleidoscope of all that was wonderful, weird, terrible, and awe-inspiring, with not a little that was beautiful and romantic.[26]

Bourke's invocation of Dante as a kind of ur-travel writer at the beginning of his own 500-page narrative deserves some attention. The allusion to Shakespeare and wry reference to Dante suggest that Bourke intends his book to be a work of literature, not politics nor even mere travel adventure, and that he considers the "frontier" he will memorialize to be a fit subject of art; he thereby attempts to elevates the region and his text above the genre already, in 1891, the purview of dime-westerns. Bourke's turn to Dante, in juxtaposition with "Uncle Sam," suggests a good-humored "Yankee" attempt to locate his text in the familiar world of belles lettres. Yet Bourke seems to forget that Dante's project was avowedly political and religious in its premises, preferring to deem both his own work and Dante's as outside of politics, as a participant in the realm of literary art, not imperialist accounting.

Bourke's opening paean to the Gadsden Purchase also signals a victory for those who had contended that its value far exceeded the ten million dollars paid for it. Indeed, Bourke's comment both summarizes the characterization of the region promulgated by its producers beginning in the late 1840s ("terrifying," "weird," "wonderful") and signals an end to their effectiveness. The Arizona landscape had been produced in the manner imagined, and a memorialization of that work could now begin via Bourke's work. In a certain sense, his opening sentences function as a marker similar to the "In Bronze" plaque that Preciado Martin lampoons. That is, Bourke's account renders the landscape historic and completed, thereby reinscribing the notion of the closed frontier.

Near the end of *On the Border with Crook,* imperialist nostalgia comes to the fore. Noting the arrival of the railroad and the transformation it had entailed, Bourke reminisces.

> Tucson had changed the most appreciably of any town in the Southwest; American energy and American capital had effected a wonderful transformation: the old garrison was gone; the railroad had arrived; where Jack Long and his pack-train in the old times had merrily meandered, now puffed the locomotive; Muñoz's corral had been displaced by a round-house, and Muñoz himself by a one-lunged invalid from Boston; the Yankees had almost transformed the face of nature. . . . American enterprise had moved to the front, and the Castilian with his "marromas" and "bailes" and saints' days and "funciones" had fallen to the rear; telephones and electric lightes and Pullman cars had scared away the plodding burro and the creaking "carreta"; it was even impossible to get a meal cooked in the Mexican style of Mexican viands; our dreams had faded; the chariot of Cinderella had changed back into a pumpkin, and Sancho was no longer governor. "I tell you, Cap," said

my old friend, Charlie Hopkins, "them railroads's playin' hob with th' country, 'n a feller's got to hustle hisself now in Tucson to get a meal of frijoles or enchiladas; this yere new-fangled grub doan' suit me 'n I reckon I'll pack mee grip 'n lite out fur Sonora."[27]

Longing and admiration structure his nostalgia.[28] And in a stinging prediction, food alone comes to signify Mexican culture—that which he finally, in concert with his predecessors, narrates as lost. Renato Rosaldo identifies this form of nostalgia as "imperial," as "nostalgia for the colonized culture as it was 'traditionally' " harbored by those "agents of colonialism" who "intentionally altered or destroyed" it.[29] What is clear from Bourke's narrative is that his nostalgia is not simply for the culture he helped destroy—he had been a member of the occupying army—but also for the particular way he had once perceived himself: it is a nostalgia for his sense of himself as superior outsider, an identity he had come to cherish. Yet the narrative of nostalgia also authorizes his own text, *On the Border with Crook,* to function as an archive, as an official memory, or as a memorial, a textual monument of sorts. For if nostalgia confirms "progress" and "enterprise," it also confirms the text itself as a signpost of modernity, as an index and icon of the very progress it signals through mourning, wonder, and melancholia.

Bourke's closing assessment of Tucson is notable for more than its imbrication in imperialist nostalgia. His comment that "Yankees had almost changed the face of nature" clearly reflects the significance of spatial transformation to colonial power and development. If, as Henri Lefebvre argues, "social movements must produce their own space," so, too, must colonial efforts produce spaces that instantiate new forms of power and mitigate dissent. Spatial structures (garrisons, corrals) disappear; technologies (railroad, telephones, electricity) transform; Mexican identity is swept into loss; Mexican labor (mining, transportation) is funneled into entertainment (marromas, enchiladas), so that what is remembered is food, music, and fantasy—not the Mexican industry that located and developed mines, and implemented the agricultural and ranching economies that made possible Anglo colonization in the first place. That Mexican institutions vanished from the landscape implies the disappearance and loss of Mexican influence and culture, as well as people. ("Samaniegos, Suasteguis, Borquis, Ferreras, and other Spanish families had withdrawn to Sonora.")[30] Bourke makes it clear, as Emory and Bartlett would only predict, that the making of place entails the production and unmaking of cultural identities, that is, their disarticulation. Such disarticulation occurs on the one hand through references to fairy tales (Cinderella) and legends (Cervantes) that render the Mexican past unreal, mythical, and imaginary—and therefore immaterial—and, on the other hand, through metaphorical displacement. The "one-lunged invalid from Boston," for instance, refers to the wealthy victims of consumption who had migrated to the Southwest and displaced the laborers like the anonymous "Muñoz," suggesting further the massive economic transformation of the region.

Mexicanos in Tucson, or los Tucsonenses, facing the onslaught of Anglo settlers and narrators, could not afford to ignore the repertoire of strategies meant to deprive them of their subjectivity, land, water and mineral rights, and political and economic self-determination. Unlike Californios or Tejanos, few Mexicanos in Arizona could be considered even remotely wealthy, with the vast majority being subsistence farmers. Little real capital flowed through the region. None possessed the massive land grants that characterized California, for example. Thus, with no material resources to draw from, they were forced to turn, as the writers of the Bancroft testimonios would, primarily to discourse.[31] The Mexicano response to Anglo incursions, however, did take numerous other forms. First off, they survived—this despite thirty years of nearly unchecked violence, what historian Joe Park calls an "undeclared war." They formed a number of mutual aid alliances. These proto-unions helped people pay funeral costs and regroup after disasters; they also created well-organized social networks that eventually served as the backbone for strikes, political campaigns, and business enterprises.[32] These alliances utilized flexibility and mobility to assist people deprived of the privileges of property and civil rights.

Mexicanos also wrote, remembered, and celebrated. Refusing the cloud of characterization that first relied on them to do the labor of producing the Arizona landscape, then erased them from that landscape or portrayed them as sleeping statues, they accounted for their labor, remembered their prior claims to the region, refused the notion of their disappearance or failure, noted and celebrated the achievements of their labor, and defied the conflation of themselves with the land that demanded so much patience and acumen from them. Yet, to find written accounts of these efforts is not all that easy. A few testimonios exist in Arizona and California archives. Families still possess letters and memories. Additionally, a series of Spanish-language newspapers were published in Arizona beginning in the mid-1870s. Other signs of the vibrant Mexicano culture of southern Arizona can be found in sometimes surprising places. These sources offer an important portrait of the varied and complex efforts of Mexicanos to combat the creation of an Anglo Arizona landscape so intensely detrimental to them.

La guardia advancada

Buried in *On the Border with Crook* is an account of a play he calls *Elena y Jorge,* which was performed in Tucson in 1870 by a traveling troupe or what Bourke characterizes as a "Mexican strolling heavy-tragedy company in its glory."[33] According to his account, the theater troupe was greeted with enthusiasm: "If there was a man, woman, or child in the old pueblo who wasn't seated on one of the cottonwood saplings which, braced upon other saplings, did duty as benches in the corral near the quartermaster's it was because that man, woman, or child was sick, or in jail."[34] Bourke's attendance estimates were undoubtedly incorrect since in 1870 more than 2,000 Mexicanos lived in Tucson.[35] Yet he was probably correct about the enthusiasm with which the community would have greeted such a theater.

The play centered on the French invasion of Mexico (1863–67), as narrated through a romance between two young Mexicanos, Elena and Jorge. Here is Bourke's description:

> It was a most harrowing, sanguinary play. The plot needs very few words. Elena, young, beautiful, rich, patriotic; old uncle, miser traitor, mercenary, anxious to sell lovely heiress to French officer for gold; French officer, coward, liar, poltroon, steeped in every crime known to man, anxious to wed lovely heiress for her money alone; Jorge, young, beautiful, brave, conscientious, an expert in the art of war, in love with heiress for her own sweet sake, but kept from her side by the wicked uncle and his [Jorge's] own desire to drive the last cursed despot from the fair land of his fathers.[36]

Ultimately Jorge defeats the "mercenary" French officer and Elena's "wicked old uncle." The play ends, according to Bourke, when the "baffled Gaul has been put to flight; the guards are dragging the wretched uncle off to the calaboose, and Jorge and his best girl entwine themselves in each other's arms amid thunders of applause."[37] For many in the 1870 Arizona audience, the play's allegorical intentions would have been clear. Elena symbolized Mexico, leveraged to the French by the Catholic Church and wealthy hacendados worried about the civil, agrarian, and land reforms initiated by Benito Juarez's government. Jorge, of course, symbolized working-class Mexican resistance to the French invasion.

Bourke mocks the play, noting its "gross violations of all the possibilities, of all the congruities, of all the unities," but also admits that it captivates him.

> I despised that French officer, and couldn't for the life of me understand how any nation, no matter how depraved, could afford to keep such a creature upon its military rolls. I don't think I ever heard any one utter in the same space of time more thoroughly villainous sentiments than did that man, and I was compelled, as a matter of principle, to join with the "muchachos" in their chorus of "Muere!"[38]

The irony of *Elena y Jorge,* its obviously dual discourse, its subtle satire and critique of invading and occupying armies appears lost on Bourke, who, having described the play, moves on to a discussion of the tamales, tortillas, and enchiladas sold afterward. Bourke might have missed the double significance of the play if he was not aware of the extent to which Mexicanos in Tucson had helped fight the French invasion of Sonora. According to Federico José María Ronstadt, Tucsonenses raised nearly $24,000 in 1865 for the purchase of ammunition, guns, and provisions in order to equip a volunteer Mexican army that was fighting to push the French out of Sonora.[39] The play probably had a far deeper resonance with its Tucson audience than Bourke knew.

Bourke's cavalry, lolling about Tucson waiting for Apache raids, was every bit the occupying, colonizing army, having arrived in southern Arizona just after the Civil War. So, of course, the traveling teatro could not afford to openly narrate Mexican opposition to Anglo occupation. Instead, they displaced their anger and resentment onto the now-defeated and long-gone French in a manner that enabled Bourke to take a stance of moral superiority and disavow his own participation in a similar process of occupation. Far from offering a mere "distraction," the play provided a political critique of imperialism and local complicity with occupying armies.

Embedded in Bourke's own patronizing narrative is a text that marks the ongoing resistance to Anglo incursion and critiques the very imperial efforts of the army Bourke memorializes; *Elena y Jorge* testifies to the extraordinary power of theater and its clear political deployment by Mexicanos resisting Anglo claims to Arizona territory. *Elena y Jorge* works as a sign that people were structuring the region and the take-over along a very different axis than Washington imagined. The teatro's implicit comparison of the U.S. Army to French invaders more than mirrors the imperialistic designs of two governments; it also indicates the extent to which, in both cases, Sonorenses were vulnerable if valuable pawns in the machinations of national governments. But by recalling the successful defeat of the French, the teatro implicitly imagined a successful defeat of the United States as well. Furthermore, *Elena y Jorge* may also be seen as a subtle critique of the tendency to produce the Arizona landscape not as a *border,* but as a *gateway*— as the entry through which more U.S. troops and colonists could pass on their way to seizing all of Sonora. Such fear was well justified. For example, before Arizona had even become a territory, Sylvester Mowry, a miner and tireless campaigner for capital investments and territorial status, declared to the National Geographic Society, "Guymas, which one day will be ours, is one of the largest ports for the export of flour on the Pacific coast north of Chili."[40] Indeed, the narrative accounts of Arizona from the 1850s through the 1870s were replete with celebratory anticipation of the day the United States would seize the state. Their anticipation was reinforced by a series of filibustering attempts that made Sonorans very wary.

That the French occupation and the deaths of the more than 50,000 people who fought them continued to preoccupy Tucsonenses is further indicated by the 1881 publication in serial form of *Juarez or La guerra de mexico* by Alfred Gassier in *El Fronterizo.*[41] In this play, Benito Juarez scolds an archbishop with the words, "Señor, México es celoso de la Independencia que ha conquistado con torrentes de sangre. Quiere guardar intacta la República, que ha sabido ganar. Si ha dado la libertad á sus esclavos, si se ha libertado de vosotros, si ha sacudido el yugo de la oligarquía militar y clerical, no es para someter su victoria al capricho del extranjero" [Sir, México is jealous of an independence gained through torrents of blood. He who wishes to keep the Republic intact, must understand this: if She has given liberty to her slaves, if She has liberated even our very selves, if She has taken off the yoke of clerical and militaristic oligarchy, it is not in order to submit such a victory to the caprices of a foreigner]."[42]

Clearly both plays served an allegorical purpose as well as an educational one. For if Gassier's play reminded *El Fronterizo*'s readers of Mexico's fight to maintain national independence, then its publication during the territorial period also served to invoke in readers a sense of both Mexico's desirability and the need to battle the ongoing encroachments and threats of Anglo filibusteros.[43] Bourke's account of the traveling teatro indicates one sign of resistance to Anglo claims to Arizona territory and suggests a far more varied and vivid cultural life than his accounts of Arizona imply.

The apparent popularity of *Elena y Jorge* and *Juarez* indicates that, contrary to the suggestions made by nearly all travel writers, Anglo troops were less than welcome by the Mexicanos caught within the stretches of the Gadsden Purchase. Given the explicit danger of openly contesting occupying armies, however, such critiques depended on covert production. For signs of Mexicano dissent, then, one must look to sources other than the written accounts of the invaders and their "ethnographying" shock troops.

Tucked away in the Bancroft Collection is a narrative entitled "The Mexican Troops Departure from Tucson as recalled by Doña Atanacia Santa Cruz de Hughes as told to Donald W. Page" and dated 12 May 1929.[44] Doña Santa Cruz de Hughes would have been six years old when northern Sonora became officially southern Arizona, but she begins her testimonio not with a discussion of the confusion, fear, or excitement a six year old might have felt at the transformation but with the comment that when the Mexican troops vacated the plaza, several Anglos had already moved to Tucson: "Cuando la plaza de Tucson fué desocupada por la tropa mexicana la verificarse la entrega del territorio a los Estados Unidos en el año de 1856 ya se encontraban algunos americanos en el pueblo [By the time the Mexican troops abandoned Tucson after verification that the territory had been turned over to the United States in 1856, you could already encounter Americans in the city].[45]

The presence of Anglos attests, she implies, to the hospitality of the Tucsonenses' and to the stagecoaches running ("Ya corrian diligencias") between Tucson and Yuma (on the California border). However, despite the presence of some Anglos, despite the history of Tucson's hospitality to Anglo visitors, the Mexicanos in northern Sonora did not feel sure that they would be similarly well-treated when the region became Southern Arizona. They had heard quite the opposite: "La mayor parte de la gente se albortó en grande escala debido a que corría la voz que la tropa americana venía ocupando todo lo que antes pertenecía a México, adueñandose de las propiedades, abusando, y hasta matando a las familias" [The majority of people were extremely upset due to the rumor that as the U.S. army took over all that had previously belonged to Mexico, it was seizing properties, abusing, and even killing families].[46]

The Mexicanos' exodus from Tucson was so thorough and rapid that newspapers as far away as San Francisco reported their departure. And if the exodus parallels the Depression-era deportations of some eighty years later, it also suggests that, despite the claims of Anglo travel writers and imperial ethnographers, the territory was far from "empty" of Mexicanos. Santa Cruz de Hughes further suggests, ironically, that if the territory had been emptied, it was "emptied" not by the force of Apache wars or Sonoran colonial failure but by Anglo aggression.

She notes that in preparation for leaving, the first order of business for women [la primera preocupación de las mujeres] was to dismantle the chapel dedicated to Our Lady of Guadalupe. This labor culminated in an incredible procession.

> Los soldados consiguieron no sé de donde un carro de cuatro ruedas con cuatro bestias, y lo cargaron con los cuadros y santos (entre los últimos el crucifijo de Nuestro Señor de Esquípulas, que hoy día está en la iglesia de Magdalena, Sonora), víveres, pastura, y todo el archivo del pueblo (que por cierto habían haber dejado, ya que de nada les servía), y asi salieron, unos a pie y otros montados, entre los últimos varias mujeres que cargaban criaturas, uno adelante y otro en ancas.
> [The soldiers obtained, I don't know from where, a four-wheeled cart with four animals, and they filled it with the paintings and statues (among the last was the crucifix of Our Lord of Esquípulas, that today is in the church in Magdalena, Sonora), food supplies, feed and the entire city archive (which they should certainly have left behind, because it was of no use to them), and thus they left, some on foot and others mounted, among the last were various women bearing children, one in front and another on the back.][47]

Doña Santa Cruz de Hughes, remembering a scene after seventy years, still suggests a kind of wonder mixed with practicality as she recalls the dismantling of the heart of her community—its religious symbols and public records, as well as food and feed. The scene begins with women caring for the communal memory that the church santos and retablos represent and concludes with women caring for the communal future, which lies with the children. Mixed into this portrait of working women are asides that suggest some doubt about the soldiers—doubt rendered in hindsight (Santa Cruz de Hughes later complains about the loss of the archives, the loss of a record of three-hundred years of Mexican work and life).[48] The parade exemplifies not only what the community valued, what it sensed it must preserve from Anglo marauders, but also what it might need to survive and rebuild. Yet, perhaps most stunning about this recollection is the portrait it provides of the other side of Manifest Destiny. For here is not the glorious march of Anglo expansionism but its dis-remembered underbelly: a community sensing itself endangered, threatened, under siege, and scared enough to walk eighty miles behind its religious and civic memory in search of safety.

Santa Cruz de Hughes interrupts herself to deny the claim that when the U.S. soldiers arrived, Mexican soldiers lowered the Mexican flag and U.S. soldiers raised the U.S. flag.

> No hubo nada del episodio de la arreada del pabellón mexicano y la izada del americano; en primer lugar porque no existía esta bandera en Tucson, y en segundo porque tampoco existía bandera mexicana que yo sepa, y tan seguro estoy de esto que ni siquiera llegé a conocer dicha bandera hasta mucho mas tarde. Todo esto yo lo ví, puesto que como muchacha de seis años anduve entre la bola, como suele decirse comunmente.
>
> [There never was an episode in which the Mexican flag was lowered and the American hoisted; in the first place there wasn't a flag in Tucson, and second, because scarcely any Mexican flags existed that I know of, and I am so certain of this because it was only much later that I became familiar with that flag. All of this I saw because I was a six-year-old girl running around with a gang as the saying typically goes.][49]

Having described a somewhat horrific scene of exilic departure, Santa Cruz de Hughes narratively slides backward to assert that no *formal* ceremony of possession or dispossession took place. Her comments suggest a desire to refute what may have been a common assumption among her contemporaries, as well as a desire to remember the anxiety the community felt about the ensuing arrival of U.S. soldiers. That is, people didn't stick around for a formal ceremony of dispossession. Her comments also suggest the complex relationship the pueblo may have had with the Mexican national government because of its status as a frontier outpost with few significant bureaucratic or symbolic ties to the central Mexican government.[50] But she insists that she saw these events as a young child, which both suggests that her recollections are naive, even innocent, and, given her self-description as running around in a little knot or ball with other children, allows her to authorize herself as a kind of *pícaro* observer. Thus, her apparent digression, rather than simply discounting a local myth, also serves to reinforce her point that people fled in haste, fearing an assault by U.S. troops. At the same time, the pleasurable image evoked by a dicho describing a knot of children roaming around town like a bouncing ball similarly recodes these activities not simply as crisis but as a form of entertainment, thereby indicating the extent to which historical memory may indeed be dependent on the whimsy of pleasure.

Santa Cruz de Hughes's vehement assertion that this ceremony of possession did not take place is countered by the testimonio of another Mexicana, Carmen Lucero, whose narrative explicitly counters this memory.[51] Recalling her mother's recollections, Lucero notes: "The day the troops took possession there was lots of excitement. They raised the flag on the wall and the people welcomed them with a fiesta and they were all on good terms." Yet whether or not a formal ceremony took place, with the ongoing threat of further U.S. incursions into Mexico and the continual arming of Apaches (by the U.S. army and settlers) to fight as a client battalion against Mexicanos, fear functioned as something of a psychological ceremony of possession.[52]

Santa Cruz de Hughes and her family did not join the exodus to Magdalena and Altar. She remained in Tucson along with her aunt and sister despite the rumors of Anglo violence.

> Mí tía le preguntó [John Capron, a stage-coach driver,] que si era cierto lo que se decía de los atropellos cometidos por los soldados americanos, y contestó que en cuanto a estos si no tumbieramos más que un pliego de papel que nos serviera de puerta esto sería suficiente mientras no dieramos lugar para que nos la rompiesen; respuesta que resolvío a mí tía no abandonar nuestra casa.
>
> [My aunt asked him if what was being said about the atrocities committed by the American soldiers was true and he answered that in regards to the soldiers, if we had no more than a piece of paper to serve as

our door, it would be sufficient if we did not give them cause to break it; with this answer my aunt resolved not to abandon our home.][53]

A threat accompanies the reassurance, making the stagecoach driver's response chilling. Rather than dismiss her fears entirely, he warns her to obey, to follow the disciplinary demands of the soldier, to not "give them cause." His answer thereby doubles as threat and prophecy; the language of "papers" foreshadows the terminology used by immigration authorities for the next 150 years to deny Mexicanos due process and citizenship. Furthermore, the stagecoach driver's response implies that soldiers might indeed commit atrocities if given cause, but as so often occurs in disciplinary rhetoric, what that cause might be is left unspoken, unspecified. Given the lack of specificity, the trio of mujeres' decision to remain in Tucson despite the exodus, despite the ambiguous nature of the soon-to-be-occupying army, indicates extraordinary strength and commitment. Their choice to stay in Tucson and not to abandon their home exemplifies a refusal "to be disappeared" either through the production of an imaginary landscape or through the machinations of an imperial army.

Santa Cruz de Hughes wryly comments that those neighbors who left with the troops went only as far as Imuris or Magdalena and that most returned after a little over a month when they saw that the U.S. troops were not committing atrocities.[54] And while ample evidence suggests that Mexicanos indeed had cause for alarm about the arrival of U.S. troops, the ragtag band of dragoons that arrived in Tucson in 1856 indicated not U.S. vindictiveness but rather U.S. ambivalence about the new territories. Such ambivalence would not, of course, continue. Over the span of seventy years Doña Atanacia Santa Cruz de Hughes witnessed an extraordinary transformation of the region. She also witnessed an extraordinary growth of Mexicano culture in Southern Arizona, a growth that her contemporaries understood not in terms of the Gadsden Purchase, nor indeed the liberation of Mexico from Spain, but in terms of the movement of the Mexica peoples from Aztlán to the Valley of Mexico and back again.

Mexicanos who were contemporary witnesses to their own disarticulation responded avidly by countering Anglo assertions that the region contained no history—indeed, could be characterized only as forbidding or terrifying or depraved. Consider, for example, Ignacio Bonillas's address to the "Club Union" on the occasion of the celebration of the sixty-eighth anniversary of the independence of Mexico. Bonillas begins his address, re-printed in *El Fronterizo,* by reminding his audience that the Greeks cele-brated their festivals in part by remembering the glories of their progeni-tors. Thus he urges his audience to celebrate Mexico's heritage by recalling the Mexica pilgrimage from Aztlán "para ir en busca de un país mejor, mas hermoso y mas fértil" (in search of a better country, more beautiful and more fertile); their eventual settlement in el Valle de Mexico; the conquest of the Américas; and the subsequent arrival of Spanish conquistadores. What might appear to be a standard recitation of Mexico's history, however, takes on local import in Bonillas's retelling.

> Las ruinas de las ciudades que edificaron en su transito, contemplamos aun en nuestros dias. En este territorio de Arizona, en Nuevo Mexico y en Sonora, tenemos muchisimas ruinas de las ciudades que muchos años ha florecieron bajo el gobierno de los antiguos Aztecas. Los habi-tantes que entonces habitaban estas regiones, eran enteramente salvajes, por consiguiente, no pueden ser los autores de los edificios que ni la fuerza de los años, ni las intemperies del tiempo, han podido destruir por completo. De esto se infiere que los Aztecas en sus peregrinaciónes las construyeron.
> [Even today we can gaze at the ruins of the cities that they built dur-ing their passage. In this territory of Arizona, in New Mexico and in Sonora, we have many ruins of the cities that flourished for many years under the government of the ancient Aztecs. The inhabitants living in these regions were complete savages and, as a consequence, they could not be the authors of buildings that not even the force of years nor bad weather have been able to destroy completely. From this we infer that the Aztecs constructed them during their long journey.][55]

Bonillas's comment accomplishes a number of subtle goals. It connects the region, largely marginalized from canonical Mexican history, to its cele-brated Aztec past. He thereby elevates Arizona from lost frontier outpost to place of origin—Aztlán, homeland of the nation itself. In so doing he transforms the landscape from neglected settlement caught in a thirty-year tripartite war between Anglos, Apaches, and Mexicanos, to a region with a glorious history. Such a maneuver connects Tucsonenses to a history ex-tending back past Anglo-colonists, past the arrival of Marcos de Niza, past

Jamestown, past Cortez and Columbus, and grants them a nearly sacred claim to Arizona. Such a connection, however, must come at the cost of constructing other peoples as "savages." This gesture thereby produces the necessary distance between those proclaiming themselves as Mexicanos and those whom they fought and disparaged. On the one hand, such a contrapuntal narrative of precolonial presence reauthorizes Mexicano claims to the area, but, on the other hand, it relies on a tired hierarchy of conquest.

Bonillas's reconstruction of history, though farsighted, is also ambivalent. He spoke, perhaps, with an eye toward the transformations the then-under-construction railroad would bring. His assertion, in 1878 no less, that Mexicanos held a 700-year claim to the region changes the angles of vision of historical memory by undercutting the proliferating narratives of Mexican disappearance and migration that have been used to disarticulate their cultural and land claims. Bonillas thereby establishes a new intellectual framework by which Mexicano presence in Southern Arizona may be understood and proudly proclaimed.[56] Interestingly, he attempts to construct such a framework by placing Mexicano claims to the land prior to the arrival of either the Spanish or the British; his strategy once again suggests the extent to which narratives of temporality frequently structure nationalist claims to land, indeed consistently structure the production of space and place.

Bonillas's speech might have been one of the earliest to use the concept of Aztlán, that is, to invoke Aztlán to gain political and moral ground in the battle for Mexicano and eventually Chicana/o civil rights. Bonillas's turn to Aztlán, one of the first references uncovered to date, baldly points toward its ambivalent value as liberatory or revolutionary icon.[57] Not only does Bonillas's centralization of the Aztec past as the standard-bearer of Mexico's pre-Cortesian history elide the complexity of Mexico as a nation of nations with distinct languages, cultures, and territories, but his dismissiveness toward local peoples with far more entrenched claims to the region (particularly the Tohono O'odham) indicates the ambivalent structure of mythical Aztlán, an ambivalence that would continue to trouble its appropriators one hundred years later during the Chicano Movimiento. Bonillas's dismissiveness presages the complexity through which Mexican citizenship would be constructed throughout the twentieth century: because he invokes a Mexican mestizaje in part by distancing it from local and present Indians, he thus simultaneously affirms, denies, and defers Mexicano mestizaje. The affirmation of mestizaje, of Aztec ancestors, depends on its deferral into the past, establishing a temporal shield of sorts through a denial of contemporary relations, of ongoing mestizaje.

Given this ambivalence, Bonillas's rhetorical strategy not surprisingly dovetails with the strategy of William Ritch, secretary of the Territory of New Mexico, who seven years later published *Aztlán: The History, Resources, and Attractions of New Mexico*. Though bent on further dislodging Hispano claims to New Mexico, Ritch similarly depends on a mythic construction of a distant past and a ruinous portrayal of contemporary Indians. As Ramón Gutiérrez explains, Ritch's use of Aztlán preyed on an "America that in the 1880s was lamenting its spiritual impoverishment and searching for new inspiration in mythology and legends" while simultaneously reducing, even decimating, local people's options, cultures, means of subsistence, and rights.[58] Narratives of Aztec possession of Arizona even earlier than Ritch's or Bonillas's can be found—for example, in Territorial Representative Charles Poston's speech before Congress in 1865.[59] But Poston, unlike Bonillas, claimed that present-day occupants were the "degenerate descendants" of the Aztecs. In all cases, references to Aztecs and Arizona-as-Aztlán are fraught with racial hierarchies.

Visible in Bonillas's invocation of Aztlán is an early indication of the uses to which the mythical Mexica homeland would be put one hundred years later by Chicanos who, as Rafael Pérez-Torres notes, would affirm a "glorious past" in order to condemn "a repressive present."[60] Bonillas's speech, coming less than twenty-five short years after the Anglo colonization of mineral-rich northern Sonora, suggests not simply the significance of the production of space to conceptions of subjectivity or citizenship, or indeed to national belonging, but also suggests that how a region is conceptualized and placed within historical, national narratives has more than a minor effect on the image of the locale itself. For if the production of space entails a production of sociality, then a counternarrative of space, in this instance, an alternative spatial genealogy, offers, again in Pérez-Torres's words, "the means of a counter discursive engagement."[61]

Yet for Bonillas, such a counterdiscursive engagement must come in terms of a reproduction of a racist sociality. Given Bonillas's long narrative of Mexica and Mexican history, from precolonial Aztlán to 1878 Aztlán, as a series of masculinist victories and defeats, complete with a traitorous Ma-

linche, his production of place (an Aztlán-ification of Arizona) entails a gendered, patriarchal sociality. Bonillas offers a characterization of southern
Arizona that is only partly in contradiction to that produced by Anglo colonialists. That is, Bonillas maintains a racial and gender hierarchy different in
details but similar in fundamentals to that constructed by his Anglo peers.[62]

Two weeks after Bonillas's speech, yet another narrative of Tucson was
printed in *El Fronterizo*.[63] The far-less-romantic essay "El Tucson" also
sought to adjust the angles of vision by which Tucson was seen by subtly
countering the narratives of mud and depravity promulgated by Anglo
writers. The author, probably the newspaper's editor Carlos Velasco, describes the city in glowing terms, citing its "rapid progress," its flourishing businesses, its technologically advanced methods of communication, its
churches, and its schools. In this account, Tucson, rather than being filled
with "desperados" and anxious about "Apache depredations," is packed with
miners and prospectors and fantasies about new and richer mineral discoveries. The mineral discoveries were so frequent, the author notes, that three
assay offices were "constantly" at work. Similarly, numerous buildings were
under construction in a city approaching 5,000 permanent inhabitants and
with countless temporary residents (*la población flotante*). Carpenters, black-
smiths, tailors, butchers, bakeries, flour mills, shoe stores, and restaurants
flourished alongside opportunities for recreation. Or, as the author puts
it, "Tampoco faltan á nuestra ciudad alegres lugares de recreo, tales como
el Pueblito donde D. Leopoldo Carillo está formando un bonito jardin"
(Our city scarcely lacks happy places for recreation such as the development
where Don Leopoldo Carillo is building a pretty garden). Carillo Gardens
would subsequently serve as an important counterpublic space for Tucsonenses, serving increasingly as the alternative site of public pleasure, particularly as Anglo colonists maneuvered Mexicanos out of all positions of
political and juridical power.[64]

The stability and development of the city is further underscored by an
account, recorded fifty years later, from a Mexicana who recalled her parents' memories of Tucson in the nineteenth century: "Life was very simple.
Each man had his little piece of land down below the walled city where he
raised beans, lentils, onions, squash, garvanzas, chili, wheat, tomatoes, and
corn. There were some fruit trees with peaches, pears, and quinces. Most
everyone raised pigs, rendered lard and made salt pork. There was no such

thing as anyone hiring a man for pay. If a man needed help his neighbors went out and helped. At harvest time many neighbors would help—some would stand guard while the others worked.[65]

If Carmen Lucero's *memoria* focuses less on urbanization and city amenities, it nevertheless underscores "El Tucson's" claim to being a city that scarcely lacks "alegres lugares." What these narratives offer, in addition to lists of amenities and suggestions of abundance, are, at least in narrative terms, the production of counterspaces bent on refusing what Lefebvre calls the "imposition of homogeneity and transparency."[66] Like Bonillas, the author of "El Tucson" looks forward to the arrival of the railroad: "Entonces el Tucson llegando al apojeo de su grandeza con los múltiples elementos de prosperidad que la rodean, vendrá á ser, no hay que dudarlo, la envidia de muchos pueblos, el punto de vista de grandes capitales, y el emporio del comercio y del tráfico de estas dilatads cuanto ricas regiones [Then Tucson will become the apex of grandeur with multiple elements of prosperity surrounding it; it will come to be, there is no doubt about it, the envy of many cities, the point of view of great capitals, and the emporium of commerce and traffic from this expansive and rich region].[67] The celebratory tone and ornate rhetorical structure mirror the type of predictions that Anglo narratives offered. But, importantly, "El Tucson" begins from different grounds—from a celebration of its existing structure and pride in its current development. Rather than denigrating Mexicanos in order to elevate Anglos, this point of view includes, even centers, Mexicanos within the portrait of a utopic transformation. By offering an alternative spatial narrative, one that pauses to note the development of Carrillo Gardens, the author critiques the prevailing Anglo effort to racialize and demonize Mexicans through the production of spatial narratives.

It is precisely around "the clash and disarticulation of peoples" that, as Fernando Coronil notes, modernity depends.[68] For Anglo ethnographers and travel writers, producing Arizona through an alchemy of wonder, race, and desire required a construction of the region that disarticulated Mexicano history and presence and narratively reduced the region to a wasteland of abandoned settlements and desperate people. On such grounds ethnographers and travel writers hoped to build their own positivist modernity. Yet for those Mexicanos combating the groundswell of disarticulation, the ethnographers and travel writers were producing a "modernity" out of a deficit, and it was that deficit they feared, not necessarily the promised modernity.

Therefore, in this crucial period of contestation, Mexicano essayists sought to produce a narrative of U.S. sociality that would highlight the failures of imperial capitalism. Through such a maneuver they attempted to gain a kind of moral upper hand in order to rearticulate a Mexicano sociospatiality that could effectively compete for hegemony over the region.

While the Anglo-Arizona landscape largely depicted a disappearing, depraved, licentious Mexican culture, an essay published in *Las Dos Repúblicas* in July of 1877 countered such assertions by arguing for a conception of Mexican culture as superior but under siege. The only manner in which such a besieged community could thrive and regain spatial control, the writer argued, was by refusing to disappear as the ethnographic alchemists envisioned. Indeed the essay, "De la discusion nace la luz" begins with this very contention.

> Entre las dos pueblos que ocupan al continente de América, los del norte gozan de un gobierno fuerte de una industria y empresa sin igual, y de todas las ventajas materiales de la civilizacion Europea. Pero á todo esto le falta alma, el principio vivificante de un sistema moral. Asi, en medio de su prosperidad, se descubren de cuando en cuando, los indicio fatales del barbarismo.
>
> [Between the two peoples that occupy the continent of America, those of the north enjoy a strong government, an industry and enterprise without equal, and all of the material advantages of European civilization. But all of this lacks soul, the living principle of a moral system. Thus in the midst of its prosperity you can discover from time to time the fatal indices of barbarism.][69]

The author argues that rather than seeing the United States as the epitome of civilization, the standard-bearer of modernity, readers would do well to look for the cracks in U.S. social fabric—cracks evinced by the development of "spiritualism," "Free Love," "women's rights," "divorce," and "mormonism." Such developments, the author contends, indicate that "moralmente el Anglo Saxon no tiene poder ni para perpetuar el patrimonio de civilizacion" [Morally, the Anglo Saxon does not have the willpower to perpetuate the patrimony of civilization]. Here the author implicitly emasculates Anglo men, stripping them of their capacity to reproduce a culture. By contrast, he argues that Mexicanos have inherited a rich civilization, indeed, "la civilizacion latina superará al fin, por la fuerza de la superioridad moral" [Latina civilization will finally succeed by force of superior morality]. Despite such superiority, the author argues for strategic realism, acknowledging that "En el choque de estas dos sociedades, nuestro poder fisico es vano" [In a conflict between these two societies our physical power is futile]. Maintaining a superior moral code, in this case Catholicism, is not enough "para lograr victoria en la batalla social" [in order to gain victory in the social battle]. Instead, the author proposes a process of transculturation in which the "Saxon" adopts Mexican customs in order to gain a soul and Mexicanos learn to take advantage of their current circumstances. For if they do not, then Anglos will "nos arrojen del pais natal, que desaparezca nuestra raza y nuestra lengua" [hurl us from our native land and cause our race and our language to vanish].

How much more forcefully could the writer state the stakes of the "batalla"? Quivira, as the author was identified, understood the intentions of the Anglo travelers and ethnographers as well as the arriving miners and capitalists: "La batalla que sostenemos aqui en Arizona en esta guerra de razas, es primero moral, y segunda fisica. De la primera dependen nuestras costumbres, de la segunda nuestra existencia" [The battle that we are enduring here in Arizona in this war of races is first moral and second physical. On the first depends our culture and on the second our existence].

Quivira saw that Anglo hegemony predicated itself on a racialized hierarchy that threatened not only a community's cultural structure but its members' very lives. The force of such language was not simply rhetorical. Throughout the 1870s the undeclared war against Mexico wrought havoc on Mexicanos in Arizona—ongoing battles over land grants, increasingly racialized laws instituting dual wage structures, obstructions to Mexican entrepreneurship, and unremitting violence clearly threatened the lives and well-being of not just Tucsonenses but Sonorenses as well. Waging an effective battle against demolition involved, not taking up arms, but rather active involvement in politics and business.

According to Quivira, as an "advance guard" Tucsonenses had to maintain their faith, customs, and language, cultivate a capitalism that would rival "El Saxon en industria," accumulate wealth, and fight "el imperio del estado" by electing officials who would enact laws that conformed to their interests and who would look after Mexicano welfare. Pursuing such involvement would help ensure not simply local survival but Latin America's sovereignty more generally: "Estamos aqui, pues, la guardia advanzada de la civilizacion latina en América y nuestro deber es mantener nuestro puesto contra el ataque de las hordas del norte" [We are here as the advance guard of Latin American civilization and our command is to maintain our position against the attack of the Northern hordes].

Quivira argues that such political involvement must be understood in the context of U.S. expansionism: "El caso es que los Estados Unidos han ya tomado gran parte de México; será por esto que debemos de abandonar el tereno, é irnos replegando paso á paso hasta que nos arrojen al oceano, como hicieron con los indígenas" [The fact is that the United States has already taken a great portion of Mexico; it will be the same for us, they will force us to abandon our land and retreat bit by bit until they hurl us into the ocean like they did with the Indians]. Quivira's rhetoric intensifies with each passing phrase, building toward the apocalyptic picture of Mexicanos being hurled into the ocean. Yet the memory of Indian genocide (a memory that ignores Spanish colonial tactics of genocide) girds this portrait, signaling the vitriolic force of imperial desire—one that Sonorans had practiced themselves. Quivira's critique of U.S. policy and his prophecy that Mexicanos would be treated "like Indians" would have had a profound resonance for *Las Dos Repúblicas'* readers because it turned a racial/social hierarchy violently enforced by Sonoran elite back in on themselves.[70]

But, interestingly, Quivira did not allow the comparison of Mexicanos with Indians to last, suggesting instead that Mexicanos learn from U.S. Southerners: "No Señor, aprendamos de los Surianos que aceptaron el juicio de las armas y se rindieron, pero solo para cambiar sus tácticas del campo de batalla á la política y á los salones del congress" [No gentlemen, we must learn from the Southerners who accepted the judgment of arms and surrendered but only in order to change their tactics from the battle camp to politics and the salons of Congress].[71] For Quivira, the South's white establishment was, as Reconstruction began to wane, reestablishing its forces through political mobility. Understanding the potential of electoral politics, Quivira maintained, would be a key component, in combination with a strengthened if conservative sociality, of surviving the Saxon onslaught.

"De la discusion nace la luz" stands out in its rhetorical vehemence from other essays published in the 1870s and 1880s in Tucson newspapers. Far more than most, it audaciously announces a crisis and a virtual state of siege. Indeed, it suggests that the crisis Santa Cruz de Hughes's neighbors feared had, if more slowly than predicted, come to pass. But, additionally, Quivira turns on end the rhetoric of barbarism versus civilization used by Anglos to characterize Mexicans and reframes the debate around Mexican superiority, suggesting that Mexicans are like Roman citizens fighting the Visigoths. Similarly, Quivira appropriates the very language of scientific racism for Tucsonenses' own nationalist ends. Quivira's gesture, like Bonillas's, depends on an attempt to hold the moral center and to reframe debate to Mexicano advantage. Yet what also seems clear more than 120 years later is how modern the author's rhetoric was and how much it anticipated the terms later deployed by Chicano Movimiento activists: he argues for the strength of Mexican culture, language, and family structure; he calls for Mexicans to become politically active; and he insists that Mexicans turn to entrepreneurship to gain financial leverage.

If writers such as Quivira argued as persuasively and clearly as possible that "Anglo Saxons" threatened the culture and life of Mexicanos, they also wrote allegorically, relying on a tradition of romance and sentimentality to convey a critique of Anglo dominance. Just as *Elena y Jorge* depicted the French Intervention in symbolic terms—Elena representing the desirable land of Mexico and Jorge its loyal, native defenders and suitors—"Sombras de Amor" (Shades of Love), published in 1877 in *Las Dos Repúblicas*, turns to the allegorical romance in order to offer an ambiguous critique of Arizona law and politics as well as of the idealization of white women.[72] The authorship of "Sombras de Amor" is uncertain—it is signed simply "A.R." Armando Miguélez argues that, given the story's romantic content, the author can be presumed to be a woman.[73] Many other essays, poems, and stories published in *Las Dos Repúblicas, El Tucsonenses,* and *El Fronterizo* during this period, however, were also signed only with initials, and men surely were as capable as women of writing allegorical romances.[74] Furthermore, as Gabriel Meléndez argues in his crucial work on Nuevomexicano periodiqueros, pseudonyms and aliases were common, a long literary convention frequently deployed in Latin American literature.[75] The gender of the author therefore cannot be presumed.

The narrator introduces the story with a dicho: "Cada casa es un mundo y cada hombre una historia" [Each home is a world and each man, a history]. The saying underscores the anonymity of the story itself, placing it within the realm of commonsense and myth. The story begins as the narrator recalls a beautiful and balmy spring night in 1863—a night when "las fuentes de sus encantos, para acariciar con ellos los ensueños de los enamorados, los recuerdos de las almas doloridas; las esperanzas de las imaginaciones exal-tadas, las ilusiones de los corazones vírgenes" [The fountains of enchantment caress lovers' dreams, the memories of sorrowful souls, the hopes of exalted imaginations, and the illusions of virgin hearts].

On just such a magical night the narrator encounters a beautiful woman at a birthday dance. Before offering a description of her, however, the narrator interjects that their meeting took place more than ten years before this re-counting of the story and asks "¿Quereis saber que significan diez años . . . ?" [Who knows what ten years mean?]. The narrator answers by arguing that ten years mean many things but symbolize in particular "una cuenta de los desengaños aumentada en una cifra fabulosa; las palpitaciones del corazon disminuidas; la fé en la amistad, menguada, la sombra de la dicha casi des-vanecida; el placer que acaba, el hastío que comienza, la alegría que muere, la tristeza que nace; un caudal en fin, de ilusiones perdidas!!!"[a story of in-creasing disillusionment, of diminishing heart palpitations, of waning faith in friendship, with the shades of happiness dissolving, the pleasure that had arrived and just begun dies, sadness is born, in the end, a torrent of lost illusions!!!].

Through a framework of disillusionment the narrator underscores the impossibility of happiness. For justification, to explain the vastness of his loss, the narrator turns to a description of "Enriqueta": "un tipo digno de un pincel maestro" [a figure who would dignify a master artist's brush]. Tell-ing readers to imagine a statue "completamente armonizada con sus formas" [completely in harmony], the narrator anatomizes Enriqueta by parceling out lavish descriptions of her eyes, eyelashes, hair, lips, and skin which he describes as "como una taza de alabastro, limpio como un cielo sin nubes, transparente como el velo de gasa de una vírgen" [like a cup of alabaster, clear as a cloudless sky, transparent as the gauze veil of a virgin]. Yet even this effusive description, the narrator laments, cannot approximate the beauty of Enriqueta.

The narrator turns to the details of their first meeting, noting the mag-netism that existed between them and the pleasures of dancing together. The two walk to a balcony where "la luna en toda la plentitud de su belleza, bañaba de llenos y perpendicularmente, el interesante rostro de Enriqueta" [the moon in its fullest beauty bathed the plain and, perpendicularly, the face of Enriqueta]. The narrator continues to celebrate the ideal, even sublime, beauty of Enriqueta, but even in the midst of such beauty begins to feel the coldness of death creeping up on him, so much so that "me abandonamba su mano, cuya frialdad era realmente cadavérica! Oh! yo hubiera querido en aquel momento prestar á Enriqueta el fuego todo de mi volcanizada de sangre!" [I dropped her hand whose iciness was in reality cadaverous. Oh how in that moment I wanted to lend Enriqueta all of the fire of my volcanic blood!].

Enriqueta slowly begins to fade, becoming more ethereal, more poetic, and, not surprisingly, the "brilliant light of day" reveals that "el baile con sus luces, su música y sus parejas, eran sombras de mi fantasía. Pasado el sueño, despierto á la realidad, y la realidad me sofoca" [the dance, with its lights, its music, its dancers, were shadows in my imagination. The dream disappeared, and I awoke to reality, and reality suffocates me]. But the illusion of the beautiful Enriqueta is so powerful, so magnetic, that "reality" becomes unbearable and the narrator in a lamenting, concluding question asks, "Será que estoy condenado á no ver ni encontrar esas creaciones de mi fantasía, á las que llamo sombras de amor, sino en mis cortas horas de ensueños y delirio? [Might it be that I am condemned never to see or find such creations of my fantasies that I call shadows of love except in the short hours of dreams and delirium?].

True to its allegorical form, out of the shadows of "Sombras de Amor" dance a number of possible interpretations. Its closing question demands interpretation, reinscribes the importance of imagination and fantasy in terms of painful social reality. Its presence on the front page of the second issue of *Las Dos Repúblicas,* alongside less ambivalently opaque discourses such as "De la discusion nace la luz," further suggest the viability of literature as a means, in Barbara Johnson's words, of doing "cultural work, the work of giving-to-read those impossible contradictions that cannot yet be spoken."[76]

What are the contradictions exposed and cultural work done by "Sombras"? "Sombras" might be read as a powerful and early, if misogynist, critique of fetishized whiteness—where the seeming transcendence and ideality of whiteness are revealed as a deathly, frigid, disappearing mirage. Already by 1877 racial discourse in the United States had clearly established the figure of the white woman to stand for whiteness as both object of veneration and as a form of property. The ethnographies and travelogues of Arizona predicated their productions of the region through the discourse of mongrelization. And such narratives clearly informed public policy. In an area like southern Arizona, where the consequences of racial narratives of degenerate mongrelization turned explicitly on the notion of racial purity (again, repeatedly invoked by the white virgin) and where such narratives were used to render significant harm, a meditation on the fourteen-year effects of the mirage of whiteness would provide the opportunity for an unusually subtle critique. "Sombras" implies whiteness as the conjured fantasy of delirium—a fantasy whose strength continually "suffocates" the present through its powerful unobtainability.

But "Sombras" offers additional possibilities. The author utilizes the romance genre to both critique the notion of romantic love by depicting the debilitating effects of such a fantasy and also to destabilize the power of "white women." In this sense, "Sombras" suggests that the fantasy has granted only a continual sense of present loss and lack, of impossibility and distance, rather than a combustive and creative sense of future pleasure. Thus, the story might be read as a critique not of whiteness specifically but of the celebration of white women as superior to Mexicanas in a region where white women were understood to be scarce commodities.

Perhaps most important, "Sombras" offers an allusion that allows a very different interpretation. The narrator introduces the story by quite specifically noting that the encounter took place in the spring of 1863 ("Estábamos en la primavera de 1863"). In 1863, shortly after the Confederate troops who had seized Tucson and declared it a Confederate territory were routed from the area by northern forces, the U.S. Congress passed the Arizona Organic Act. Passed amid much controversy, the Organic Act divided the territory of New Mexico in half, thereby establishing two territories destined for statehood: New Mexico and Arizona. Dividing New Mexico effectively handed control of what became the territory of Arizona to mining interests. It also changed the juridical and political power dynamics—Nuevomexicanos could no longer curtail Anglos' racialized designs on Arizona. In some sense, this act was the teleological culmination of years of Anglo narrative production and a seal of approval, as it were, on the landscape eagerly anticipated by so many colonial enthusiasts. The Organic Act, in other words, provided the opportunity to begin full scale work on the Anglo Arizona landscape.

It might be helpful to understand the Organic Act not simply in terms of the practical organization of an empire (dividing New Mexico involved dividing a territory more than half the size of Europe), but rather in terms of its importance to establishing Anglo hegemony in the state. Arizona was created, over the objections of nearly half of Congress, because its proponents claimed that Anglos could not flourish in a region governed by New Mexico. Implicit in their arguments was the notion that due to the existing colonial structure Anglos would have to submit to (Nuevo) Mexicano judges, governors, and police, something Anglos maintained was beneath them. Congressional opponents of the Organic Act were not concerned with such racism but rather with the lack of Anglos living in the region. As one leader of the opposition to territorial status put it, "This government never organized a Territory for so small a white population as even the maximum in Arizona."[77] Beyond the difficulties of traveling 400 miles to court and the state house, Anglos in Arizona understood that they could not control the region and impose anti-Mexican policies as long as Mexicanos in New Mexico maintained some political strength. The passage of the Organic Act made it possible to establish what would become apartheid-like conditions for Mexicans in Arizona. Such conditions included differential wage scales, prohibitions against Mexicans starting or maintaining mines, various English-only initiatives, disenfranchisement of Mexican voters, and so forth.[78]

By locating the encounter with Enriqueta shortly after the Organic Act was established, "Sombras" offers an elusive commentary on the production of Arizona as the Anglo complement to the Nuevomexicano other. Additionally, it suggests in less generous terms that the celebratory narrative of what territorial status would offer to Mexicanos had been nothing more than "la brillantez á la par que el cansancio de la mirada de un calenturiento" [the brilliant mirage seen by an exhausted victim of heatstroke]. Upending the "foundational fiction" by revealing how "erotics and politics" had always already "join[ed] forces" in the production not just of Arizona but of the United States, "Sombras" suggests that the symbolic heterosexual union of racialized other and whiteness could not indeed function as foundational, could not overcome ethnoracial-economic roadblocks, for exposure to "la brillante luz del día" revealed it to be the product of delirium.[79] In this manner, the allegory refutes a romance of nation and expresses nothing but regret, loss, and dismay over the effects of the Organic Act's intervening fourteen years. Increasing violence, increasingly intractable dual wage structures, and the closure of the courts and legal and political systems to Mexican participation ensured that, as A.R. suggests, the story of Arizona territorial status was indeed one of "increasing disillusionment, diminishing heart palpitations, of waning faith in friendship, with the shades of happiness dissolving."

Thus, A.R.'s "Sombras de Amor" considers the emergence of Arizona as an illusory promise: Mexicanos will not "possess" the region symbolized by Enriqueta, just as they won't possess the seeming enchantments of citizenship reserved for Anglos, just as in the years after the French Intervention the Mexican working classes were more and more dispossessed of the land symbolized by the figure of Elena. The American rhetoric of inclusion and democracy collides with the ideology of Saxon racial superiority and manifest destiny, revealing the first to be a delusion and the second to bring the coldness of death. The plaintiveness of "Sombras" folds into the anger of Quivera's critique, printed on the subsequent pages; as a pair, the two texts offer imposing indices of the future critique of Anglo hegemony that would emerge in Arizona.

Patricia Preciado Martin's "The Journey" concludes when the narrator discovers a flower growing through a crack in the asphalt covering her Tía's razed home:

> "Ah, mihita," she says at last. Her eyes are shining. "You have found out the secret of our journeys."
> "What secret, Tía?"
> "Que las flores siempre ganan. The flowers always win."

While this moment may be read as an overly sentimental attempt to put a hopeful spin on a very painful story, the scene also suggests a determination born of surviving the onslaught of violence. The flower poking through the asphalt indicates not just the strength of nature, but given the importance of gardens to Tucsonenses, the strength of the Mexicano legacy and will to resist disappearance and defeat.[80] In this sense, "The Journey" stands also as a memorial to the extraordinary efforts of Tucsonenses in the nineteenth century to battle their obliteration. Furthermore, reading this contemporary story in terms of its archived predecessors illuminates the extent to which the landscape that "The Journey" contests emerged not through consensus and rugged individualism but through conflict and repression. Yet if Anglo colonialists thought they had razed Arizona, they failed to understand a cultural project with very tenacious roots.

It was still necessary then, more than thirty years after the publication of "Sombras de Amor," for Anglo capitalists to assert their control of the region continuously. The grand buildings such as the El Paso and Southwestern Railroad Depot built at the edge of the Gadsden Purchase signaled their triumph but also warned against the efforts (actively championed by Mexican revolutionaries) to deprive them of their control of the region. Not surprisingly, the U.S.–Mexico border became once again crucial as a place of contest and coercion, resistance, and critique.

2

Double-Crossing la Frontera Nómada

Frida Kahlo's 1932 painting "Self-Portrait on the Border Line Between Mexico and the United States" narrates national difference through a visual depiction of temporal disjunctures.[1] Kahlo's self-portrait divides the painting into an uneven diptych. On her right side, Mexico is represented by the partially excavated ruins of a temple. Pre-Cortesian deities and stone rubble fill the barren ground as a fiery sun and enraged moon battle each other. At the bottom, lavish flowering plants crowd the frame, their roots extending downward, mimicking the thunder striking the temple above. On the smaller, U.S. side, skyscrapers and a Ford factory fill the area. In contrast with images of deities, robotic air ducts crowd the foreground; a U.S. flag emerges out of the puffing exhaust from the Ford factory smokestacks. A generator supplying electricity to the U.S. industrial complex is plugged into the roots of one of the Mexican plants and the base of the border monument. This electrical connection between the body-border monument, the Mexican plants, and the industrial complex dramatically illustrates how U.S. capital depends on both the natural resources of Mexico and the very border between the two nations.

By rendering her body as the border, or rather by rendering her body as an extension of the boundary marker on which she stands and thereby echoing the odalisque boundary markers built long before border fences were in place, Kahlo suggests that it is at the scale of the body that nation-states most effectively police and direct their economies and resources. She reinforces that position by portraying herself in a long, pink dress, typical of the style worn during the late nineteenth century—the period of Porfirio Díaz's dictatorship. This anachronistic fashion detail ironically and subtly alludes to Díaz's sanctioning of U.S. capitalists' aggressive exploitation of Mexico's natural resources.[2]

The painting plays with stereotypical representations of both nations. The heat lamp in the corner of the U.S. section is the counterpart to the sun in the opposite corner on the Mexican side. The artifacts, temples, icons of

Mexico suggest the violence of its conquest, but they also render Mexico as static and ancient, thereby placing Mexico, in the language of stereotypes, outside modernity, outside the swirl of progress. On the other side, *en el otro lado*, burgeoning industrialization creates a robotic, jammed space, thereby placing the United States, in the language of stereotypes, at the pulse of modernity, in the vanguard of progress.

"Self-Portrait on the Border" satirizes as it illustrates the effects of modernity's structural separation of space and time into a dialectic that encourages a linear narrative of national development: nations emerge along a linear spatial-temporal continuum that begins with feudalism and ends with cosmopolitan modernity. Borders serve, in this narrative, as the container for the territorial-temporal state. Nation-states can thus be understood, according to Neil Brenner, as "the politico-geographic blocks in terms of which the temporal dynamic of modernity [is] widely understood."[3] According to this logic, each nation occupies its own spatial-temporal field, and thus each understands itself according to its own temporal scale as it anxiously, repetitively strives toward a slippery modernization, ambiguously understood as the fulcrum of progress.[4] Crossing the border in this logic involves crossing from one temporality to another.[5] Built into the loose term *border* is a static, modernist concept of difference that depends on the veiled separation of time and space.

National borders utilize the fantasy that a nation on one side of the border exists in one phase of temporal development while the nation on the other side functions at a different stage. Moreover, borders simultaneously produce and elide this difference between nations, implicitly suggesting that a person can be formed in one temporality but when he or she crosses a border that person transmogrifies, as it were, into someone either more or less advanced, more or less modern, more or less sophisticated. The simultaneous transparency and solidity of this disjuncture between space and time is essential to understanding the ontology of the U.S.-Mexico border; to tracing what labor the border performs; to interrupting its alchemy, which works in part as an abjection machine—transforming people into "aliens," "illegals," "wetbacks," or "undocumented," and thereby rendering them unintelligible (and unintelligent), ontologically impossible, outside the real and the human. The border, of course, accomplishes more than this alchemy. It labors to define two nations in geopolitical and socio-imaginary terms, and it labors to erase the signs of its labor. It functions excessively as more than a site, a metaphor, a location, an image, or a fantasy. Emerging through the violence of its policing and through discursive maneuvers (ranging from memoirs to magazine covers to museum displays), the border exceeds understanding as a mapped geographic terrain, an economic or contact zone, or a region repeatedly represented as posing unremitting terror and danger to the "nation's interior."[6] It works, in other words, as a complex system with multiple and diverse nodes of production and reproduction.

As a number of Chicana critics and writers have noted, the border looms large and figures mightily in the production of identities. Although it does not approach what Henri Lefebvre defines as monumental space—it does not, for example, "offer each member of a society an image of that membership, an image of his or her social visage"—the border, like monumental space, has more than a single signified tied to it.[7] In this vein, the border can more properly be understood to have a "*horizon of meaning:* a specific or indefinite multiplicity of meanings, a shifting hierarchy in which now one, now another meaning comes momentarily to the fore, by means of—and for the sake of—a particular action."[8]

Because of its near monumentality within the national image repertoire, not all of the border's meanings can be grasped from a single vantage point. This multiplicity of meanings gives the U.S.-Mexico border a remarkable instrumentality, serving various functions, operating now as the forgotten and settled edge of a nation, now as the harbinger of crisis. Thus, Ronald Reagan could vaguely point toward the border in 1984 and say, "The simple truth is that we've lost control of our own borders and no nation can do that and survive."[9] Similarly, Texas ranchers, complaining in 1996 about the ineffectuality of the border patrol, argued that, "It's we private citizens who have upheld the integrity of the border . . . and we can't do it anymore. We're losing America."[10] These declarations attempt to carry a rhetorical weight of history, as loss and containment work together to punctuate fear. The border is produced through a nostalgia that imagines its (former) tranquillity and that necessarily belies the three centuries of conflict that have engulfed it. In other words, these border narratives depend on an understanding of space, of place, as immobile and fixed not as process.

Chicana/o writers are not, of course, unaware of the multiple uses of the border. Although the border-crossing scenes discussed here largely take place in "the past"—that is, before the militarization efforts initiated by Jimmy Carter and Ronald Reagan—the scenes themselves were largely writ-

ten while Reagan's crisis-oriented words echoed across the frontera, en-
couraging writers to produce what Carl Gutiérrez-Jones calls a "historically
layered inquiry" of the border's production.[11] Taken together these border-
crossing narratives ironically tackle the mechanics of the border as an abjection machine. They also collectively reveal how the system that is the
border produces more than abjection. Indeed, they reveal that the border
might be understood more fully as a state-sponsored aesthetic project. By
this I mean that the state has a stake in producing places as events, as projects
that only seem to be naively aesthetic; or rather, while ostensibly divorced
from the political, such projects or events augment the images and activities of the state and lend credence to the state's claim to objectively uphold
"the law." Understanding the border as a state-sponsored aesthetic project
implies that the border is a system whose ends and methods and effects are
far more caught up in the swirl of histories, temporalities, and narratives
than any simple glance would suggest.

Not surprisingly, Chicana border-crossing narratives typically refuse a
temporal economy in which Mexico is equated with a static, ancient order
and the United States emerges as a vibrant, pulsing arena for change and
transformation. Similarly, these narratives work against the power of the
border to function as an abjection machine because they understand that
the border is a system, not merely a site, a place, an image, or a fantasy.
These narratives simultaneously demystify the border and extend a critique
of its nation-making, people-making functions by excavating the border
in discursive and essential terms. Furthermore, by narrativizing the moment of "crossing," Chicana writers invoke a spatiohistorical conception of
subjectivity-in-process. For "crossing the line" involves more than movement in formal or informal terms; it involves recognizing a set of historical narratives, of family memories, of vectors of various national fantasies
that have an effect on identity and agency and on the formation of subjectivity. Border-crossing scenes suggest that "mestiza consciousness"—Norma
Alarcón's particular formulation of a racialized, gendered subjectivity-in-
process—emerges in relationship to spatiality, to the ongoing production
of places, to the buried and entangled relationship between time and space.
For just as subjectivity-in-process implies that subject formation involves
multiple temporalities, these crossing narratives also indicate the extent to
which the production of space—in this case, the production of a particular
national border—entails the production of subjectivities. Making identi-

ties is integral to making places; places get made in part through identity-making activities.

The border system attempts to disarticulate people from the signs of their subjectivity, to deprive them of meaning and identity. More than simply producing people as "abnormal" and "horrifying" because "aliens" or "mojados," the border system produces abjection by simultaneously focusing on the very subjects, the "aliens," who the system would master and dismiss, even though they are supposedly outside and beyond it. Julia Kristeva suggests that abjection is produced through "a failure to recognize its kind" and that "in this misrecognition of what is most near, all is rejected and a 'territory' is created edged by the abject."[12] The border system depends on the repetition of estrangement. Abjection functions through dis-remembering and dismembering. The abjected "aliens" are fundamental to the creation of insider/outsider, citizen/interloper, nation/not-nation. In the crossing scenes that follow, people tangle with the system that would abject them and thereby manipulate that system into nearly misrecognizing itself—abjecting itself rather than them. For, to produce abjection, the system depends on a willed unknowability of the abjected. These scenes illustrate how subjects rendered abject may turn that strategy in on itself.

Crossing scenes in Chicana/o literature often explore the desire to double-cross the border—to trick the extensive machinery of containment, of discipline, and of exploitation that has historically made the border a proving ground not simply for citizenship but for humanness as well. Chicana writers insert into their texts the means to identify social relations, to critique the minutiae of gender oppression, cultural imperialism, and racism. But here they write from the vantage point of trying to get over, to identify the machine, to acknowledge its prowess, and yet create social locations not only from which to critique the border-as-system, but also from which to partially escape it, to step aside, even for the moment, from the ongoing effects of domination.

Splitting Tongues

The work accomplished by the border system is revealed in part by the claims made on behalf of it and by what is at stake when the term *border* is invoked. What becomes clear is that *border* is an elastic referent—its meanings splitting and twisting in strange ways. On the one hand, the materiality of national borders—a materiality described, invoked, and parodied in Gina Valdés's work, as well as in contemporary advertisements—appears to anchor the term, naturalizing an array of methods used to maintain a border's geopolitical efficacy, to ritualize its crossings, and to produce a series of border subjectivities. On the other hand, precisely because it appears anchored, *border* also works as a floating signifier for contemporary critical theory, which, in a consensual fashion, has settled on *border* to suggest an array of nebulous states.[13]

There Are No Madmen Here, Gina Valdés's 1981 collection of interwoven short stories, closes with a border-crossing scene that illuminates the border's significance to the juridical production of identity and its value to the regulation of commerce and labor.[14] The collection traces the experiences of a family that obtains extra cash by illegally importing tequila and selling it at a profit in order to pay for college tuition, weddings, and rent. Their trans-frontera import business reflects their ambivalent relationship to a discourse of nation and citizen that would seek to construct them as aspiring members of a U.S. middle class, just as Valdés's collection as a whole traces the various experiences of discrimination that mark the contradictions of the state's offer to provide a clear path to such middle-class status.

The family circulates throughout the borderlands, and the collection stages their multiple crossings as largely prosaic. At one point, the central figure, María, goes so far as to claim, "In a way the border is invisible" (85). In "disappearing" the border, María rejects national claims to figuring identity and, to the degree that the border can be made invisible, temporarily and partially constructs her own sense of identity as apart from the monolingual, nationalist model of identity formation. María invokes the border's metaphoric significance, an invocation that both parodies and denies the border's materiality. By declaring that the border is invisible, she is also declaring independence from the historical legacy that the border implies, including the history of cultural degradation and asymmetrical labor practices; her declaration is also aligned with Chicano cultural politics. As one Chicano Movimiento newspaper, *Sin fronteras,* prophesied, the political border between the two nations would eventually be seen as an "artificial creation that in time would be destroyed by the struggles of Mexicans on both sides of the border."[15] Yet if María's declaration is similarly utopian, her desire to negate

Double-Crossing la Frontera Nómada

the border disavows its importance, for it is precisely the maintenance of the border that makes possible the family's *chamba* (easy money).

While María's erasure of the border might contain the hope of threatening the discursive underpinnings of the nation-state, the final border-crossing scene in *There Are No Madmen Here* exemplifies how the containment mechanism of the border system jerks into action when its juridical apparatus actually registers such defiance. On the eve of his retirement from the smuggling business, María's brother, Ramón, makes one final trip to obtain tequila. Before he returns, he buys six parrots for $60 which he plans to resell in the United States for more than $1,200. Ramón's and María's sister, Emilia, gives the birds tequila so that they will be quiet during the border-crossing check.

> The parrots were silent, "Dead to the world," thought Ramón. He thought about his retirement from the tequila and about the extra money. "A thousand extra . . . no, twelve hundred . . . for each parrot. . . ." He smiled at the police officer and the officer smiled back.
>
> "Bringing anything from México?"
>
> "Just this hat for my wife."
>
> (Viejo cabrón)
>
> "What was that?"
>
> "What was what?"
>
> "I thought I heard something."
>
> "I didn't hear anything."
>
> (Viejo cabrón)
>
> "It sounds like a woman's voice."
>
> (Viejo cabrón)
>
> "It sounds like it's coming from the back of your camper," said the officer as he walked toward the back of Ramón's car.
>
> (Viejo cabrón)
>
> The officer stood in front of Ramón and asked him to unlock the back of the camper. Five of the parrots were completely passed out, but one of them was pacing his cage, drunk, repeating what was apparently his favorite curse. (150–51)

The parrot double-crosses Ramón, unmasks his smuggling operation, and the parrot's curse results in Ramón's temporary incarceration *not* in a romantic reconfiguration of power structures. Yet the parrot's curse is more than simply the comical fury of those in powerless positions forced to conform to the terms set out by those in power. And it is more than an anguished moment of frustration with the representative of bureaucracy or the local machinery that power uses to instantiate itself. While the parrot's curse does not actually transform power relations, it does serve to remind readers, and even the border patrol guard, of the degree to which the border functions not simply as the line between two nations but also as the producer of a constant reenactment of historical divisions, conquest, and control. And this historical reenactment continues to reproduce and further stratify all kinds of relationships, including those understood in terms of labor and ethnicity.[16]

The parrot's curse mocks the self-importance of the border and the bureaucratically determined rituals for crossing (and producing) it. If the parrot speaks Ramón's secret thoughts, it also voices the desire the system itself produces: defiance guarantees the crossing guards' jobs and ensures systemic permanence. The bureaucratic and technical apparatuses surrounding customs stations create the very border they serve to guard. They exist with a melancholic faith that the border, their border, actually exists somehow outside of and apart from the control techniques neatly delineated in manuals or signaled by border patrol uniforms and guns. At the moment of "crossing," the non-site of the border—a line occupying no space but spatially determined nonetheless by juridical-national discourses—becomes an enclosure where identities are constructed precisely because of their bodily location at that particular site.

Ramón's encounter with the customs agent indicates how influenced the ritual of crossing (and of double-crossing) is by the catholic confessional. With a ritual set of questions that always include "What is your citizenship" and "What have you purchased?" (as well as, perhaps, "where are you going?"), the performance of the crossing sanctioned as "legal" depends on a known set of priestly-parishioner relationships. Secrecy and revelation structure one's confession as citizen-consumer (or not-citizen/laborer/tourist), and the anxiety of secrecy, of revelations withheld, of secrets to be uncovered structures each encounter, just as the terror of secrets left undiscovered produces the crossing-repetition effect. That is, secrecy helps to structure the repetition of border crossing and, through that repetition, underscores the sedimentation of the border as "natural."

Valdés's narrative reinforces this slide between secrecy and revelation. On a first reading, one might assume that "Viejo cabrón" is merely Ramón's own thought: only in the moment of revelation does the reader discover who actually "says" the words. By delineating the curse not with quotation marks but with parentheses, Valdés places the words outside "normal" speech but within the legible, causing a reader to shift reading practices in order to imagine the squawking parrot within the interstices of the dialogue. The pacing, drunk bird produces the abjection the border desires. So if the parrot unmasks Ramón's attempt to simply pass over the border, disrupts his methods of betraying the system, it nevertheless reveals the structure of production at work on the border.

Gina Valdés continues her meditations on the border in her poem "Where You From?" in which the speaker stands defiantly before the border declaring,

> I didn't build
> this border
> that halts me
> the word fron
> tera splits
> on my tongue.[17]

The poem itself crosses the border, moving "from here and from there" in a recognition of the border system that the speaker articulates as "soy de aquí / y soy de allá." These multiple locations, which could translate as "I am from (of) here / and I am from (of) there," do more than visually represent or invoke national interstices—they work to ironically answer the poem's title. The question implies the extent to which an originary location is always assumed to be singular. Similarly, with its suggestion of colloquial informality, the title question also refers to the frequently hostile question Chicanas/os hear when we are under suspicion of not belonging (here/there). The speaker's answer to this question works through negation. By refusing to answer the question directly, the speaker draws attention to the border's splitting effects.

The border is not invisible in this configuration. Rather, it affects the speaker bodily: her tongue feels the fissure. The schism occurs "on" her tongue. In pointing to the tongue, the speaker highlights the schism between Spanish and English that "monological" national discourses insist on.

57

The alternation between "border" and "frontera" emphasizes that split, just as the orthographic splitting of frontera, without the bridging dash, visually forces the reader to experience the split. The eye falls into the interstices. The poem thereby points to the constructedness of the border, but the speaker asserts a distance from that construction even as she implies the extent to which the border continues to construct her.

"Where You From?" offers an allegory of the struggle between the constructed and the essential, the material and the metaphoric. It plays with the limits of both, their mutual contingency—the border has no prior materiality apart from its appearance in discourse; after all, maps, treaties, speeches on the Senate floor, newspapers, ethnographies, and housing developments produced and reproduce the border. At the same time, the border is, following Judith Butler, an "elusive referent" whose materiality (including fences, night scopes, rivers, deserts, holding cells) shifts away from a precise claim to discursive constructedness alone.[18] The border stands between its transparent ontological status and "the real" of metal fences with edges so sharp they sever the fingers of those forced to climb them.

"Where You From?" suggests that the border draws its power from its hold on both the real and the discursive, from its play with the limits of its discursive construction, and from its slippery dance with the various referents deployed to capture its materiality. The poem offers an important contrast to broadly deployed uses of the border that have emerged recently. By questioning its ontological function, Valdés draws attention to the extent to which the border depends on a material/metaphoric division that is both "false" and "real." And through the narrator's anger and passion, Valdés draws attention to the border's affective power and destructive potential. In this sense, "Where You From?" challenges the popularity of the border as a key term in many contemporary theoretical projects.

Border has gained a currency that enables it to perform a variety of theoretical labors; it functions, for example, as a term that describes a personality disorder ("borderline"), the effects of split-subjectivity, the liminal space between binary categories, or the potential complexities of relationships where difference is central to the narrative of those relationships.[19] The interest in borders has flourished alongside the proliferation of the prefix *post* (postcontemporary, postmodern, posturban, postfeminist, and on and on). *Post* is always here a temporal term and border a spatial one. Of course, the temporal post's homonym is rather a spatial term (e.g., army post, lookout post). This elision of *post*'s spatial valence in contemporary usage may give us a hint as to why *border* has come to appeal so thoroughly to many critics. Or, one might say, it is from the vantage point of a border that theorists of the temporal *post* wish to operate.

This recent turn to the border is illuminating because, first, it suggests the continuing attraction to terms that seem all-enveloping but don't disclose the limits of both discursivity and materiality; and second, its multiple uses as a metaphor in theoretical discussions suggest new ways to understand the discursive field out of which the U.S.-Mexico border emerges. In contrast Chicana crossing narratives expose how the gap between the material and the discursive that borders appear to bridge is less a gap and more of a relay charged with a critical power to delineate difference.

Not surprisingly, the growing popularity of borders accompanies the continuing transition of capitalism from its base in the material resources of the nation-state to its dependence on worldwide flexible accumulation. This transition has increased the focus on national borders as sites of violent conflict. The appearance of borders in academic journals echoes their appearance on the nightly news where border skirmishes provide compelling footage whether they take place in Tijuana, Korea, or the West Bank.

Yet scholars and journalists are not alone in finding borders attractive. Throughout 1996 Taco Bell, for example, ran an ad campaign with the slogan, "Make a Run for the Border."[20] As part of the campaign, Taco Bell also published an employee newsletter, "The Border," which included headlines such as "Keep on Taking Back the Border!" "Re-Energizing the Border: U.S. Invasion," and "Strengthening the Border." One issue of the newsletter, for example, encourages employees to cut production time, offers profiles of newly promoted managers, and under the category "Expanding the Border" describes the merger of Taco Bell and Kentucky Fried Chicken.

For Taco Bell, the U.S.-Mexico border symbolizes not only the fast-food chain's seemingly enticing food but also its market share. Yet the newsletter's militaristic allusions also point toward the fortressing of the border taking place alongside its capitalist dismantlement. In one easy and almost parodic gesture, Taco Bell captures both the contemporary nationalist anxiety about what borders signify within a national image repertoire and their seeming irrelevance but utter importance to capitalism. Furthermore, Taco Bell's campaign—like "Where You From?"—indicates the value of the border's ability to shift between metaphoric and material status. It is this shifting capacity that finally makes *border* so appealing a term to critics seeking to describe contested and nebulous conditions. The term functions precisely because it is fraught with a violent materiality that such critical discourse can simultaneously invoke and disavow through generalizing operations.

Border Amnesia

As the twenty-first century begins, it might appear that earlier national contests waged over the border's production in geographic terms have been forgotten even though anxieties about the border continue unabated, the border being always already under siege. Yet such a formulation, if invoking a number of anti-immigration campaigns that call for "Lighting up the Border" (as if it disappears in the dark), is too simplistic. The border functions through strategic forgetting and remembering, for the border system's economy of memory encourages a violent amnesia, erasing cultures, identities, and differences, while simultaneously producing subjectivities, differences, and cultures in terms of itself.

Rather than take the border as transparent, as a given, in contrast to Taco Bell, or indeed in contrast to many contemporary theorists, Montserrat Fontes, in *Dreams of the Centaur* (1996) evokes the border as a "site of memory," to borrow a phrase from Toni Morrison.[21] She performs the "kind of literary archeology" that Toni Morrison suggests is almost mandatory for anyone "who belongs to any marginalized category, for, historically, we were seldom invited to participate in the discourse even when we were its topic."[22] Thus, Fontes returns to an earlier, pre-Taco Bell stage in the border-as-system's construction. In an effort to rethink the terms of its formative discourse, Fontes excavates the border's particular system of disassemblances and resemblances and the contrapuntal dynamics of translation and forgetting that structure it.

Set at the turn into the twentieth century in northern Sonora and rural Arizona, *Dreams of the Centaur* unveils a series of border-crossing scenes giving closure to the narrative. With these scenes, *Dreams of the Centaur* offers both a complex metaphor for U.S.–Mexico relations and a prophecy of the emergence of the borderlands as dependent on multiple erasures: "[Felipa] notices the difference in border stations. Americans have an adobe single-room low structure. Mexicans have a wood kiosk. Thirty meters separate the stations. She wonders what country claims that land."[23]

The crossing begins with a comparison between the two stations—where the structures might function as synecdoches for the two nations. More to the point, the border here serves to highlight difference even though the presence of the "border stations" reveals that for both nations the border works as a revenue-producing zone. Furthermore, Felipa's glance alludes to the region as "nepantla"—the land in the middle—which both Pat Mora and Gloria Anzaldúa explore. Her glance also draws attention to the constructedness of this particular border, indicating that if it may be contested and claimed, then it has a history; rather than being a static locale, it is a process. Finally, Felipa's query—"what country claims that land"—implies that the region functions as a "no-man's land," which, as Joan DeJean explains, originally "stood for a spatial paradox, a territory defined by its lack of definition."[24] Felipa's observation suggests the extent to which producing the border also produces estrangement.

The party's interrogation by the Mexican officer at the "wood kiosk" is quite brief, and he waves them through without requesting papers. Yet his apparent informality does not erase his purpose as guardian who patrols who enters and who exits. Charco, the son of Felipa's deceased husband and a Yaqui laborer, hides his Yaqui identity by removing the sandals that would mark him as enemy-Other. As the novel explores, Yaquis had been declared enemies of the state, and Mexican officials were arresting and deporting them to work in forced labor camps in southern Mexico. Charco's simple trick to pass as Mexican illustrates the dissassemblances that the border enforces, as well as his resistance to a Mexican nationalism that would depend on the assimilation of Yaqui culture into an undifferentiated mestizaje.

Having passed through one check station, Charco reclaims his status as Yaqui by putting on his sandals (exemplifying the extent to which race and citizenship function through visuality). Felipa subsequently turns her attention to the U.S. officer.

> Slowly they move toward the American side, which has several officers working. The line barely moves. Americans ask more questions, she notices. She sees them checking wagon beds. For what?
> She sees Pimas and Opatas crossing the border in both directions.

Some carry chickens, others herd goats. Neither border station seems to notice them.

No Yaquis. . . .

The American sees Charco's sandals. "You Yaqui?"

"Yaqui, yes," Charco answers.

The officer points to the sandals. "Did the Mexicans see those? Yaquis and Mexicans—" With his index finger, he makes a dramatic cutting motion across his throat. He walks to Felipa's side. His eyes engage hers, then comb her face and stop at her breasts. "You're no Yaqui," he says heavily, and leans toward her. (339)

The officer's heavily breathed "You're no Yaqui" illustrates the intertwining of race with desire and the danger of sexual exploitation that awaits women, in particular, as they cross the border. Note too that the officer's interest in Felipa follows the violent gesture toward Charco. By linking genocide and sexual exploitation, especially the threat of rape, to border crossing at the point of its early institutionalization, *Dreams of the Centaur* uncovers one way in which violent, state-sanctioned desire shapes the border as a zone of terror that, as Carl Gutiérrez-Jones points out, is "critical to the manufacture of social and cultural dependency in the United States."[25] After a few moments of interrogation in which the men with Felipa attempt to assert their claim to her (indicating the extent to which women easily become commodities within the border economy), a senior border patrol officer comes over to see what the confusion is about.

"What's holding you up?" asks another officer. He's younger, but clearly the officer in charge.

"Why would Mexicans claim to be Yaquis?" asks the red-faced man. "They're enemies. Blue-eyed Yaqui landowners with a high-bred, un-branded stallion. Don't you think that's strange?"

"We can expect a lot of them. Some battle happened. Nogalitos is full of them. If they have no weapons, let them through. Yaquis, Mexicans, what's the difference?" (340)

The senior officer dismisses the other officer with an act of conflation: "Yaquis, Mexicans, what's the difference." For this officer there may exist differences, but these do not matter to him or, by extension, to the nation. The border patrolman's conflation comes at the end of a novel that has explored in detail the cultural autonomy of Yaquis and the evolution of their status as public enemies within Mexico. *Dreams of the Centaur* works hard to show difference and to explore how the Diaz regime exploited and then sought to destroy these differences. The crossing guard's conflation of Yaquis with Mexicanos indicates the relatively small role within the symbolic economy that the United States is willing to assign either group. The mestizaje that postrevolutionary Mexico would celebrate is here ironically and schematically produced through a border guard's cynical dismissal. The border thus enables and even encourages a violent forgetting or erasure of culture, identity, and difference.

A subsequent crossing scene parallels Felipa's experience and further underscores the extent to which the border depends on forgetting differences while simultaneously installing them. The narrator describes a group of Nimipu who moved back and forth across the border in an attempt to elude U.S. soldiers who plan to incarcerate them. But the Nimipu are not visible to the U.S. army as Nimipu, because they are only seen as "Indians" (Pima, Opata, Yaqui); the army depends on spotting their "spotted" pinto horses in order to distinguish them from other Indians. So the Nimipu disguise their horses by painting them "a solid color with a mixture of charcoal, iron shavings, oil, and vinegar" (344). Both Charco and the Nimipu survive by manipulating the signs of their abjection, turning the border's dependence on estrangement into the source of their own subterfuge. Furthermore, the novel's description of the Nimipu's efforts, as well as the earlier description of the Pimas and Opatas crossing the border without garnering attention, highlights that the establishment of the U.S.-Mexico border divided not just Mexican land but the lands of a range of nations including Pimas, Tohono O'odhams, and Opatas as well. This significant division is often subsumed into and forgotten in the dominant narrative of U.S.-Mexican relations.[26]

By drawing attention to the subterfuges people employ to rework the border for their own needs, Fontes invokes the historicity of the border, emphasizing that its presence stretches further back than the crisis-ridden calls that drive contemporary campaigns to police the border. Not surprisingly, the production of the border with Mexico has preoccupied the United States from its infancy. As early as 1786 essayists began calling for efforts to obtain Florida and Louisiana, as well as Mexico. During the next sixty years, the drive for greater territory was fueled by continual calls to obtain, by force or treaty, the wealth and lands of Spain and newly independent Mexico.

Neither the 1848 Treaty of Guadalupe Hidalgo nor the subsequent Gadsden Purchase squelched the U.S. desire to push the boundary with Mexico farther south from Washington, although the 1848 treaty is often credited with providing closure. Throughout the 1850s, for example, Congress and diplomats continually urged Mexico to sell additional territory and threatened the nation with renewed war if it did not.[27] These official attempts to gain new territory were accompanied by a number of filibusters, armed incursions into Mexico by U.S. citizens who wanted Mexican lands for new colonies and protectorates. As Luis Zorilla explains, the United States continually threatened Mexico with a version of extinction if it did not cede new territory: "En otras palabras: para que hubiera armonía entre los dos vecinos era necesario que uno estuviera alimentando cada vez durante espacios más cortos, con parte de su propio organismo, el apetito insaciable del otro" [In other words, if harmony were to exist between the two neighbors, one had to nourish the insatiable appetite of the other with part of its own organism, in shorter and shorter intervals].[28] Zorilla's graphic depiction of the transformation of the border at the expense of Mexico captures the border dynamics in which relations of exploitation and domination characterize the two nations' histories.

The Civil War interrupted the rush to produce a new border, but calls to expand U.S. territory and renegotiate the border resumed again shortly after the war's conclusion and continued throughout the 1870s and 1880s as the land boom in southern California came to a close.[29] Indeed, even as the physical boundary between Mexico and the United States was being established, it was being contested. William Emory, the first U.S. boundary commissioner to successfully map the border from Brownsville to San Diego, noted in his report to Congress that, since the boundary markers were almost immediately torn down and disassembled after their erection, he had commissioned drawings of the topography of every point along the southern border where a marker had been placed. Plates of these drawings were filed in vaults in both Mexico and the United States, and Emory's report included copies of these drawings in an effort to capture the illusory border in visual-legal terms.

If Apaches and others perceived the border as temporary, so did filibusterers hungry for the rich agricultural lands of Sonora. They continued to campaign for funds and manpower under the banner of an ever-larger American empire. Although rumors of filibusters were more common than actual filibustering attempts, such attempts did continue, with both rumors and attempts tacitly sanctioned by the government. Indeed until late in the nineteenth century when the solidity of the U.S.-Mexico border helped produce enormous profits for U.S. capitalists, the government did nothing to discourage filibustering, because such campaigns continued to reinforce U.S. efforts to maintain its identity as a nation that defined itself in part through its ability to choose its own territorial borders.[30]

Almost immediately after the new boundary line was drawn, both Mexico and the United States began establishing customs stations.[31] As early as 1853, the Treasury Department hired sixteen mounted inspectors to police the customs district at Brazos de Santiago, Texas (near Brownsville).[32] Mexican officials similarly called for help to limit the increased smuggling the territorial changes had engendered. The citizens of Ures, Sonora, argued in 1856 that the money Mexico received for the Gadsden Purchase should be applied to the policing of the border to prevent further battles with Apaches, as well as American incursions.[33] Throughout the period between 1853 and 1890, skirmishes about the location of the border occurred in part because people destroyed the boundary monuments or moved them.[34] By 1887, after several violent encounters between U.S. sheriffs and Mexican police, Mexican officials called for "neutral zones" encased by steel fences between border cities. The United States followed suit a few years later.[35]

By the 1890s territorial boundaries began to appear more or less permanent and more or less inviolable and with this change a new phase of the production of the border began: its institutionalization. So although the Mexican Revolution gave newspaper editors yet another chance to fantasize about additional territorial gains, and despite an Arizona senator's annual resolution to Congress to purchase the state of Sonora (submitted five times between 1915 and 1940), the focus on the border shifted from changing its location to policing it.[36] An 1893 report to the secretary of the interior from the territorial governor of Arizona hinted at the transformation to take place over the next century.

> The border of this customs district to be guarded is 450 miles in length, the line traversing a mountainous and desert country sparsely

populated throughout the entire distance. Crossing this line is one railroad and about a dozen wagon roads and innumerable pack trails, besides which there are several long level stretches, over which wagons or pack animals can easily make their way without following any public path. It is an ideal region for smugglers, and that the facilities it offers for carrying on of clandestine trade are very largely taken advantage of by a lawless border element can not be doubted. To guard this long line but nine inspectors are employed, giving to each an average section of fifty miles in length to protect.

It is generally believed that a large amount of illicit trade is carried on at different points along the line. An increased force of line riders would add considerably to the duties, as opium, mescal, sugar, and other foreign commodities are believed to be smuggled to a large extent. It has been frequently found that quantities of opium have been landed at Guaymas. At one time the shipment reached the point of 30,000 pounds. What became of it is not known. It is believed, however, to have been brought into the States. . . . Attention is also called to the fact that many Chinese are smuggled through this line. At one time no less than thirty were captured in one batch, and were returned to China at great expense to the Government. From the best information I can gather this illegal traffic is continued without abatement.[37]

Change the language of this message slightly and this statement could have been written at the end of the twentieth century rather than the end of the nineteenth. The governor's message works almost as a prophecy of what would become standard, bureaucratic border anxieties. These border thematics have repeatedly and anxiously appeared throughout the twentieth century: the hundreds of miles of border are nearly always characterized as impossible to police or surveil adequately; the smuggled commodities result in lost tax revenue; the movement of opium threatens the nation's moral well-being; and the opium is followed by the threat of Chinese workers also clandestinely crossing the border—not a surprising claim, given the long history of symbolically linking opium with Chinese immigrant workers.

In 1893 as in the late twentieth and early twenty-first centuries, "narcotics" and "aliens" constituted the ultimate twin threats to the border, to national sovereignty. The combinatory Othering achieved by their twinning—a hybrid super-Other—underscored the extent to which the impregnability of the border functioned as a nationalist fantasy and the pregnability of the border worked as a nationalist nightmare. The nightmare served to inculcate terror; terror was subsequently combated by increasing police forces and militarizing the region. And that terror obscured the border's function of producing revenue for the state; policing it more effectively, as the territorial governor explained, "would add considerably to the duties." That the value of border policing lay in its revenue producing was underscored nearly thirty years later when, in congressional hearings to establish a unified border patrol (combining the work of customs and INS), U.S. Navy Captain John P. Jackson urged Congress to increase patrol funding by pointing out the "advantages to the Government, from a revenue producing angle alone, of establishing an effective patrol."[38]

The territorial governor tells a story of gnawing, omnipresent border anxiety where losses—lost money, lost sovereignty, lost knowledge—remake the border and transform it into a zone of erasure, of unknowing, of dispersal and disappearance. It is precisely because the theme of loss voiced here by the anxious, pacing state official has persisted for more than a century that a kind of border melancholia has emerged. Border melancholia is further underscored by the border patrol's various highly publicized "operations" to seal the border. Their titles—Operation Wetback, Operation Hold the Line, Operation Restore, Operation Gatekeeper, Operation Safeguard, Operation Blockade, Operation Alliance, Operation Rumpunch—all suggest that efforts to guard the border are doomed to endless and even uncanny repetition.[39]

The names of these operations reveal, as does even a cursory glance at the hundred-year congressional discussions of the border, that guarding the border or sealing it is, in effect, an impossible task. From its inception, the border patrol has apparently recognized that its stated goal cannot be realized. The border's miles and miles of walls, installed to forestall these losses, have failed to relieve border melancholia, the anxiety that the "integrity of the border" is disappearing, despite the government's best efforts. The fences keep the anxiety of loss, the phantasmatic possibility of unwanted invasion in place, so that rupture and the horror of invasion (predicated on a nationalist desire to be desired) continue to structure the production of the border. And thus, what these "Operations" and the melancholy that surrounds them finally reveal is that the work of the border patrol is something other than its officially stated purpose. Writing about the fortressing of fourteenth-century France, Joan DeJean explains, "On the one hand, the impregnable fortress suggested that all those inside its invincible barriers would be safe from all enemies. On the other, the image served to refine the concept of enmity."[40] As the titles of the U.S. operations suggest, then, what is at stake is not the pregnability of the border but the production of enmity.

Prior to its fencing, the border was demarcated between El Paso and the Pacific Ocean by odalisques placed every thirty to two hundred miles along the border. (Inscribed at their base was a warning that destruction of the monument was a crime in both the United States and Mexico.) During the period between 1848 and 1910, several joint U.S.-Mexico survey teams placed and replaced these monuments as the two nations argued over inches and acres.[41] For example, boundary surveys were initiated in 1882 and again in 1891 in response to complaints from customs and army officials. Merchants took advantage of the ambiguous boundary system to the frustration of the government. At one saloon built on the borderline, customers paid for cigars inside U.S. territory, then walked to the back of the saloon to pick them up in Mexican territory, thereby avoiding paying taxes to either nation.[42] After the Mexican Revolution the United States began to install fences, first barbed-wire then chain-link.

The most recent fortification of the border has largely coincided with the slowdown and demise of the Cold War. In the mid-eighties, the Reagan administration, in declaring a renewed war on drugs, began to advocate the use of the military and military techniques to guard the border, and Congress began to demand that action be taken to "seal" the border. Since Reagan's 1986 declaration, the border has undergone a profound physical transformation.

Agents have planted nonlethal landmines along a mountainous route in southeastern Arizona to terrorize travelers.[43] In San Ysidro and Calexico, California, as well as near various border cities in Arizona, the government erected what a spokesperson called a "steel curtain," massive walls built from steel landing mats left over from the Vietnam War.[44] The INS has built miles of concrete-lined ditches, some fourteen feet wide, five feet deep—what an assistant attorney general characterized as a "buried Berlin Wall." The marines have also deployed spy drones, radio-controlled planes that send out a stream of video images of the border region.[45] The Pentagon and the Customs Service experimented with massive blimps designed to survey the airspace a hundred miles into either side of the border. When the first balloon was deployed the task force imagined that a series of sixteen blimps would create an "impenetrable 'electronic fence'" along the border.[46] The blimp experiment failed (because they were mysteriously unmoored and allowed to float freely away), but the INS continues to be attracted to new electronic technology that might complement its existing system of underground sensors.[47] Such fortifications are not the first experiment the military has made with technology in an effort to police the border. Indeed, in 1885 Brigadier General Nelson A. Miles, believing the border to be so significant, attempted to build an elaborate system of communications using a telephone system and a heliograph (a system of mirrors established on border mountain peaks) to police the movements of Apache communities.[48]

Yet if the multiple constructions of the border have shown anything, it is that their symbolic content remains significant. The story of fences includes a new installment, what might be characterized as a "kinder, gentler" chapter.[49] At one border checkpoint the INS spent nearly a million dollars to erect a fourteen-foot-high wall designed, as the government contract specified, to allow "light and a feeling of openness to be present along the perimeter of the barrier."[50] This "friendly wall" contrasts oddly with the hundreds of miles of steel-landing-mats-turned-walls that have been built along the border. Its salmon and blue colors quote the traditional architecture of custom's houses. Glass inserts suggest friendliness, belying the reinforced steel interior of the walls, which were designed to meet the government's requirements that the new barrier withstand, "repeated physical assault by means such as welding torches, chisels, hammers, firearms, climbing over or penetration with vehicles."[51] Alongside the glass planes are ceramic tiles meant to someday bear local children's artwork. The wall echoes both mall architecture and the fences surrounding suburban gated communities, thus effectively rendering the border as familiar and anesthetizing its militarization. Other border cities may also receive such a wall.[52]

In contrast to the "friendly wall," or as a weird continuation of that project, the border patrol has also announced that it will build desert "stations" to "assist" crossers. Responding to the unprecedented number of deaths in the arid Arizona desert (where migrants have been forced to cross because various operations have made traditional crossing points more vexed), the border patrol plans to install six poles, topped by strobe lights, that will flash when a red button is pushed, thereby signaling the border patrol office in Yuma, Arizona. Obviously, the border patrol will deport whoever they find at the stations as well as, one would hope, assist them.[53]

Such "friendly walls" and stations depend on a certain amnesia. They depend on forgetting that walls between the two nations are a relatively new phenomena. They depend on forgetting that the border fences may keep people in as well as keep people out. But at the same time, the friendly wall and the strobe lights make it nearly impossible to forget that the border itself is a state-sponsored aesthetic project. The wall, especially, represents an attempt to mute the politicality of the border, by rendering the site and the attending methods of discipline and control attractive and desirable—pretty, aesthetically pleasing, and thus "naturally" outside the political and the contested.[54] Erected not far from where Charco and Felipa cross the border, the friendly wall participates as aesthetic acts do in the effort to shape how people remember, contesting the terms of memory that *Dreams of the Centaur* asserts as essential to recognizing the labor the border performs. The wall and assistance centers work to suggest the benevolence of the state and the natural evolution of its protective structures. But such an ideological project fails to obtain its desired naturalized status when Montserrat Fontes remaps the border system's memory so fundamentally. If the friendly wall would withdraw the border from memory, Fontes's novel restores the border as a resource for political contests.

Like *Dreams of the Centaur,* Norma Cantú's "autobioethnography," *Canícula* (1995), works partly as an archaeology of the border by engaging the border's history.[55] *Canícula,* however, moves the border history forward to the era of repatriation campaigns and then past those campaigns to post–World War II Texas. Through a series of vignettes and discussions of photographs, some reprinted, others only described, Cantú recounts a fictionalized biography of a woman growing up in the borderlands of South Texas.

One of the first vignettes, "Crossings," describes *Canícula's* protagonist, Azucena, and her family as they cross from Mexico to the United States. This particular crossing invokes the stories of a different type of crossing—the forced deportations and repatriation of Chicanos throughout the Southwest during the Depression.[56] Azucena describes how her grandparents, "crossing from one Laredo to the other," lost all they possessed to corrupt border guards: "Tía Nicha still talks of how weeks later she saw a little girl wearing her dress—a mint green dress she'd hemmed herself with pastel blue thread."[57] The theft of the dress neatly mirrors the theft of their status as U.S. citizens. For the young child, the dress worn by another symbolized her own displacement; for the elderly aunt recalling that loss, discussing the dress reinforces the materiality of her memory. And the mint green of the dress recalls the economic motives behind their deportation, providing a powerful image of the U.S. effort to create a class of surplus labor for which neither the state nor capital would feel any obligation to bear the costs of reproduction. That is, the circulating mint-green dress neatly anticipates and mirrors the mobile capital of the contemporary post-Fordist era even as it recalls a crisis in the process of solidifying a Fordist economy.

The deportations and disenfranchisement of tens of thousands of U.S. citizens have gone largely unrecorded in canonical U.S. histories, but they reveal the extent to which borders serve to establish stratified networks of laborers. The Depression-era deportations solidified the largely informal systems of apartheid labor already in place throughout the Southwest. By emblematizing the state's and capital's need to control who could cross, when and how, and who could be "sent back" and why, the U.S.-Mexico border served (and serves) not simply to highlight inclusion and exclusion but also to regulate the uneven development of wealth and labor.

In "Crossings" the narrator deploys a "local history" to make the broader point that such state-sponsored crossings remake the border, just as the border reconstituted her family. Their move back across the line, thirteen years later, appears bittersweet: "Crossing meant coming home, but not quite" (5). The border implies the distinction between home and exile—it embodies loss. "Crossings" closes by putting pressure on "home" and leaves the reader with an underexplained interrogation of the concept of home. The family cannot afford to believe in a stable concept of home or nation; to feel that they "belong" is to heighten their own vulnerability. The border signals their exile on either side of the line.

The next cuento, "On the Bridge," describes the experience of walking the bridge over the river that splits the city of Laredo, one side belonging to México, the other to the United States. A description of a particular photograph of the narrator with her sister and mother frames the story of their multiple crossings. In this narrative, crossing is both celebrated as an opportunity for adventure and marked as prosaic. The narrator describes shopping at the mercado; moving from stall to stall; picking out meat, sweets, fruit ("he extracts the pits so we can legally cross them to the United States"); stopping to go to the bathroom, to get shoes shined; and then, "We walk, cross the bridge, resting every half block or so, resting our arms, sore from carrying the heavy redes. We take the bus home" (8). Their shopping is marked by the agricultural restrictions established to protect U.S. avocado farmers. But more important, the description of the merchant's treatment of the aguacates, "which he carefully cuts in half . . . and closes them again, like fine carved wood boxes" (8) alludes to the children's own sense of fractured identity—the split, pitted avocado echoes the schism of Gina Valdés's tongue.

In this narrative, the border, here marked by a river and navigated on foot over a bridge, separates economic regions and emerges through the consumption of various commodities. The narrative further intensifies the link between the border and the economy through attention to the labor of the narrator's father when she explains that in the photograph her mother is anxious because her father is away working construction. He will return to obtain a job at a nearby smelter. That work, which might pay fairly well, carries the risks of periodic layoffs and "during those times, the trips to Laredo, Mexico, are put on hold; only for emergencies do we cross—to see the doctor, to visit an ill relative, or to pay a manda at Santo Niño de Atocha Church. Tino and I miss our adventures, our sojourns al otro lado" (8). Once again the linguistic switch to Spanish serves to emphasize and mark the discursive effects of the border.[58]

Crossing here signifies relative economic well-being. The border itself becomes a marker between the shifting periods of poverty and plenty. Crossing the border takes on additional significations: the "other side" figures early in the narrative as a space for familiar and repetitive adventures. But at the narrative's close, la frontera becomes a gendered zone navigated only with parental mediation. Not simply the source for pleasant food and the site of religious and familial obligations, the border zone offers the commodities necessary to reinforce patriarchy. Having almost joyfully recounted her and her brother's joint adventures al otro lado, the narrator gives a new and even more gendered distinction to their crossings: "Now Papi takes Tino to get haircuts and shoes shined while Mami and I buy *Confidencias,* a women's magazine I'll read a escondidas, during siesta time. Hiding in the backyard, under the pirul, I'll read 'cartas que se extraviaron,' and pretend the love letters are for me, or that I wrote them, making the tragic stories mine. I pretend I'm a leading star—María Félix, Miroslava, Silvia Pinal. During recess, I retell the stories to Sanjuana and Anamaría, embellishing to fit my plots" (8–9).

The frontera becomes a distant and public space, reinforcing the hetero-sexualized production of spatiality. Crossing the line entails a certain nor-malization, with the border subsequently functioning as a signifier of gen-dering, of the two children's emplotment in heterosexual cultural scripts. Tino and Papi perform rituals of "manhood" together. Azucena and her mother purchase the cultural commodities that offer instructions and ex-amples for the gendering process that will try to interpolate her as a proper Chicana wife and mother. Yet, as the narrative concludes, Azucena suggests that she still retains agency—she takes the *Confidencias* and remakes their stories. She does not simply memorize and internalize them; she transforms them, "embellishes" them to fit her own plots. Nonetheless, such efforts at subversion must first take place privately, hidden away "under the pirul."

Cantú's border triptych concludes with "The Flood," a description of a massive flood that wiped out the bridge. The flood forces Azucena's family to evacuate their home and destroys the homes of many of her relatives across the river. "Crossing" subsequently becomes possible only when they "brave a bridge that swings, made of wood and rope" (9). This experience of crossing the "toy bridge" is far more frightening and dangerous, and Azu-cena recounts her grandmother's chanting prayers and calls to the child, "te quedes" (stay with me) and her response "ay voy" (I'm coming). The flood brings typhoid, polio, and other diseases. The photo (again, not reprinted) that accompanies the narrative depicts the family visiting a shrine in grati-tude for their safety. The destruction of the bridge reminds them of what they could have lost.

Cantú's triptych takes apart the commonplace notion that borders simply binarize. As the portraits suggest, the multiple crossings create not pairs but systems. Cantú does not provide one single photograph of "the border" itself. Constituted through text, through the text of the multiple narra-tives that make up *Canícula,* the border emerges not as a stable line, river, or bridge, but as a shifting locus of identity and displacement. In other words, in *Canícula* it is not just text, nor just text and photos that makes up the border—it is text, photos, and photos displaced into narrative. The bor-der is constantly evoked and disappeared; this strategy parallels the slippage between the discursive and the material that Gina Valdés's work invokes.

"Still Trembling"

Taking the border's history into account, reconceptualizing it as process, denaturalizes it and makes visible some of the operations that work to sustain it. As *Dreams of the Centaur* and *Canícula* highlight, by exploring the history of the border, it is possible to see how the border works to produce gendered and sexualized, eroticized and racialized identities that reinforce and reinscribe state power by centering that power as determinative. Yet if these two texts make this process visible, they do so in part because a discourse that figures the border patrolman as hypermasculine has flourished throughout the twentieth century. As the site that supposedly threatens the innocent inner reaches of America, the border becomes a zone for proving masculinity, for homosocial bonding in which the nation's desire to be desired is visibilized through the anxious energies of men (and boys) proving their masculinity by preventing other men from penetrating the nation. Adventure stories set on the border depend on the economy of border erotics just as Arturo Islas's novel *Migrant Souls* satirizes it by drawing attention to the freighted, theatrical rituals that rely on the hyper-masculinized agent of the state.

Freemont B. Deering's *The Border Boys across the Frontier* (1911) and Gerald Breckenridge's *The Radio Boys on the Mexican Border* (1922) paint idealistic portraits of young "American men"—their masculinity, athletic prowess, intelligence, and earnest will displayed on each page. They are the white sons of wealthy entrepreneurs with "business interests" in Mexico and along the border. Both novels rely on obvious stereotypes of Mexicanos and stage the border as a buffer zone between an idealized United States and a plotting, turbulent Mexico.

Border Boys follows the adventures of three young men when they join an archaeological expedition in New Mexico to search for the signs of human sacrifice among a "vanished race."[59] The "boys" accidentally get caught in the middle of a gun-running scheme operated by supporters of Francisco Madera; the boys not only stop the scheme but subsequently save a gold mine and its cache of $20,000 in gold bullion from the "insurrectos." In Breckenridge's novel, the "Radio Boys," as they call themselves, also travel from the East Coast of the United States to New Mexico, but in this case they hope to foil a plot by the "Octopus" (a thinly veiled depiction of the

Standard Oil Trust).[60] They become embroiled in an attempt by revolutionaries and their German sympathizers to draw the United States into a war with Mexico in order to overthrow General Obregon. Mexico's revolution is invoked as a threat to American capital, and the border functions as a buffer and military theater. Mexican masculinity is declared inept in this border region—young, inexperienced white boys successfully tackle smugglers and revolutionaries.

In both novels, the border becomes a place to prove white masculinity against what are portrayed as the shortcomings of Mexican masculinity.[61] For if, as Amy Kaplan argues, earlier romance novels depicted white masculinity proving itself for domestic female consumption, these subsequent narratives display boys' masculinity largely for the consumption of other white boys.[62] In this manner, the border is imbricated in a queer reading economy that displaces homoerotic energy onto the representation of racial conquest.

Young, white adventurers use their wits and muscle to protect U.S. capital against Mexicans whose "Indian" ancestry is exemplified by certain skills: "Moreover, those of them who dwell along it know the border far better than any white could ever hope to."[63] Mexicans are further viciously stereotyped by alternate references to their "cunning" or their "aversion to work."[64] Boys outwit and outmuscle experienced Mexican soldiers: "But whatever the Mexican might have been able to do with knife or pistol, he was no match for the muscles of the American lad."[65] One revolutionary leader sums up this attitude by noting, "I see it is useless to fight against Young America."[66] Spoken by a veteran soldier about adolescent boys, the comment rings as a disciplinary warning to those who would oppose U.S. economic interests and as a disciplinary invitation to those who might seek a model of white masculinity in an era of segregation as well as industrial and imperial expansion. That these young men are the sons of scions of industry further suggests the ideological link between narratives of masculinity, race, and economy, between the nation as imperialist economic power and young men as its allegorical embodiment.

This tradition of hypermasculinized border heroes suggests that one of the vectors of desire that produces the border, or the desire that the border itself produces, is a queer desire, carrying a homoerotic charge in which anxiety about penetration implies an immanent desire for it. In another boy's adventure story, *Pagan: A Border Patrol Horse* written by Sterner St. Paul

Meek and published in 1952, border patrolmen and their horses round up laborers crossing the border informally, solve a murder, and help to disband a marijuana and opium smuggling network. The homoerotic energy imbricated in the hypermasculine model erupts at a crucial moment in the narrative as border patrolmen arrest suspected smugglers: "His skilled hands went quickly over the four men in turn. He gave a glance around to make sure the Mexican crone was not in sight, then turned again to the prisoners. 'Remove your clothing!' he snapped. There was a moment of hesitation but as Ramon moved forward with a threatening air, the *mojados* removed their shirts. 'Turn around, Felipe,' Ramon said in a deceptively soft tone. 'Now, stand just so while we admire your manly beauty'" (55).

Pagan underscores the potential erotics of power as an arresting officer commands his captives; the border becomes a region of crisis, terror, *and* desire. Desire, not surprisingly, is racialized. Ramon is everywhere described as a Chicano whose "superior" tracking skills are attributed to "an inheritance from his Indian forebears." If his queer performance is carried out at least in part for his Anglo partner (and readers), it is nonetheless because of his racialized identity that such queerness does not threaten the image of the border patrol's heteromasculinity. And it is this heteromasculine hero, a discursive maneuver underscored by cinematic depictions of border patrolmen, that the children's books so carefully inscribe.[67]

Such patriarchal, if not homoerotic, narratives of the border are elaborately satirized in Arturo Islas's novel *Migrant Souls* (1990).[68] *Migrant Souls* moves between migration and immigration, between the sense that, as the borderlands dicho goes, "We didn't cross the border, the border crossed us!" and the understanding that this knowledge, this history of invasion and conquest, is largely deemed irrelevant by many who patrol and produce the border. *Migrant Souls* further suggests the significance of cultural rituals for producing U.S. citizens—the "migrants" and "immigrants" of the borderlands—and subtly links these rituals to crossing the border itself, revealing how seemingly disparate events and practices (in this case celebrating Thanksgiving and crossing a bridge) reinforce each other and the nation. As the novel implies, it is through its repeated, ritual crossings that the border is naturalized; calling attention to such rituals displaces the effects of its naturalization, produces it, following Renato Rosaldo, as a theater, "simultaneously symbolic and material, constructed and violent."[69]

In *Migrant Souls,* Eduviges Salazar decides to cook a traditional Thanksgiving meal despite her husband's objections in order to please her children who have been learning about it in school. " 'Eating turkey is going to turn my girls into little *gringas*. Is that what you want?' " Sancho Salazar argues (22). The ritual won't, of course, have transubstantiating effects, but it will reinforce the message of his daughters' education and the dominance of amnesiac cultural traditions; Sancho also recognizes the extent to which the repetition of ritual freights these cultural traditions with truth-effects.[70]

Sancho ultimately concedes to his wife's plan and the family crosses from "Del Sapo" to Juarez in search of a turkey for their dinner. They anticipate their trip to obtain and smuggle a turkey with a discussion replete with fear of the border patrol's powers of incarceration and the anecdotal knowledge that moves that fear from paranoia to common sense. They remember, for instance, that neighbors, U.S. citizens, are repeatedly picked up and deported because they "appear" Mexican, and they remember the humiliating strip searches their friends have undergone. As the narrator remarks, "The Angel children were brought up on as many deportation stories as fairy tales and family legends" (23). The family also remembers the numbers of people who die attempting to cross the border, suggesting that the border also serves as a tomb.[71] Like "fairy tales and family legends," deportation stories function, then, to socialize the children, producing contradictory and split subjects capable of self-policing and of critiquing the mechanics of the border system.

Sancho prepares his daughters: " 'Now remember, girls,' Sancho said, wiping his face. 'I'll do all the talking at the bridge. You just say "American" when the time comes. Not another word, you hear?' " (28). Sancho's participation in the crossing ritual begins with these instructions—instructions parents regularly repeat to children "to avoid trouble" everywhere along "the line." Sancho knows that a caustic or sarcastic answer to the agent's query about citizenship will create problems if the agent feels annoyed or threatened or disrespected—in other words, he tells his daughters to memorize their lines for the play. Ironic as claiming *American* as opposed to *U.S.* citizenship may be, Sancho understands its value: " 'Serena,' he said, 'I'd hate to lose you because of this stupid bird but if you open your mouth except to say "American," I won't be responsible for what happens. Okay?' " (28). Sancho thus reminds his daughters of the "proper" answer to the ritual question, "What's your citizenship?" This question is paired frequently with "Where are you coming from?" and "Have anything to declare?" Like a catechetic ritual ("Who made you?" "God made me."), the border patrol agents' standard questions reinforce their power to include and exclude, to grant status and to deny it.

Despite the girls' knowledge of their script and the "fact" of their citizenship status, their symbolic status within the United States nevertheless remains in question as long as the nation continues to conflate citizenship with having an Anglo appearance. As the family drives toward the bridge, one daughter asks "her father if they were aliens" (29). Her question emerges from her anxiety over their crossing and from her experience of being called an alien at school. " 'That's what they call Mexican people in the newspapers. And Kathy Jarvis at school told me real snotty at recess yesterday that we were nothing but a bunch of resident aliens.' " Sancho responds with a vehemence that startles his daughter. Having already reminded her that " 'We are not aliens. We are American citizens of Mexican heritage,' " he continues, " 'The next time she tells you that, you tell her that Mexican and Indian people were in this part of the country long before any *gringos,* Europeans (he said 'Yurrup-beans') or anyone else decided it was theirs. That should shut her up. If it doesn't, tell her those words are used by people who think Mexicans are not human beings' " (29).

Sancho here challenges the normative script of the border and its symbolic role in dehumanizing people. Sancho's rebuke intertwines the history of genocide, invasion, and colonization with a critique of the discursive production of the border system's work as an abjection machine: "Don't you see, Josie. When people call Mexicans those words, it makes it easier for them to deport or kill them" (30). Sancho's deconstruction of the border project entails laying bare the interaction between naming and policing. By explaining the political uses to which abjection can be put, he underscores the complicated systemic workings of the border.

Sancho curses as he, the two young girls, and the turkey draw close to the crossing guard, "Oh shit. . . . I hate this goddamned bridge" (34). Sancho's hatred is probably less for the bridge itself than for the border stations that crown either end of the bridge and that mark history as catastrophe, to paraphrase Lisa Lowe.[72] In other words, the bridge exemplifies the trope of difference used to justify the invasion of Mexican territory and the subjugation over the next hundred years of the remnants of the population who remained in their ancestral lands. Thus, Sancho's curse, "I hate this goddamned bridge," focuses on a space that must be understood in multi-dimensional and multitemporal terms. Norma Klahn points out that the border emerges as a means "both to delineate and to inscribe" difference — as though the border naturally implies, "Where the line is delimited, the 'other' begins."[73] Sancho's curse points to the uneven effects of this line and the violence that its banality hides. His curse echoes the border's seemingly benign spatial function, one that repeatedly reinforces and inscribes sub-jugation at the same time that it naturalizes the national narrative of an exceptional United States preserving democracy and freedom.

While the family drives toward the border, the turkey (who had been placed in the back of the truck in a covered crate on which Serena sits) is silent. But when they slow down to wait in line and then pull toward an agent, the turkey starts gobbling. As the turkey's gobbling grows louder "in a long stream of high pitched gurgles" the border agent takes notice and starts to search the truck. "Behind them, Serena began gobbling along with the bird and it was hard for them to tell one gobble from another." Serena attempts to mask the turkey by performing as a turkey. Instead of remaining silent, instead of confessing only her citizenship status, she erupts into babble. Excess covers excess, so to speak. Behind Sancho and the girls, in the family's car, is their mother. She sees what is happening and reacts quickly: "Their mother pressed down on the horn of the Chevy and made it stick. Eduviges was ready to jump out of the car and save her daughter from a fate worse than death." Eduviges can perceive the risks, her anxiety about a fate worse than death reminding readers of the stories about border patrol agents who have raped women and children in custody (a history that Fontes similarly recalls):

> In the middle of the racket, the officer's frown was turning into anger and he started yelling at Serena.
>
> "American!" she yelled back and gobbled.
>
> "What have you got there?" The officer pointed to the plastic covered crate.
>
> "It's a turkey," Serena shouted. "It's American, too." She kept gobbling along with the noise of the horn. Other drivers had begun honking with impatience.
>
> The patrolman looked at her and yelled, "Sure it is! Don't move," he shouted toward Sancho. (34–35)

Serena throws the confessional scene of the border crossing into confusion by confessing their secret cargo—revealing the secret—and by parodying the narrative of national belonging (indeed her claim that "It's American, too" recalls Ben Franklin's efforts to declare the turkey the official symbol of the United States). Like parrots, avocados, and horses, the gobbling turkey suggests that what gets "crossed" are above all economic commodities and that the agent, whose primary role is to produce revenue for the state, can be tricked.[74]

Eduviges, realizing the extent of the crisis, builds on her daughter's performance. For if her daughter has slipped out of speech, she slips into hysteria: "Eduviges had opened the hood and was pretending not to know what to do. Rushing towards the officer, she grabbed him by the sleeve and pulled him away from the pickup. Confused by the din, he made gestures that Sancho took as permission to drive away. 'Relax, *señora,* and please let go of my arm'"(35). In resorting to a hysteria that moves the agent into a patriarchal and protective pose, Eduviges demonstrates a spontaneous ingenuity, manipulating the codes that establish his power by enacting the role assigned her. In a different version of the story, Islas adds a line to this scene that reinforces the narrative of patriarchal protectiveness that Eduviges so brilliantly maneuvers around. Having gained the patrolman's attention, "Eduviges tightened her grip, buried her head in his jacket and made sobbing noises that took him off guard. 'Don't cry, *señora,*' he said. 'It's only your horn. I'll fix it in no time at all.'"[75] In so doing, she calls on the border patrol agent to enact the gendered role prescribed to him both as a man and as an agent of the state. Furthermore, both Eduviges and Serena turn the abjection machine in on itself by performing the very abjection it desires; by moving outside speech, they might appear to disarticulate their own subjectivity, but instead double-cross the system that would define them:

> In the truck, Sancho was laughing like a maniac and wiping the tears and his nose on his sleeve. "Look at that, Josie. The guy is twice as big as your mother." She was too scared to laugh and did not want to look. Several blocks into South Del Sapo, she was still trembling. Serena kept on gobbling in case they were being followed by the *migra* in unmarked cars. (35)

Largely powerless, the family resorts to charades, mimesis, and hysteria to outwit the armed and annoyed agent. Yet the two girls' reaction also suffuses the moment with the bitter irony of terror. Although Sancho sets the rules, it is Eduviges who pulls off the ruse—suggesting the subtle linkages between patriarchy and nation-making. Eduviges understands that "following the script" won't work. Or, rather, she understands that one patriarchal script can be used against another. The family's seemingly playful encounter engages the serious work of nation-making at its most banal level. Their refusal to consent to the regulations that the border agent enforces and that contrive to structure relations of power is, in this case, a minor rebuke. Yet, juxtaposed with the long tradition of Thanksgiving and with the devastation and genocide the holiday enshrines and mystifies, this turkey crossing takes on broader significance. How precisely might the young girls now interpret the Thanksgiving ritual and its role in reinforcing an ideology that has made the border an omnipresent zone of terror for them? *Migrant Souls* anatomizes the border as an erotic theater where actors both wittingly and unknowingly enact prescribed roles. Such an anatomy reveals that manipulating a state-sponsored aesthetic project requires ingenuity and wit, as well as, it would seem, a sense of history.

"Wide Gaps of Unguarded Stretches"

The preceding border-crossing narratives invoke the border system's power but situate it as contested; refuse it the status of given or natural; and underscore its productive capacities—capacities that these narratives alternately satirize and defy. By producing different conceptions of the border, they unfix its ability to sediment identity; indeed, they betray its skill at abjection through a political imaginary that refuses the system's gestures toward a kind of omnivorous monumentality. These textual critiques are not, of course, the only critiques available; a wide range of retablos, corridos, rock music, and performance art also turns to the border—or overturns it.

Yet it would be naive to understand these efforts to betray the system, to double-cross it, as functioning completely outside of the border system. The work of Cantú, Islas, Valdés, and Fontes considers the border system not as a symbol or a stable, guarded line but as productive (especially of enmity). While they disclose the border systems' contradictions and the various dis-identifications that it necessarily produces, they nevertheless continue to do battle within the system itself, even as they imagine the route outside. If I seek here to be less than utopic about the possibilities of these texts' radical potential, it is not because I do not admire their imaginative maneuvers. Rather, I want to suggest how such border betrayals emerge as contingent to the ideology of nationalism. During its first century, the United States defined itself in part through its refusal to acquiesce to something like "natural borders"; it defined itself through its insistence that as a nation it could pick and choose and settle on its own boundaries. By 1926, when Captain Jackson, charged with policing the borders, complained to Congress that smugglers "cross the borders in the wide gaps of unguarded stretches" and that he therefore requested additional personnel and technological assistance to police those gaps, this lynchpin of national self-identity had been lost.[76] A new national self-identity emerged, one which depended not on forever pushing the borders of the nation; not, as historian Zorilla might say, on nourishing its insatiable appetite for land; but on transforming the now-permanent border into something like Fortress U.S.A., making the nation "impregnable." The "crisis" over the border is an inevitable outcome of this gnawing loss of nation-making, boundary-producing, national self-understanding. As Jackson himself acknowledges, the "sealing of our borders against illegal entry is very much more far-reaching than would at first be suspected."[77] Although Jackson not surprisingly proceeds to argue that without sealed borders the nation-making process must devote itself to the internal cleansing of its apparatus by identifying the "public charges," "criminals" and "political agitators," who would endanger the "general morals" of the nation and "menace the health of counties," having freely entered through the gaps—an argument that, as Lisa Lowe has so effectively shown, forms the concept of citizen through the production of "alien"—what might actually have been more "far-reaching" is the crisis that the loss of such a foundational narrative has engendered. These texts respond to that loss, exploiting and stabilizing it.[78]

In a similar manner, the preceding double-crossing scenes refuse to establish the border as either outside time or as a marker of time. Instead, they emphasize the process of bordering and of the labor that borders perform, as well as how such labors may be undermined. The crossing narratives also suggest the extent to which sexuality and borders intermingle both through threat, interdiction, and the creation of the abject, as well as overt desire. Finally, they indicate the extent to which Chicana/o writers have studied the mechanics of a border that is neither static nor monumental but is instead a process implicated in terror and revenue collection.

3

Intermarginalia: Chicana/a Spatiality

and Sexuality in the Work of Gloria Anzaldúa

and Terri de la Peña

If, as Chicana border-crossing narratives point out, the U.S.-Mexico border is both a system with multiple and slippery meanings and symbologies
and a state-sponsored aesthetic project whose crossing and ongoing production involve contradictory and ambivalent historical narratives, family
memories, desires, and national(ist) fantasies, then to meditate on "borders"
is no simple, naïve, or clichéd task. Gloria Anzaldúa's *Borderlands/La frontera*
further underscores this point through a theoretical discussion of borders
that moves, from multiple vantage points and through shifting genres, to
tackle the sliding tensions between border meanings and effects.[1] Layered
into the text are a series of repeating terms that link ideas and establish
contradictions as well as continuities. Many of these terms have a spatial
valence—border, interface, margin—that help to emphasize the text's keen
investment in understanding spatiality, in the discursive power of producing borders of various kinds, and in the near-monumental powers of the
U.S.-Mexico border to organize knowledge and to foster desires. In other
words, the text explores the spatiality of desire—how the social production
of space involves desire as well as desirability.

This interplay between space and desire becomes particularly clear in
the poem "Interface," a biting critique of the sexual politics of what could
be called a spatial-visual matrix.[2] A "lesbian sci-fi love poem," as Yvonne
Yarbro-Bejarano calls it, "Interface" tells the story of a love affair between
a human and an "alien" and concludes the section of poems Anzaldúa titles
"Crossers y otros atravesados."[3] *Atravesados* is slang for *queer,* so the implied translation "Crossers and Other Queers" suggests the interplay between movement and pleasure. More particularly, it calls attention to the

way sexuality and desire may be referenced with a spatial shorthand. Yet if this is a playful title, the quote that follows from Isabel Parra is less so: "Al otro lado está el río / y no lo puedo cruzar" [On the other side is the sea/ I cannot cross (bridge) it]. This quote seems to assert the impossibility of crossing and bridging. The speaker knows of the existence of the other side of the river but claims, "I can't cross it." Crossing is suspended between the knowledge of and apparent desire for an "other" side and the prohibitions or difficulties of getting there—crossing thus signifies a melancholic sense of inability. The poems in that section trace, sometimes with exquisite delight, the memory of a love affair ("Compañera, cuando amábamos") or the pain of love lost and loneliness ("En mi corazón se incuba"); they also describe vicious hate crimes ("Yo no fuí, fue Teté") and racialized and homophobic police violence ("Corner of 50th St. and Fifth Ave."). Not surprisingly, given the heading "Crossers," several of the poems place queerness in the street— where violence occurs, as well as where "Mano en mano nos paseabamos por las calles" [Hand in hand we wandered the streets]. "Interface" concludes this series of intimate poems about the experience of being queer in the world, of crossing rivers and categories and norms, by questioning the very worldliness of queerness.

In 1987, when *Borderlands* was first released, *interface* might have evoked relationships between computer components (parts that "interfaced" could "speak" to each other) rather than the word's nineteenth-century geometrical definition ("a surface lying between the two portions of matter or space, and forming their common boundary"), but the word's spatial (and outer-spacial) valences murmur throughout this playful, narrative poem.[4] Written in first person, the poem begins with the narrator recounting how she began to "see" her lover "at the edges of things . . . / Where before there'd only been empty space."[5] In keeping with Cisneros, Ponce, Montiel, and Cantú, Anzaldúa's narrator works to push past the limits of an ideologically imposed vision (of what she has been taught one can possibly see). As she allows her vision to "blur," and thereby to transform the harsh edges and see into the interface (between the material objects and the space that surrounds them), she discovers that at least initially "it was hard to stay / on the border between / the physical world / and hers. / It was only at the interface / that we could see each other."[6] Unlike the melancholic tone set by Parra's epigraph at the outset of the section, "Interface" suggests that contemplating the space between—indeed, discovering the largely hidden surface lying between two portions of matter or space—and then falling into that space, opens whole new arenas for desire, pleasure, and transformation. In this sense, too, the poem continues the argument made throughout *Borderlands/La frontera* that categories do disciplinary work with spatial effects—that a whole range of categories work to place people and limit their movements, desires, economies. Critiquing those categories, looking past their edges, changes what you can see, who you can love, and who can love you.

The narrator describes her efforts to communicate and touch her emerging and barely visible queer object of desire. As she does so the two begin to experience each other's presence: "We lay enclosed   by margins, hems, / where only we existed."[7] Anzaldúa leaves a gap between *enclosed* and *by,* visually emphasizing the erotic-spatial work of margins. Yet *hems* changes the argument by suggesting that a slipped enclosure is almost protective or by suggesting instead that the couple is "hemmed in" or locked into a limited maneuverability that conditions their possibilities.

The narrator continues throughout this long stanza to describe the growing "physicality" of a "human" and "noumenal" love—a physicality that is made even more tangible when "Leyla," as the narrator calls her, enters with an icy chill "in / and in and in," after which "I started hurting a little / When I started cramping / she pushed out / her fingers, forearm, shoulder. Then she stood before me."[8] The narrator gives birth to her lover; but this surprising turn is less important than Leyla's next phase of embodiment. Having been born, Leyla gets to work learning "to pass" (although she can alternately make herself invisible). Leyla's process of learning to pass (as human) underscores the poem's critique of the categories that define human acceptability and the codified behaviors that make people visible and invisible in public places. Like those laboring under the strictures of alien citizenship-status, Leyla protects herself and her lover by adapting the unacknowledged— hence banal, hence nearly invisible—norms of public behavior reinforced through, for example, the courtesies of commercial interactions or "appropriate" dress and gait. Leyla's education hides her "alien" status, and in this playful manner reminds us that other kinds of "aliens" must learn similar tricks if they are to avoid the gaze of the INS. On the other hand, the ability to operate outside those guidelines is made possible by the guidelines' own rigidity, as Leyla suggests when she walks, without a plane ticket, past a flight attendant, then comments "humans only saw what they were told to see."[9]

The possibilities of alien love entail understanding the failure of borders or, alternately, understanding how borders structure possibilities. For Leyla and the narrator, *alien* signifies not codified legal behavior but the failure of categories to contain; that is, it suggests that along the edges of categories so neatly defined and smugly presented and so powerfully wielded by the state lay alter-narratives. As the poem concludes,

> Last Christmas I took her home to Texas.
> Mom liked her.
> Is she a lez, my brothers asked.
> I said, No, just an alien.
> Leyla laughed.[10]

The play between *lez* and *alien* implicates both in systems of management and matrices of knowledge. In this rendition, the spatial aspects of *alien* are made clear because they suggest how movement—Who may and may not move freely about the country? Under what conditions? Where, when? When can such a status be revoked?—can be regulated through the naming process. This alternative structure of being does not fit easily into existing city spaces, as is detailed in the poems preceding "Interface," which depict the violence and hostility awaiting queers on the streets. Indeed, these poems make it clear why Leyla requires an education in passing: so that her citizenship status may not be questioned. If she can pass, no one will ask her for her papers.

Under the guise of a science-fiction love story, "Interface" links border-making to the less spatially marked category of citizenship. In indicating the spatiality of citizenship, the poem participates in Chicana feminists' broader effort to reconsider the status of citizen, a reconceptualization, Chela Sandoval argues, that has been made necessary as a strategic response to the movements and vicissitudes of power. A reconstituted understanding of citizenship would be based not on a unitary sense of self but rather on a "self-conscious flexibility of identity."[11] Cherríe Moraga's play *Heroes and Saints* (1994), Tish Hinojosa's album *Frontejas* (1994), and Lucha Corpi's novel *Cactus Blood* (1995) all challenge the grounds on which citizenship is constituted by calling into question how subjectivity is authorized and on what terms history can be deployed by the state.[12] Terri de la Peña's novel *Margins* (1992), extends this critique of citizenship by interrogating its limits in sexual and racial terms.[13] *Margins* explores how the construction of regulatory arenas such as cities, universities, convents, and cemeteries work in tandem with public discourse to force Chicana lesbians to feel like interlopers. At the same time, the novel also shows how race and sexuality are used to stabilize the distinctions between "the public" and "the private," and by extension, citizenship.

Citizenship has been a central concept in the development of the modern nation-state.[14] The structure of citizenship has depended on a unitary (white, male) subject and has been held together by a gendered and racialized spatial framework. The unitary (male) subject-citizen functions as an agent who moves easily between the so-called public and private spheres. Feminists theorizing the production of space have turned repeatedly to an analysis of the microphysics of public and private spheres to explore how women experience space differently; how they negotiate choices between work, housing, recreation; and how the gendering of public and private spaces works to reinforce power relations. These analyses reveal that the "social process of symbolic encoding and decoding produces 'a series of homologies between the spatial, symbolic and social orders.'"[15] Until recently, however, such spatial analysis has not considered the degree to which constructions of race and sexuality further constitute and hold together the distinctions between public and private spheres, nor has it taken into account that the obverse operates as well, because spatial distinctions help to structure sexuality, race, and class.[16]

Margins offers a provocative opportunity to examine further the complex interplay between sexuality, race, gender, and the regulation of space. The novel follows Veronica Melendez as she recovers from a near-fatal car accident and mourns the death of her lover, Joanna Muñoz, in that accident. A graduate student in UCLA's English department, a struggling fiction writer, and closeted to her family, Veronica attempts to create a series of short stories describing her six-year relationship with Joanna. As she struggles with the recovery and writing process, she becomes involved with René Talamantes, spends time at her Carmelite sister's convent retreat house, comes out to her family, and completes drafts of her stories. The rapid movement of the plot is accompanied by an equally rapid, if not dizzying, tour of southern California. By utilizing a series of specific spaces including Santa

Monica, UCLA, and Santa Barbara, the novel moves beyond simply mapping, charting, or repossessing land with all of their mimetic assumptions and notions of spatial transparency to the complicated process of narrating the impact of space, its aliveness rather than its inertness. Veronica must negotiate in and around a labyrinth of spaces, few of which are truly welcoming and most of which would either disavow or consume her texts. *Margins's* compelling survey of geographic semiotics re-visions the overdetermined sites of the university, the convent, and the grave, while also repopulating a white-washed city with Mexican Americans.

PoMo S.M.

The city, perhaps more than any other public space, has been narrated as male (the locale for flaneurs and industrialists among others) and as a network of public spaces enclosed by private spaces through which (some) men may dance with impunity. Anthony Vidler argues that the production of this narrative has involved psychic projections of fear and displaced anxieties. While it is apparent that "modernist space, and its late twentieth century extensions, are for the most part constructed by and for men," these erections are "inevitably riddled with rejection, suppression, anxiety, and phobic fear."[17] Twentieth-century Euro-American theorizing of the metropolis developed out of earlier conceptions of the city as harboring "dangerous diseases, epidemics, and equally dangerous social movements," as well as the newly discovered nervous diseases formulated by mental- and social-science movements.[18] Pathologies of agoraphobia and claustrophobia were identified as gendered "urban phobias," inciting architects and planners to call for open, thoroughly transparent, garden-like cities that radiated harmony.[19] Demand for these imaginary cities, according to Vidler, grew out of an anxiety that people in cities were "prone to neurasthenic disease— the 'weak,' the 'enervated,' the 'over-stimulated,' the 'degenerated' and the 'bored'—[these] were bound to succumb to mental collapse, and first in line, for the psychologists and psychoanalysts, were women and homosexuals."[20]

The problem for modernist planners was that they thought homosexuals, in particular, thrived on the closed and closeted spaces of cities, their alleys, and shadows, and anonymity. The antidote, they decided, would be to create the open spaces of gardens and glass buildings, seeming anathemas to homosexuals who would then be unable to run for cover. According to this narrative, the spaces of the city—that is, the spatial organization of urban social relations—actually produce a nonheterosexual sexuality that predicates heterosexual anxieties about its own systemic equilibrium. Such "founding" narratives of contemporary city planning conflate homosexuality with mental "abnormalities" and make homosexuals a threat to be eliminated or managed along with neurasthenic diseases. In this context, Anzaldúa's "Interface" takes on new significance. If read as an allegory about the threat that the marginalized poses to the production of the normal, then "Interface" can be seen as an enactment of the fears that city planners had fantasized about. In other words, Anzaldúa's poem is in a kind of concordance with the planners: it is out of the (narrow, crowded) spaces between sanctioned sites (i.e., the alleys, riñconcitos) that non-normative desire can flourish, if one can grasp the presence of such edges in the first place.

More than a century after planners offered their theories of sex in the city, the coding of cities remains an ambivalent one for gay men and lesbians. And this coding has very precise effects in the battle over civil rights—over who may be deemed a proper subject by the state, what that citizenship can mean, and what protections it ensures. Contemporary documentaries such as *The Gay Agenda,* produced by the Christian Antelope Valley Springs of Life Ministries and released at nearly the same time as Seal Press released *Margins,* visualize the city as insidious, confusing, and hyperstimulated, thereby establishing a narrative about dangerous city life that hardly differs from the anxieties expressed by nineteenth-century planners and economists. *The Gay Agenda* is a study in the cinematic screening of space, taking advantage of bad lighting, unfocused and jumpy shots, and visual stereotypes to suggest a kind of out-of-control simultaneity that somehow threatens a fundamentalist desire for hierarchy and order. In other words, the video productively draws from the still circulating master-narratives of the city even if they are no longer openly couched in the language of criminology and sexology.

The film begins with a male voice-over worrying that a stronger battle must be waged against "homosexuals' larger plan" to gain "special minority rights." It uses California's battle over legislation that would have made discrimination on the basis of sexuality illegal (AB101) as a framing device, beginning with the state-wide protests over Pete Wilson's veto of the bill and concluding with his approval of a similar measure the next year. Within the frames of this debate over citizenship, the film counterposes interviews with "former homosexuals," ministers, and psychiatrists alongside shots of Los Angeles gay pride parades, bars, and festivals. The interviews attempt to serve as stable and rational sites of containment, thereby highlighting the seemingly frantic scenes of dancers and marchers. The cameras repeatedly pan across buildings and cars and back to the marchers in order to contextualize gay activity by underscoring its status as public. In this manner, *The Gay Agenda* endeavors to reconstitute power relations by creating anxiety over the ruptured distinctions between the public and the private. Realizing that the binary no longer operates effectively to contain queer activity and that its rupture destabilizes a heterosexual regime, the film narrates the city as crisis-ridden in order to again assert a claim to police space and social relations. Through the visual narration of the city as implicitly dangerous for heterosexuals (perhaps especially so for young, white men), the film calls for the renegotiation of citizenship laws; "special minority rights" entail, the film repeatedly suggests, access to public space and to an identity readily translatable as queer. Controlling the category of citizen involves not only governing access to public spaces, including streets and parks, but also controlling how those spaces may be structured and produced.

What *The Gay Agenda* portrays as scary and dangerous emerges in a queer imaginary geography as compelling and potentially liberating, if ambivalently so. The move from the rural to the urban is a common trope in lesbian writing, which frequently suggests that only by moving to larger cities can women find the opportunities, partners, and evidence, as it were, for less restrictive outlets for their desires.[21] In many such narratives, the bar and the university provide nodules of mildly liberated space.[22] These regions or zones of otherness—warehouse districts, "bad neighborhoods"— may be heavily surveilled by police yet pocketed away and slightly off-center from the surveillance of normalizing (white) heterosexuality. That is, because the logic of uneven development encouraged the creation of something like "the other side of the tracks," queer clubs situate themselves as sexually transgressive but enabled by the contradictory practices of capitalist development. Gay bars and cafes flourish, according to Larry Knopp because a "plethora of othernesses that have emerged in the 'postmodern' era owe their independent existence to the mobility of capital and the universality and sociality of money."[23] To a certain extent, then, predominantly gay male locales and, to a much lesser extent, lesbian sites are tributes to "capital's immense power (and current need) to appropriate almost all alternative coding and symbols and to construct them as new othernesses that become constituent elements in the creation of new economically productive places."[24]

Margins does not offer a wholly liberatory view of the city, although its claims are directly contradictory to *The Gay Agenda*. While taking place in Los Angeles and Santa Monica, *Margins* virtually ignores the gay center of West Hollywood that the film so deplores. Characters move, often uncomfortably, among dances, working-class bars, women's bookstores, pharmacies, beachfront cafes, and coffeehouses. The lack of representations of gay student organizations, queer dance clubs, or something like a gay center attests not to their absence in Los Angeles, but rather implies a critique of such groups. Such centers, the novel hints, are more likely to have been designed to appeal to white, gay men with more financial and political resources than women of color. But if capital seeks out its familiar agent, that does not mean queer women of color have been rendered passive. Rather, as Yolanda Ritter explains, women of color in Los Angeles have worked hard to develop queer centers designed for people of color, and she notes the continued strength and vibrancy of a few of these, as well as the more frequent commercial failure of others.[25] That history is absent in *Margins,* reflecting Veronica's general sense of alienation from a larger queer community and the geographically dispersed quality of queer groups of color within Los Angeles itself.

Not surprisingly events in *Margins* are far more likely to occur in places designated as straight rather than queer. As the narrative moves back and forth between the ostensibly private spaces of homes and apartments and the public spaces of restaurants and street corners, it calls attention to the degree to which public and commercial spaces are structured as heterosexist. For example, late in the narrative René Talamantes eagerly pursues a somewhat ambivalent Veronica Melendes. Having acted badly at an earlier meeting, René sees Veronica and, in a stunning parody of courtly love, kneels before her "in a supplicant's pose, hands crossed madonna-like over her breasts, dark head bent" (159). This scene takes place not in the sanctioned sites for gay activity but in a medical building's pharmacy. Predictably attracting attention and disapproval, the two women negotiate their complicated desires and the spatiality that makes such queer behavior "inconsiderate" and spectacularized (158–60). Their transgression simultaneously queers a pharmacy and reinforces the heterosexist imperative to police public space. The defiance of their gestures enacts Eve Kosofsky Sedgwick's assertion that the public/private binary functions not because any such pure places exist but because some people can claim the mastery of moving back and forth, using the private for public business and the public for the most intimate of matters, thereby delineating the meanings accruing to such places.[26] René and Veronica must contend with the stares of the pharmacist and the criticism of two other customers, reinforcing their sense of being "poachers," to twist Michel de Certeau's term.

An earlier moment in the narrative bolsters the importance of informal mechanisms that regulate space in order to police sexuality. At a restaurant, on what turns out to be a first date, Veronica and her neighbor Siena are sent drinks. When they reject the drinks and move to leave, their would-be suitor accosts them. Veronica resists his flirtations with Siena, but he responds, "You going to stop me, dyke?" (32), and shoves Veronica. While the man cannot control the women's access to space, another significant technology of control, he still attempts to maintain spatial dominance along two vectors—physical and verbal. Physical violence not surprisingly follows a verbal movement that dredges up hate speech. Veronica here threatens his sense of control and challenges his claim to a white female body, one that continues to function as the "repository of heirs to property and power," in Hazel Carby's terms.[27] What doesn't get questioned here, as it did in the pharmacy, is the man's ability to exert his presence. A consensus on the uses of space sanctions his sexuality, and he responds violently to its rupture.[28]

By dramatizing the complex multiplicities of city life for Chicana lesbians, *Margins* attempts to unplug the master narrative of the city from its "dirty secret." In this sense the novel performs what Françoise Lionnet calls "a discursive practice that encodes and transmits as well as creates ideology" and thereby functions as a "mediating force in society" because it produces "images that both participate in the dominant representations of their culture and simultaneously undermine and subvert those images by offering a re-vision of familiar scripts."[29] *Margins* suggests in these two scenes that queerness disrupts the presumed heteronormativity of public places by calling attention to it through queer contradiction. Furthermore, by focusing on activity at seemingly straight venues, the novel partly disconnects itself from the dominant white, gay, male coding of the city that Knopp identifies as a beneficiary of "capital's immense power." At the same time, it illustrates the very behavior *The Gay Agenda* militates against; by representing young Chicana dykes as actively claiming the full guarantees of citizenship, it does indeed threaten the homophobia that structures the management of the urban, transforming "special minority rights" (in all the racist regalia that the term implies) into the norm of an inclusive citizenship.

If *Margins* displaces a heteronormative concept of spatial management, it also ruptures the racialized narrative of Los Angeles history by re-placing Chicana/o communities in West Los Angeles, an area more typically represented as white and wealthy. It thereby reveals neighborhoods hardly surviving freeway construction and gentrification.[30] Raúl Villa argues that a whole generation of Chicano writers emerged in part as a response to the devastating history of freeway construction in Los Angeles County.[31] *Margins* is both a part of that effort and slightly distant from it, because it re-writes an L.A. script that usually locates "authentic" Chicanos in East Los Angeles and the San Gabriel Valley where much of the freeway construction has occurred. This relocation disrupts the symbolic system that has obliterated Santa Monica's Chicana/o history.[32]

The Santa Monica area was once a beach resort and low-cost neighborhood for Mexican American and African American families working as maids and gardeners for entertainment industry scions, as well as the birthplace of the modern aerospace industry and the expansive military-industrial complex.[33] Its Mexican American population once filled the regions between Olympic and Pico Boulevards, but that barrio was eliminated to make way for the Santa Monica freeway (I-10), which was officially, and without any irony, designated the Christopher Columbus Transcontinental Highway.[34] I-10 was constructed in the late 1950s and early 1960s, because the county's mass-transit system was being eliminated and the freeway was meant to serve as the major artery necessary for L.A.'s massive postwar growth.[35] The path through the barrio was chosen as a cheaper route than the more logical Wilshire corridor. Repeating patterns all over Los Angeles, thriving neighborhoods made up of Mexican Americans were dismantled and displaced to spur an economic growth cycle that would largely exclude them.[36]

The Santa Monica–Venice region—between Sunset Boulevard to the north and Venice Boulevard to the south—that *Margins* traverses exemplifies contemporary spatial trends. This area encompasses the Wilshire corridor, in which Santa Monica is the well-dressed junction "in the zone stretching from downtown to the ocean and branching south to the airport (LAX) [where there] are over sixty major corporate headquarters, a dozen banks and savings and loan companies with assets over one billion dollars, five of the eight largest international accounting firms, two-thirds of the 200 million square feet of high-rise office space in the region, a battalion of corporate law offices unrivaled off the east coast, and the national nucleus of the American military-industrial complex."[37] Within the shadow of the Wilshire high-rises, just to the south of this corridor, lies the Oakwood neighborhood, one of the poorest neighborhoods in Los Angeles County. The region thus embodies what Edward Soja refers to as the complex dynamics of intensification and extensification, part of the "crisis-generated attempt by capitalism to restore the key conditions for its survival: the opportunity for gaining superprofits from the juxtaposition of development and underdevelopment in the hierarchy of regionalized locales and amongst various productive sectors."[38] The characters in *Margins* cross these juxtaposed regions giving evidence to a spatial literacy that goes unacknowledged.

Santa Monica is also, like most of the southern California coastal cities, home to professional and managerial classes and corporations with vast assets. The area thereby reflects one of the "major changes in the structure of urban labor markets. . . . Deeper segmentation and fragmentation is occurring, with a more pronounced polarization of occupations between high pay/high skill and low pay/low skill workers, and an increasingly specialized residential segregation based on occupation, race, ethnicity, immigrant status, income, lifestyle, and other employment related variables."[39] This tendency results, Soja argues, in the increasing state-surveillance of low pay/low skill workers and the deepening wealth of high pay/high skill workers.

Margins maps the wage/occupation relationship described by Soja. Veronica's brother, Frank, a structural engineer, lives in a condominium on Santa Monica Boulevard, a transition street between the $11 million apartments on Wilshire and the older "single-family" neighborhoods south of Olympic. Veronica's parents (her father is a city-works crew supervisor) live in one of the few remaining Mexican American neighborhoods between the freeway and Rose Avenue in Venice. René and her mother, Guadalupe, a seamstress, single mother, and immigrant, live in the Oakwood area. *Margins* thereby develops the nuances between labor and identity, between access to higher wages and mobility, and between the continuum of skin-color and education. Indeed, the novel uses the fictional form to make an argument consistent with Cheryl Harris's assertion that whiteness has achieved a property value in U.S. jurisprudence, having gained the right to police and judicial protection.[40]

The novel traces the productive effects of such valuing via the forced negotiations of characters like Guadalupe and René. In charting the stratified relationships between labor, allocated living space, and self-identity, the novel illustrates how spatiality operates as a "set of relations between individuals and groups, an 'embodiment' and medium of social life itself."[41] In tracking the narrative and economic dynamics of "the urban," the novel suggests how intricately enmeshed in the geography of the everyday are the methods by which citizen is normalized as straight and white and middle class. Challenging that structure entails more than simply moving through it unnoticed, more than simply developing a spatial literacy that enables one to move across competing zones; for if the novel narrates what Soja calls "the instrumentality of space," it also suggests that refusing to capitulate entirely to the spatial narratives underlying capitalism can modify, if not stave off, the attendant disciplinary effects.

Terri de la Peña first read from her newly published first novel on UCLA's campus on 29 April 1992, only a few minutes after the verdicts of the Simi Valley jury were read. Word of the jury's acquittal of the policemen who beat Rodney King spread throughout the room and lingered as de la Peña proudly read from a text invoking the campus where she works as an administrative assistant. In the days that followed, as UCLA was engulfed in student protests and activist efforts to pressure the first Bush administration to bring the policemen to federal trial, the critique of the racialized, gendered, and heterosexist spatial structure of citizenship that *Margins* had launched was repeatedly manifested on the streets and in the academic commentary that followed. And although *Margins* did not predict the L.A. rebellion, it did implicitly suggest the formulation of resistance and anger that the mass uprising—which stretched from Pasadena to Venice and thus beyond the perimeter of the novel's geography—made visually clear to a confused television audience and an even more confused cadre of political leaders. In other words, de la Pena's novel, in its narrative of spatial practices, anatomizes much of the social and economic hierarchy that Los Angeles citizens rebelled against. It is not surprising, then, that one of the significant contributions of *Margins* is how it links a number of seemingly disparate sites in its examination of spatial instrumentality and disciplinarity. For example, universities have been crucial to urban transformations in the postwar period; so, not surprisingly, the novel devotes considerable narrative energy to the "place" of the university.

Surveying Campus

If attending a university is a major sign of access to the privileges of citizenship, then it is also one of the major mechanisms for interpolating students as proper citizens. *Margins* provides a metacommentary on this process by narrating Veronica and René's activities as UCLA graduate students and by suggesting, in the margins of the plot, the battles over who constitutes a proper university student, what texts should be promoted and by whom, and how seemingly alternative university venues fail in their claims of inclusivity. A contemporary research institution such as UCLA relays circuits of data, knowledge, and capital. Funded by a complex formula that includes government spy agencies, defense contractors, insurance and pharmaceutical firms, charity foundations, tax dollars, and, increasingly, student tuition, UCLA might easily be considered a significant exchange nexus (a file-server of sorts) for the contemporary movement of flexible capital, an arena for ideological explorations and battles over representation, as well as a producer of knowledge and the disciplined laborers necessary to further reproduce a multifaceted social system.

UCLA's site reinforces the complexity of the university's relationship to contemporary economic, political, and social relations. A massively landscaped, though architecturally dull campus, it commands a view of the ocean and mountains. More important, it is surrounded by one of the most expensive housing developments in the country (Bel-Air) and some of L.A.'s most prosperous neighborhoods (Westwood and Holmby Hills)—all these lending a country-club atmosphere to what is really an urban, commuter campus with what was, in the early 1990's, one of the most diverse student populations in the country. Thus, in *Margins*, René's twenty-minute drive from her Oakwood apartment to the borders of Bel-Air (the film school is roughly five blocks from Ronald Reagan's home) takes her from one end of the racially and financially segmented labor and housing markets to the other end of the hierarchy. Her trip mirrors the contemporary dynamics of global capitalism.

Margins similarly mirrors contemporary debates over the content of disciplinary canons. It opens with an exchange of texts between Veronica and Camille Zamora, a professor of literature: "With her index finger, Veronica Melendez shoved the paperback volume of Latina short stories across the table's weathered surface. . . . Camille Zamora outlined the pre-Columbian motif on the book's black and gold cover. 'What did you think of the cuentos?' " (3).

Along with the novel's dedication to Sandra Cisneros, Helena Viramontes, Gloria Anzaldúa, and Cherríe Moraga, the ritualized exchange of *Cuentos,* the first anthology of short stories by Latinas published in English, highlights the loose contours of the contemporary Chicana canon. Additionally, the exchange alludes rather neatly to the close relationships between Chicana poets, fiction writers, and scholars.[42] These relationships have been forged not simply through informal networks and ties, but also through annual events such as the meetings of the National Association of Chicano Studies and Mujeres Activas en Letras y Cambios Sociales. Chicanas' exclusion from academic discourse, both bodily and textually, has brought them together in a joint venture to disclose, however incompletely, "the barbarity implicit in the cultural documents encased and replicated by the university."[43] At the same time, this mutual effort has enabled them to believe, in the words of de la Peña's dedication, "que si es posible." Imagining possibilities has meant maneuvering, in scholarly and fictional terms, on the very terrain that has defined their experiences as marginal.[44]

De la Peña positions the novel with a nod toward its literary context through an opening dedication to other Chicana writers: "For the Chicana writers who by their example and work showed me que si es posible: Gloria Anzaldúa, Sandra Cisneros, Cherríe Moraga, y Helena Maria Viramontes" (iv). With this gesture de la Peña creates a set of literary comadres. Other acknowledgments of a self-conscious relationship to Chicana writers appear throughout the text. For example, Veronica mentions Viramontes's *The Moths* and later comments, "besides Cherríe Moraga and Gloria Anzaldúa, who else writes about Chicana lesbians nowadays?" (271); she also jokes about "becoming the next Sandra Cisneros." But just as *Margins* marks out a narrative community, it simultaneously suggests the fragility of that community and notes its exclusions. The very act of identifying other writers implies the limited number of contemporary writers and the relative anonymity of most in this writerly community. Indeed, with the exception of Cisneros, none of the writers mentioned had been published by a large New York press when *Margins* first appeared. The wry fantasy of becoming the "next Cisneros" further reinforces how excluded Chicanas have been from the racialized attention of commercial and academic presses.

The novel's dedication self-consciously places it within the context of a Chicana feminist movement, just as the exchange of texts that inaugurates the plot alerts readers to a foundational text within the contemporary Chicana literary tradition. Another exchange late in the story returns to this theme. Having triumphantly completed her stories and come out to her family, Veronica meets with Camille Zamora, gives her the new stories, and happily agrees to work as Zamora's teaching assistant for the coming term.

> "I'm including Audre Lorde, Sandra Cisneros, Mitsuye Yamada—Native American, Jewish and lesbian writers, too. Interested in being my T.A.?"
>
> Veronica crossed her left leg over her right, her fingers instinctively outlining the scar. "Sounds challenging. Why didn't you offer this course when I was an undergrad?"
>
> "What a difference tenure makes, verdad?" Camille laughed. "For one thing, we have a new department chair this year—he claims he's all for innovation and diversity." (314)

Given the constant references to the politics of publishing and Veronica's status as an aspiring writer, such a scene must be understood as more than a metacommentary on *Margins*'s own production and potential reception. Clearly a critique of the process of canonization, it also suggests the extent to which universities vet citizenship. And within such a spatially sensitive novel, this critique suggests how canon-making may be a spatial practice as much as a literary pursuit. In other words, the organization of national literary histories is frequently sedimented into a geopolitical history with grave consequences. When U.S. survey courses, for example, begin with the Puritans and progressively move both temporally and spatially to Bret Harte and "Western" literature, they participate in the cultural and spatial production of the U.S. that naturalizes one form of domination and, frequently, excludes the contests waged against it. In this manner, the university reinforces the system that established its role as an arbiter of citizenship (cultural and otherwise). To contest this role or the contents of the canon, as do the writers invoked in de la Peña's text, is to simultaneously advocate for an alternative spatiality. For to transform categories of citizenship would require the restructuring of spatial practices.

Another moment in the text further underscores Chicanas' ambivalent relationship to the university. It occurs at the campus movie theater after a screening of another Chicana lesbian's first film, *Tortilleras,* where René and Veronica meet for the first time. This meeting begins the novel's consideration of the complex interplay between race and desire:

> [René] squeezed Veronica's fingers. "So you're Chicana, too. Que suave! I got jazzed seeing you in the audience. Usually I'm the only brown woman in sight."
>
> "I know the feeling." Veronica met her compelling gaze. (99)

The visual pleasure René feels in seeing another "brown woman" is heightened by her own sense of scarcity. By remarking on their visual rarity, as it were, she both offers a political gesture of solidarity and implies a critique of the uneven educational opportunities for students of color. At the same time, this conversation allegorizes the lack of representations of Chicana graduate students within the symbolic economy as well as within the educational system.

This scene suggests, though it does not anatomize, the interplay between racialized status and desire. It does not explain, for example, how the two women's desire for each other might be inflected by the knowledge of their "singularity." That their meeting occurs on campus highlights a number of things. First, it emphasizes the important link between the construction of Chicana lesbian identities and universities.[45] It also contains a subtle critique of Chicano university politics: their meeting takes place not at a Chicano-sponsored venue, not at a site organized for Chicano networking such as a library or research center, but at a campus theater. And the women's relative isolation on campus indicates the extent to which Chicano cultural nationalism has refused to accommodate challenges to its alignment with heterosexuality. As Carla Trujillo argues, "The issue of being a lesbian, a Chicana lesbian, is still uncomfortable for many heterosexual Chicanas and Chicanos, even (and especially) those in academic circles."[46] Yvonne Yarbro-Bejarano takes this point further, noting that the nationalism that still frequently structures Chicano studies programs "can simultaneously reinscribe the functions of the state within its own narratives of resistance, by prescribing its own ideas of the ideal social formation and the ideal subject and setting the parameters for acceptable forms of images of national identity."[47]

In combating this ongoing effort to reinscribe "self-imaginings" into an institutional setting in which "patriarchal and heterosexist moulds" work to "resist the possible gamut of roles for women *and* men," Chicana feminists, as they work to consider applications of intersectionality, have addressed themselves to the range of exclusions that such reinscriptions foster.[48] One of these efforts has entailed the forging of the term *Chicana lesbian,* an arduous task with inestimable productive consequences. At the very least, its creation helped establish a distinct organizational category working as a form of disidentification, as José Muñoz describes it.[49] "Chicana lesbian" became a powerful framing device for subsequent narrative events such as *Margins* and anthologies like *Chicana Lesbians: The Girls Our Mother Warned Us About.* Yet this merger of two antihegemonic labels — *Chicana* and *lesbian* — that serve as signatures of distinct critiques of contemporary U.S. politics of citizenship also suggests the exclusions operating within each critique, or perhaps more specifically, suggests the abundance of experience overflowing rigid categories.

The process of molding both terms in this plastic dyad emerged as a response to a series of liberation movements: the Civil Rights movement, Chicano nationalism, feminism, and gay and lesbian activism. But as a number of histories and critiques explain, all of these liberation movements and their accompanying signatures have been fueled and held aloft by various exclusions and presumptions, a trumpeting of orthodoxies, and repressed collisions. The conjunction of *Chicana* and *lesbian* makes their respective containment strategies obvious, destabilizing each term's claims to any version of universality, or at least to their claims to being a transparent or uncontested billboard for identity. While these points may be obvious, it is worth recalling that the forging of either term has not been easy, nor their union simple and predictable.

"The appropriation and recodification of the term Chicano from oral culture," Norma Alarcón explains, "was a stroke of insight precisely because it unsettled all of the identities conferred by previous historical accounts."[50] Yet as Angie Chabram-Denersesian has so eloquently described it, and as Alarcón acknowledges, the production of the category "Chicana" was not an inevitable development from Chicano nationalist politics. Chabram-Denersesian delineates the contests that wrestled this term from the masculinist ideologies that buttress national movement politics, by adroitly showing that "Chicano nationalism was also predicated on the necessity of mimesis: a one-to-one correspondence between the subject and its reflection in a mirror-like duplication."[51]

The power within the hard-won and still-contested term *Chicana* lies in "the consideration of the excluded evoked by the name Chicana," according to Alarcón, because Chicana serves as "the name of resistance that enables cultural and political points of departure and thinking through the multiple migrations and dislocations of women of 'Mexican' descent." The term thereby "provides the position for multiple cultural critiques."[52] Important and multiple as these critiques are, somehow the production of the term could not also accommodate a critique of heterosexism. The heterosexism of the term is not all that mystical. Serving as the counter to the Chicano part, *Chicana* replicates the hetero dyad. That is, *Chicana* cannot simultaneously enact a critique of the presumed heterosexuality of *Chicano*. And this is important. Because *Chicano* presumes straightness, *Chicana* necessarily mirrors this message. The sexual politics of the terms extend beyond sexism. "O/a" relies on the imbedded heterosexist dyad male/female, duplicates the ideology of complementarity. Hence, the necessity of the appellation *lesbian* or *gay* to specify identity invokes the confluence of race, class, and sexuality, yet inevitably seems to mark their distinctiveness as well. In other words, *lesbian* is far more than an addendum to *Chicana*. It functions to disrupt the implicit heterosexism of the term *Chicana,* but like any fender bender, it does not total the homophobic vehicle. If the confluence of *Chicana* with *lesbian* marks lesbians' exclusion from the naming practice of *Chicana*, it clearly also indicates the exclusion of Chicanas from the naming function of *lesbian*. Thus, at this juncture, it might be useful to renominate cultural productions like *Margins* and "Interface" under the category "Chicana/a."

Rewriting Convent(ionality)

The university and the convent: the novel draws these two institutions together seamlessly and in doing so alludes to their powerful combinatory history as producers of a regulatory discourse on subject-citizenship. Yet the novel also suggests that the two institutions form contradictory identities ("modern university student-feminist" versus "traditional, loyal Catholic daughter"), which contemporary Chicanas negotiate often with the knowledge that both identities were formulated through their explicit exclusion. By weaving events in the novel around these institutions and focusing on Chicanas who have been variously interpolated by them, the novel neatly ties them together even as it ruptures a tradition, dating back to Sor Juana Inez de la Cruz, in which Latinas find ambivalent solace from the university and the city in the convent.

Given the importance of Catholicism's role in defining and restricting Chicana sexuality, Veronica's "vacation" at a convent is ironic. Partly as a result of a family conspiracy, she goes to the convent to visit her sister Lucy. This conspiracy echoes the long history of Catholic families containing their daughters' errant sexuality or misbehavior by removing them to the convent. Significantly, Veronica visits a Carmelite convent, also the order of other errant writers, including Santa Teresa de Avila and Sor Juana Inez de la Cruz. Like they were, Veronica has been asked to curtail her activity, but the convent fails to contain her sexuality. In a dramatic moment of reappropriation, Veronica transforms the convent into the place where she gathers the courage to write stories expressing her sexuality and establishes the voice to articulate this sexuality to her family.

Catholicism is critiqued throughout the novel, but nowhere so blatantly as in the convent scenes, which begin by suggesting the church's flagrant alliance with colonial powers and entrenched wealth: "The Carmelite convent and neighboring retreat house resembled a Spanish colonial compound, while its outlying bungalows and dormitories reflected a similar tradition. A decade earlier, a wealthy Santa Barbara family had donated their estate to the Roman Catholic Archdiocese with the intent of keeping the grounds intact. The church hierarchy had opted to conduct spiritual retreats and related activities in that secluded setting" (240). In a few short sentences the narrative reveals the tangled interconnection between money, the church hierarchy, and lush retreats for the brides of Christ. The architecture of the building memorializes and romanticizes an imperial conquest in a region in which the Catholic missionaries were particularly brutal to the Chumash communities. Similarly, the detail that a wealthy family had donated the land to the church reinforces Catholicism's complicit and contradictory relationship to capital. This brief description also draws attention

to Catholicism's power to produce and interpret space. From the sanctioning of land as holy, as a site of divine transcendence, to the removal of land
from public access (cloistering, for example), to the ideological centering of
churches in relationship to homes and other workspaces, Catholicism has
indicated its awareness of and commitment to controlling the relationships
between space and social power.[53]

The wealth of the setting overwhelms Veronica until she spies a "tile mo-
saic of Our Lady of Guadalupe." This "familiar Mexican icon" makes her feel
"at home" (241). The complexities of such a feeling can only be wondered
at—how ultimately welcoming is such an icon? What kinds of psycho-
logically transformative powers does it have? The invocation of the family
romance ("familiar" and "home") suggests the possibility of irony. On the
other hand, it also suggests that the family romance remains a compelling
paradigm for even those artists most bent on resisting its legacy. Furthermore, la Virgen actually signifies the contradictory power inherent in the
ideology of the convent (as well as the church and the family), as René notes
when she meets Veronica's sister, Lucy: "I've always been curious about
monjitas, sabes? Here you are, a woman of color living in a community
of predominantly white women, subject to a patriarchal hierarchy, and—"
(242). René pointedly marks the contradictions indicated by Lucy's and la
Virgen's presence; both have been appropriated in order to further Catholicism's claim to universality.

René's political critique only hints at the more painful confrontation
awaiting Veronica: her subsequent conversation with Lucy. Lucy, wrapped
in an itchy brown habit, signifies patriarchal religious control of the female
body. Given its position within the plot, the two sisters' discussion seems
to be the turning point for Veronica's writing efforts. Not until she openly
confronts her sister and powerfully argues for the validity and integrity of
her sexuality can she exert the kind of energy necessary to write openly lesbian stories. Their conversation raises the issue of their family's dependence
on silence about sexuality; it also raises the issue of patriarchal control embodied in both church and family, or as Sara Melendez, Veronica's mother,
later says to Veronica, "Quieres vivir en pecado mortal?" (281).

Lucy's and Veronica's conversation is provocative from yet another angle.
Both women have opted out of the traditional female role, although both
were raised to be wives and mothers. Of course, Lucy's choice is culturally sanctioned and religiously honored. Veronica's is not. Thus, Veronica's

command of her arguments, her refusal to endorse simplistic definitions of lesbian sexuality, and her readiness to challenge Lucy in terms of the bible culminate in Veronica's transforming assertion of a subjectivity contingent on choice: "I pick and choose what I want from the Church and from la cultura" (249).

Viewed from yet another angle, their conversation offers what might be termed an anticonfession. Michel Foucault argues that contemporary discourses of sexuality are deeply indebted to Catholicism, in particular to the spatial and social institution of the confessional. The development of a technology of confession around and in this closetlike apparatus put sex into discourse. The confessional became the primary means for the construction of an individuality through the contrapuntal interplay of guilt and absolution. Foucault argues that the discourse of sexuality developed in the confessional not through the rigidity of the taboo or the regime of repression, but rather through the explicit and detailed description of sexual acts, fantasies, and desires so that the father-confessor-voyeur "was not simply the forgiving master, the judge who condemned or acquitted; he was the master of truth".[54] A language of sex developed out of the mystical-juridical environment of church governance. Forbidden yet known in excruciating detail, sex had to be detailed, "tracked down, as it were, by a discourse that aimed to allow it no obscurity, no respite".[55] Modern Euro-American technologies of sexuality—medicine, criminology, psychology—are the direct inheritors of the legislated confessional's discursive creation of sex.

Lucy's and Veronica's discussion registers this history in a number of ways. First, Lucy acts as agent of the church, not unlike the confessor-voyeur's more sanctioned role. Second, Lucy serves as family mediator (like la Virgen whose religious titles include "mediatrix"), passing the information to her mother and father and receiving Veronica's statement with the threat of a critique. Third, Veronica refuses the church's approval and delegitimates it by dismissing its validity and authority. In this sense, she turns the frame of the confessional, as a discursive stage, on end—she demands that the Church accede to her perspective rather than that she acquiesce to its rules. So, if the traditional sex-confessional narrative begins with the appeal to the forgiveness of the f(F)ather, moves to a narrative of sexual transgression, and concludes with absolution and the assignment of penance, *Margins* imitates and parodies that structure right down to Lucy's final blessing (having pledged her own penance to respect her sister Veronica): "Y que Dios te bendiga, hermanita" (251). Clearly, Veronica's discussion with Lucy and subsequent writing stand as a direct challenge to an overwhelmingly influential institution. The novel thus directly challenges the ideology that has kept women lighting candles, wearing mantillas, and saying rosaries for their sons while themselves struggling to survive oppression.[56]

By placing this conversation on the grounds of the convent, in the heart of Holy Mother Church's sanctum for unwed women, the narrator commandeers the institution that would prefer to ignore her presence. Veronica's successful completion of the first drafts of openly lesbian short stories while staying in the convent's bungalow further underscores *Margins*'s explosive subversion of geographic semiotics. The (white) convent becomes a newly claimed sitio for the (Chicana) lesbian writer.[57]

"Parking Near Joanna's Grave"

Weirdly enough, what frames the movement between the university, the city streets, and the convent is a local cemetery. The cemetery scenes tie the novel's plot together, for it is in these moments that Veronica reveals her ongoing anguish over the death of her lover, as well as her struggles with the strictures imposed by her closeted status. Revealed mostly through Veronica's nostalgia and painful memories, Joanna serves as the background —the victim of a tragic accident, the dead lover, the daughter, and the friend. It is at the cemetery where her memory is most frequently evoked. It is also at the cemetery where Veronica and Joanna's mother meet to share their grief and to battle over how to remember the dead woman. The conflict over the memory of Joanna serves as the crisis of the narrative plot. But this is a conflict over Joanna's decomposing body as well. Had they acknowledged their daughter's sexuality, Joanna's orthodox Catholic family might not have been able to bury her in the local cemetery. So, just as the novel challenges the traditional significations of the convent, it calls attention to another powerful discursive site: the grave.

The representations of Joanna most clearly and frequently presented to the reader belong to Veronica. Veronica struggles with this imaging, her writing being an attempt to remember, to textualize, by placing Joanna into discourse. For Veronica, such an effort requires coming to terms with the prohibitions against writing about sexuality. Given the paucity of writings by Chicana lesbians—"Anyhow, besides Cherríe Moraga and Gloria Anzaldúa, who else writes about Chicana lesbians nowadays?" (271)—Veronica must encode her own experiences and imagine others with few examples of writers with similar experiences. For a beginning writer, a lack of role models makes the terrain all the scarier.

Veronica's habit of "parking" near her dead lover's grave obviously plays with the lost sexual relationship, even as parking doubles back to suggest an adolescent experience of sexuality, recalling as it does the pleasure of surface tensions and sexualized oppositions like front and back seats. But Veronica's parking by her lover's grave additionally reinforces writing's melancholy attempt to regain what has been lost, to return to the mythical originary text, to recreate by repeating words, images, wisps of desire. The gap, the distance to be traversed, between the moments of "parking" and of arriving at the headstone on the grave, between memory and the absent signifier now a rotting corpse, suggests the intangible fragility of what had been a closeted love between two young Chicanas. For Veronica, the texts she struggles to write, her autobiographical stories about their love, narrate and fill this gap, but do not eliminate it.

The cemetery, a heterotopia, signifies the cursing abandonment of love lost to memory.[58] Foucault argues that such sites offer a kind of counterspace—*real,* yet unreal, because they are not the sites for everyday living. Thus cemeteries overflow with meanings that cannot be channeled into something like a daily tedium. Such heterotopias juxtapose "in a single real place several spaces, several sites that are in themselves incompatible."[59] The cemetery Veronica visits has the suggestion of a park, lined by trees and with carefully maintained grass. It similarly resembles a museum of local history, with a catalog of "vital information" about previous inhabitants of the Santa Monica area. The cemetery also serves as a strange kind of map, not with an easily mimetic relationship certainly, but one that highlights the physical aspects of visuality by enshrining the loss of the body. Ironically, the cemetery in lies quite close to the Christopher Columbus Transcontinental Highway (I-10)—the construction of which wiped out the homes and neighborhoods *Margins* remembers. Thus, this particular cemetery operates as an isolated marker of a disappeared community.

But struggling to co-opt Joanna's memory with equal tenacity and with the strength of la cultura behind them are her family and the neighborhood boys. As Carla Trujillo notes, "Chicana lesbians are perceived as a greater threat to the Chicano community because their existence disrupts the established order of male dominance, and raises the consciousness of many Chicana women regarding their own independence and control."[60] Isabel, Joanna's mother, patrols the cultural fences, guards her daughter's grave, in an effort to maintain this patriarchal status quo.

Isabel's and Veronica's first meeting at Joanna's grave reveals the intimate and interanimating alliance between the closet and the grave. The initial scene begins with Veronica's anguish as she examines what has been left out of the engraved inscription, "Nuestra Hija Querida, Joanna Maria Nuñez" (108). What "remained unsaid, untold" is Joanna's role as Veronica's lover. Judith Butler offers a point that may allow further articulation of the engraved tombstone: "Here oppression works through the production of a domain of unthinkability and unnameability. Lesbianism is not explicitly prohibited in part because it has not even made its way into the thinkable, the imaginable, that grid of cultural intelligibility that regulates the real and the nameable."[61] These "abjects" must remain within the realm of the unthinkable, because to think them might mean challenging the oppression that holds them as unnameable. As Veronica reads the inscription on the tombstone, she must once again, as she has for so many previous months, confront the covert oppression that keeps her relationship with Joanna in the "domain of unthinkability and unnameability." Reading the tombstone, Veronica must insert the additional signification of their relationship, this time in the form of "tears splashing on the rose granite stone" (109).

For Isabel as well, "that grid of cultural intelligibility that regulates the real and the nameable" works to oppose and thereby repress what she suspects as the truth about her daughter and her daughter's "best friend." Isabel opens her conversation with Veronica by noting that she has found her letters to Joanna. Her articulation of her knowledge requires, it would seem, that she and Veronica keep the secret, maintain the silence: "If you want them, Roni, they're yours. No one else has seen them." But Veronica seizes the moment to address Joanna's sexuality, acknowledging their closetedness and hence their love: "We didn't want to shock anyone. It was between *us*— no one else." The revelation of that love motivates Isabel to acknowledge that she had wished to destroy the evidence of it: "I was going to keep quiet and burn [the letters]" (110).

Isabel struggles with her daughter's departure from what Alarcón calls "woman's overdetermined signification as future wives/mothers."[62] In her conversation with Veronica, Isabel reveals her allegiance to "a cultural order that has required the masculine protection of women to ensure their 'decency,' indeed to ensure that they are 'civilized' in sexual and racial terms."[63] She asks Veronica if Joanna "had ever been with a man"—a sure indicator of normalcy. When Veronica negates this, Isabel wonders if it was a "passing thing," thereby rendering lesbian desire wavering and momentary, an unstable and unlikely threat to patriarchy (111).

Having removed the buttresses from what Alarcón calls the "symbolic contract," Veronica names her relationship with Joanna—"Joanna was a lesbian, and so am I"—and Isabel cringes. Turning, perhaps to her last defense against the reality of this sexuality, Joanna's mother wonders, as Veronica's father later would, "Do you think it was because of something *I* did?" (112). Now, with her relationship out beyond the "domain of unthinkability and unnameability," Veronica must begin to help Isabel negotiate her newly challenged, and rendered lacking, "grid of cultural intelligibility"—for this grid cannot account for the image of Joanna as a lesbian. Yet to do so, Veronica must, following Alarcón's incisive cultural reading, argue for the viability, the civility, of living as a woman out from under the sign of masculinity, detached from the phallus. But the site of this conversation, like the genre of the novel itself, still locates these questions in the tradition of romance, of the rancheras that mourn dead lovers.

It seems painfully ironic that the final conversation between Veronica and Isabel again takes place at Joanna's tomb. The confrontation is framed in terms of religion; Isabel has apparently wrestled her memory of her daughter away from her identity as a dead lover by characterizing Veronica as the aggressive seducer, the serpent keeping her daughter from the Kingdom: "All you ever wanted was to touch her—ruin her. She's burning in purgatory now because of you!" (235). No longer the translator or explainer, Veronica can only refuse to accept Isabel's characterization and demand that she return her letters. But Isabel has burned them so that her husband might not see the erotic content of the letters, suggesting women's willingness to protect patriarchy. Isabel fends off the disruption represented by the letter, burns and erases the blasphemous desire. The maze of discourses competing for Joanna results, in some sense, in immolation; already entombed, the sign of Joanna's sexuality—the letters that mark her as vendida, unnatural, blasphemer—now signify not love or desire, but a third term in the patriarchal dialectic—one that must be returned to the silence of the closet, the tomb.[64]

Plots That Plot

Margins concludes as Veronica begins to read her new short stories before a small audience in a women's bookstore close to campus. Having "come-out" to her family and established a new relationship, Veronica turns her attention to "being-out" as a writer. The novel suggests that the bookstore works as a staging ground for a wider assault on the literary canon and the structures containing citizenship within a white, middle-class, and hetero-sexual norm. Whether or not women's bookstores were effective staging grounds for writers of color remains to be explored more thoroughly, but *Margins* suggests their significance as an alternative to the institutions that more typically mediate citizenship such as the church, the university, and the family.

By reclaiming the body—what it can be used for, how it may be represented, what desires it may explore—and tying this maneuver together with the appropriation and analysis of space—where one can move, how one may act, how space itself can be understood—the novel challenges the theoretical grounds of citizenship, dependent as it has been on a universal, bodiless, unlocated subject. This challenge takes place through the plot of the novel, which is itself a plotting of sites and institutions. But this activity of plotting or mapping is centrally concerned with the production of a self-conscious vantage point, one aware of its own peripherality to the regions charted. It is an awkward movement to be sure, for the novel does not provide a steadily located central space from which distances are measured, as maps traditionally do. Indeed, the central plotter, Veronica, moves about so much that the spatial vantage point shifts and shifts, implying that plotting takes place along the edges, at the margins, from the hem.

The plot of the novel moves rapidly between one site and another, around one region and another, through one institution and another. This movement may or may not be transparent to readers: for a reader without geographical knowledge of southern California and especially West Los Angeles the novelistic plotting may be invisible or meaningless; the sometimes dizzying details might just float by. On the other hand, for a reader who knows where St. Mark's church and La Cabaña restaurant are, the novel's tour would potentially produce a double-effect: the "concrete" places might concretize the fictional narrative, thereby making the characters and events seem more real. In this sense, the novel relies on the reality effect of the spatial; it utilizes it to naturalize queer desire and thereby reinforces the concept of place as transparent and static. If *Margins* attempt to subvert heteronormativity through claims to the real, it may be that the fictionalized portrayal of Chicana lesbians pursuing their pleasures and imaginative impulses, in public, at known venues would transform how the reader understands these sites. In this second response, the fictional transformation of places, whether they be university theaters or busy intersections, might enable the reader to imaginatively jump scales. In other words, because the characters do not confine their activities to secret and hidden spaces or to "known" venues for queer activity, indeed to the interfaces alone, they enlarge the scale through which queerness may be experienced, normalizing it as public and mobile and grand, rather than private, restricted, confined, tucked away, hidden.

In this way, *Margins* makes new claims on the possibilities of citizenship and thereby participates in what Renato Rosaldo identifies as the "dissident traditions of struggle for first-class citizenship."[65] Furthermore, the novel may be understood as yet another form of "Latino cultural citizenship," illustrating as it does "the way that claims to citizenship are reinforced or subverted by cultural assumptions and practices."[66] For, in keeping with this broader effort, *Margins* claims public rights such as access and freedom of movement, even as it charts the uneven distribution of resources, both material and cultural, and illustrates their instrumentality. In this sense, the novel emplots citizenship in both economic, spatial, and cultural discourses so that by charting them in terms of each other their mutual productivity becomes clear. This fundamental reconceptualization of citizenship, space, and the body should not be ignored. And one can hope that if *Margins* were to fall into the hands of Gloria Anzaldúa's "Leyla" the alien-lover might imagine that she need not "pass"—or perhaps might understand that the terms and terrain of her education in passing could be shifted, challenged, and broadened.

If *Margins* and "Interface" plot and map space and sexuality, race and spatiality, Sandra Cisneros's collection *Woman Hollering Creek and Other Stories* may be said to offer an antiplotting through its rupture of narrative conventions. But like *Margins* and "Interface," *Woman Hollering Creek* deepens the collective Chicana critique of the terms by which spatial (and thereby racial and sexual and gendered) production takes place.

4

Sandra Cisneros's Contrapuntal

"Geography of Scars"

Driving down streets with buildings that remind him, he
says, how charming this city is. And me remembering when I
was little, a cousin's baby who died from swallowing rat poi-
son in a building like these.

   That's just how it is. And that's how we drove. With all his
new city memories and all my old. Him kissing me between
big bites of bread. —SANDRA CISNEROS, "Bread"

The conclusion of Sandra Cisneros's "Bread," a story from *Woman Hollering
Creek and Other Stories* (1991) in which the narrator remembers an afternoon
spent in a car with a lover, suggests that our perceptions of space evolve out
of complex and disjunctive interpretive processes.[1] As a mobile memory, a
kind of drive-by narrative, the brief sketch moves toward this interpretive
aporia and past it, implicitly critiquing the tendency to romanticize poverty
and destabilizing *charming* as a value-laden spatial descriptor. Beyond suggesting that disparate interpretations of particular spaces emerge from different viewpoints or class positions, "Bread" implies that spatial narratives
help to sustain class structures, allowing rat-infested buildings to be seen as
"charming" homes. This interpretive disjunction also illustrates the impulse
to produce charming landscapes that erase labor and minimize capitalist exploitation by placing the landscape in a time frame different from that of its
observers.[2] Characterizing the story's neighborhood as charming threatens
to shift it into a different temporal modality.[3] The narrator of "Bread" lyri-
cally refuses to surrender her memory of dangerous tenements to a romantic
spatial construction that erases the consequences of uneven development.

   As "Bread" indicates, much is at stake in the representation of space. Cindi
Katz argues that "social power is reflected in and through the production

and control of space."[4] Space is not a transparent or irrelevant backdrop for history; the production of space is part of the production of history.[5] Therefore, although the spatial is often equated with the material and placed outside the social, Doreen Massey argues that it can be more accurately conceptualized as "social relations stretched out."[6] Power accrues to those who exercise control over the environment; similarly, power adheres to those who produce narratives that sustain and naturalize places as opaque, natural, or fixed, and thus beyond contestation or negotiation.

Rather than assuming that time is boundless while places are defined by immobile boundaries, Massey argues that a trenchant conception of places imagines them as "articulated moments in networks of social relations and understandings." Places are not frozen in time; rather, "places are processes, too."[7] Massey's reconceptualization refuses romanticized attachments to places as refuges from change, static signs of a heritage, or locales with a "real" meaning. Conceptualizing place as process draws attention to ongoing contests over the production of space and the struggle to control its representation—to determine how social existence will be "spatially inscribed."[8] Any dominant claim to public space must contend with repeated challenges; as Gillian Rose says, it must also police bodies in order to discipline "every new body" to "guarantee" the ongoing construction of public space.[9] Such disciplining includes not only mundane city ordinances about nudity, urination, and advertisements but also the broad cultural meanings allowed to accrue to state-protected monuments and symbols. Tremendous energy is expended to remind the public that "all the world's a stage" (and merely a stage) and thus to mask the "relations of power and discipline" concretized into "the apparently innocent spatiality of social life.[10]

Woman Hollering Creek is an extraordinary example of a text that considers the shifting terrains of power and makes explicit some of the terms of contemporary spatiality through both its narrative style and content.[11] The collection explores how "spatial control, whether enforced through the power of convention and symbolism or through the straightforward threat of violence" fundamentally constitutes various axes of identity, carrying out what Michel de Certeau calls "a labor that constantly transforms places.[12] Cisneros's stories perform their critique of the production of space in multiple ways, within individual stories, and through the interplay between and among them.

La vida de loiter–ia

The spatial narrative strategies of *Woman Hollering Creek,* perhaps surprisingly, resemble those of contemporary gay literature, or "loiterature," as Ross Chambers calls it. Chambers defines loiterature as a "genre which, in opposition to dominant forms of narrative, relies on techniques of digression, interruption, deferral and episodicity . . . to make observations of modern life that are unsystematic, even disordered, and are usually oriented toward the everyday, the ordinary and the trivial (what is called 'flaneur realism')."[13] Like flaneurs, loiterly narrators walk around, observing, pausing and commenting, instigating, and joking. Loiterature works as an "oppositional comment on the ambitious pretensions of aesthetic sublimity, and on the blindness, rigidity and exclusionary formalism of disciplined and systematic modes of knowledge."[14] Loiterly writing is spatial writing—tricky in its use of juxtaposition and humor, and wry in its cruising observations on the spatial inscriptions of social life. The stories in *Woman Hollering Creek,* like loiterature, explore the links between wandering around and unauthorized desire, between ruses and prohibitions, playing with episodicity and digression to make observations on contemporary Chicana life and to bring "the everyday" into sharp focus. Yet if these stories defy narrative postulates by relying on seemingly unsystematic asides and digressions, they also shrewdly exploit complex relationships between reader, narrative voice, text, and spatial gestures. Out of these relationships emerges a stunning portrayal of the manner in which spatial differentiation affects social processes.

Many of the stories (e.g., "Eleven" and "Mexican Movies") defy, or at least ignore, the conventions of storytelling. In less than a dozen sentences, "Salvador, Late or Early" offers a portrait of "Salvador inside that wrinkled shirt, inside the throat that must clear itself and apologize each time it speaks, inside that forty-pound body of boy with its geography of scars" (10). Without the soothing structure of a beginning, middle, or end, without a goal to tug a reader through the plot, each of these brief stories emphasizes through contrast the predictability of conventional narratives. These stories also function as momentary interruptions of the flow of the collection's more conventionally structured stories.

Most of the stories include teasing, flirtatious exchanges, joking asides, and minor secrets; some make deadly serious revelations. Their digressive and fragmentary nature highlights minor details and experiences, but more importantly it forces the reader to look around, to linger and remember. Like the ex-votos (prayer-petitions appended to the walls and statues of churches) that compose the first half of "Little Miracles, Kept Promises," Cisneros's digressions are social. They play with relationality and take social strictures seriously; their turn to ruses and episodes masks the production of a social identity that can be "a pertinent micro-level political contingency," to use Phillip Brian Harper's words, for those who have been largely outside "the historical distribution of the power to conceive of oneself as a centered, whole [storytelling/history writing] entity."[15] Cisneros's narrators suggest the significance and sophistication of their heretofore ignored and invalidated knowledge, conceptualizing alternative epistemologies as they offer asides and digressions that refuse or challenge systematization—all the while appearing simply to loiter.

Often a conversational tone belies the disruptive revelation toward which the narrative meanders. Near the end of "Remember the Alamo," for example, the narrator reveals a young boy's sexual assault: "Sweating, pressing himself against you, pink pink peepee blind and seamless as an eye, pink as a baby rat, your hand small and rubbing it, yes, like this, like so, and your skull being crushed by that sour smell and the taste like tears inside your sore mouth." Yet the next sentence negates this revelation: "No. Tristán doesn't have memories like that" (67). The narrative rushes past the disclosure, nearly erasing the volcanic memory by denying it. In brief asides, narrators of other stories in the collection reveal instances of violence and abuse that similarly jerk their narratives. In "My *Tocaya*," Patricia nonchalantly mentions that her friend's father "*was* mean" and "Maybe [he] beat her," distancing herself from these bitter revelations by speaking in the mocking tones of a belligerent teenager (36–37).

These parenthetical declarations, like the narrator's pause to describe her mother's violent murder in "Eyes of Zapata," function both as counterpoint to the lyric descriptions and jumbled lists found throughout the stories and as a strategy for making dangerous revelations. Such revelations, the narratives imply, cannot yet be the subject of a story, or rather, they can be the subject only by being masked as asides. So, while the stories may be loiterly, they are neither naive nor invested in the production of nostalgic fantasies. Instead, they use contrapuntal techniques to rupture themselves, turning lyric moments into caustic humor, forcing a gap, like an exposed cut, between humor and bitter revelation.[16]

Though the loiterly story "Anguiano Religious Articles" purports to offer only gentle parody of the commercial aspects of Chicano Catholic culture, a quiet aside draws it into the matrix of the collection's broad critique of repressive social norms. This two-page monologue meanders through an account of an errand, pausing occasionally as the narrator looks around: "A statue is what I was thinking, or maybe those pretty 3-D pictures, the ones made from strips of cardboard that you look at sideways and you see the Santo Niño de Atocha, and you look at it straight and it's la Virgen, and you look at it from the other side and it's Saint Lucy with her eyes on a plate or maybe San Martín Caballero cutting his Roman cape in half with a sword and giving it to a beggar, only I want to know how come he didn't give that beggar *all* of his cape if he's so saintly, right?" (114). This passage plays with religious campiness as the narrator invokes the regal sweetness of the child Jesus and the solemnity of the Virgin, both of which are humorously contrasted with the grotesque image of "Saint Lucy with her eyes on a plate." In a manner typical of other narrators in the collection, she then concludes with a question that interrogates the logic of a narrative heretofore taken for granted. The ostensible digression turns a religious story typically used to encourage self-sacrifice into a means of questioning received pieties.

Cisneros's seemingly straightforward narrative style masks its shrewdness by deploying childlike or nonchalant voices to destabilize the apparent solidity and neutrality of the built environment. Loiterly narrators are attuned to the changeable nature of space because they are busy pausing, noticing, and digressing. The stories in *Woman Hollering Creek* rely on common spatial denominators but interweave them with memories, prohibitions, and anxieties that make space *felt*. Acknowledging the emotion-laden aspects of spatiality undermines the positivist tendency to treat the material as objective, largely unchanging, and outside the vitality of living, sociality, and relationships. Cisneros's stories resist the tendency "to think of space as an abstract, metaphysical container for our lives," suggesting instead that space functions in relation to identity and agency.[17]

Most of the stories' narrators presume their audience's familiarity with particular sites (as indicated by phrases like "you know the one"). Rather than including lengthy descriptions, the narrators refer to stores, streets, buildings, restaurants, and other geographic markers in asides or as part of a gesture of connection. Often reworking her lyric descriptions of sites into the stuff of humor and imagination, Cisneros establishes an important theoretical insight through her construction of an audience familiar with the communities in her narratives. Location is integral to the construction of identity and community. References to places are frequently gestures of intimacy. Local knowledge works as an exchange, an invocation of shared knowledge and inclusion that suggests places are produced out of and through relationality.

The stories therefore invoke their audiences—as well as the sites of their telling—with brief, conversational gestures: "You must've seen her in the papers" (36) or "You know that religious store" (114). Some stories, particularly "One Holy Night," "*Bien* Pretty," and "Remember the Alamo," don't identify an audience; nevertheless, they emphasize their orality, their spoken status, challenging the reader to hear the narrator rather than simply read the text.[18] The emphasis on monologue and dialogue makes the reader the other half of a conversation, thereby establishing a sense of community and intimacy. Or, alternatively, the monologues and dialogues turn the reader into a kind of *metiche* (busybody), who takes pleasure in overhearing someone else's conversation. When the narrators become gossipy performance artists, they reveal the short stories as scripts.[19]

The narrators themselves are alternately *chismoleras* (gossips) and metiches whose performances imply the participatory nature of storytelling/ listening and the communal aspects of meaning-making. When they assume the mantle of chismolera, the narrators underscore the pleasures, tensions, and power imparted in making revelations. "My *Tocaya*" and "*La Fabulosa: A Texas Operetta*" are told entirely in the form of *chisme* (gossip). A typical teenage question, "Now why didn't anyone ask me?" initiates "My *Tocaya*" and indicates the narrator's sense of holding undervalued, ignored, and even maligned knowledge. Gossip functions through its apparent informality and portability, as well as through its reliance on anonymity, voyeurism, and distance from authoritative textuality. Gossip also assumes an oppositional relationship to official discourse, to sanctioned categories of knowledge and methods of acquiring information. It can, as Lisa Lowe argues, satirize private life and official discourses even as it pillages them. Gossip is powerful because it "derides the separation of 'public' and 'private' spheres, transgressing these separations symbolic of bourgeois order."[20] According to Francine Masiello, by blurring the line between fiction and reality gossip can "challenge the uses of language in relation to the authority of the state."[21] *Woman Hollering Creek* laces together its critique of spatial relations through its nuanced and elaborate uses of the comparative strategy inherent in gossip.

English and Spanish are used contrapuntally throughout Cisneros's collection.[22] Spanish words appear in place of English words, sometimes translated literally and sometimes not at all. The musicality of one language rubs against the cacophony of the other. At times, the English translation of a Spanish word follows it or vice versa, creating redundancy and emphasis. Often a narrator will obviously mistranslate a Spanish idiom. In *"La Fabulosa,"* for example, the narrator mimics the speech of a lively gossip but also undermines it with too-literal and thus mocking translations: "Yeah, sure, he was her sometime sweetheart, but what's that to a woman who's twenty and got the world by the eggs" (62). Rather than rendering the vernacular Spanish *huevos* as the vernacular English *balls,* the speaker translates the word literally as *eggs.* This satirical double joke alludes simultaneously to the complexity of translation and to the range of meanings opened by fluency in two languages.

These multiple and flexible comparative strategies invite the reader to conceive of space, in Kristin Ross's words, as "active [and] generative," and thereby "to experience space as created by our interactions, as something that our bodies reactivate, and that through this reactivation, in turn modifies and transforms us."[23] Because a contrapuntal technique relies on interaction, it underscores this revised concept of space as interactive. Thus, contrapuntal narrative strategies work well with the insistently voiced style of the text to reinforce its spatial critique. In other words, Cisneros's narrators deconstruct the built environment by "talking about things" as they wander into stores and bars or past public monuments, by slyly pointing out differences and alluding to contrasting experiences and epistemologies—that is, by casually pointing out the power relations that streets, stop signs, and walls make concrete.

Shaping Public Memories

"Every history," according to Philip Fisher, "has, in addition to its actual sites, a small list of privileged settings."[24] These privileged settings play key roles in the emergence and transformation of a national imaginary. The meanings allowed to accrue to "actual sites" and "privileged settings" can therefore be fiercely contested, since the maintenance of spatial dominance relies in part on the "power to narrate, or to block other narratives from forming and emerging."[25] Conversely, public memory can be very effectively shaped through the construction of particular places.[26] Thus, when counterpublics create counterspaces or counternarratives of public monuments, according to Henri Lefebvre, they not only challenge the dominance of an only seemingly unified public memory but also shake "the existing space to its foundations, along with its strategies and aims—namely, the imposition of homogeneity and transparency everywhere within the purview of power and its established order."[27]

Four stories in *Woman Hollering Creek* interrogate the production of two well-known shrines: Tepeyac, site of the basilica dedicated to the Virgin of Guadalupe in Mexico City, and the Alamo in San Antonio, Texas. Complicated and seemingly oppositional, both sites play significant roles as commodified symbols of nationalism, although their complex positions in Spanish and Anglo imperialism have been muted and stabilized through triumphalist rhetoric. Both serve, in Bill Brown's phrase, as "prosthetics of empire," their meanings and interpretations vigorously protected by state ideology.[28] Both encode gender assignments. Both emerge through complex formations of race and sexuality.

According to Sahagún, one of the chroniclers of the Spanish conquest, worship of la Virgen de Guadalupe initially centered at El cerro de Tepeyac, a hill north of Tenotchitlan where the Mexica had "a temple consecrated to the mother of gods, called Tonantzín, which means, 'our mother.'"[29] Sahagún argues that Tonantzín and Quetzalcoatl were the Aztecs' principal creative forces and should be considered the premier "couple" in their pantheon. In 1531 the Virgin appeared numerous times to Juan Diego and, speaking in Nahuatl, requested a shrine in her honor at Tepeyac.[30] The mass veneration that quickly emerged there was initially contested by many clergy, who argued that it was simply a clever means of continuing to worship Tonantzín. Others saw the transformation of a pre-Cortesian site as an effective tool for converting the populace.[31] The Virgin also became a favorite with the Creole classes, who quickly began to resent both Spain and the *Peninsulares* sent to govern the colony because the Peninsulares repeatedly invoked Europe's superiority to America.[32]

Not surprisingly, two Guadalupan traditions emerged. One developed among the Creole ruling classes, to whom the Virgin appealed as the primary means to distinguish Mexico and ultimately to elevate the colony above Spain. "Among the Indians," however, "the cult found devotion because the Virgin's message in the *Nican Mopohua* was specifically directed to them and their misery, a plight that troubled Hispanics, whether Peninsular or Creole, far less."[33] The two traditions became so widely disparate that two separate Guadalupan festivals were apparently celebrated, and eventually two distinct accounts of the Virgin were published, one in Spanish, the other in Nahuatl.[34]

The Spanish version, Miguel Sánchez's 1648 *Imagen de la Virgen Maria, Madre de Dios de Guadalupe, milagrosamente aparecida en la Ciudad de Mexico,* recounts the history of devotion beginning with the apparitions in 1531. Sánchez weaves stories about the Virgin that had been appearing on ex-votos at the Tepeyac shrine together with myths and legends, legitimizing them all by casting them in the language of the bible. In an extraordinary rhetorical maneuver, Sánchez claims that the Spanish Conquest had only one purpose: to prepare the way for the Virgin's appearance.[35] This argument pleased the Creole classes and initiated Guadalupe's role in a nascent Mexican nationalism, because, as Margarita Zires explains, Sánchez was appropriating the Spaniards' most sophisticated spiritual weapons.[36] Sánchez thus initiated a political project that gave Mexico an identity not as a colony of Spain but as a "Tierra Santa," a holy land, and the Mexicans an identity as "un pueblo elegido," a chosen people.[37]

One year later, Luis Lasso de la Vega published *Huei Tlamahuiçoltica Omonexiti.* This text combined two documents: one narrated the Virgin's apparitions, and the other described the miracles attributed to her.[38] These texts, also culled from ex-votos and circulating narratives, were polished in an eloquent Nahuatl by an anonymous writer who invokes Nahua, rather than biblical, religious symbolism and language, and emphasizes the Virgin's empathy for the suffering of the Mexica peoples at the hands of the Spanish.[39] Thus, the Virgin is identified as "She Who Banishes Those That Ate Us" and "She Who Crushed the Serpent's Head."[40]

The Virgin of Guadalupe emerges then not only as a means of evangelization and domination and as a mechanism through which the Creoles appropriated the Christian symbols and religious power of the Spanish, but also as a symbol of defiance and resistance to whom *corridos* would eventually be sung hailing her as the "Queen of the American Indians."[41] A symbol both of conquest and resistance, the Virgin's flexible historical trajectories make available a pre-Cortesian past as well as a post-Cortesian history of struggle.[42] As Norma Alarcón explains, "her invention was underway as the national Virgin Mary and goddess only twelve years after Cortes' arrival," and she became "capable of alternatively evoking the Catholic and meek Virgin Mother and the prepatriarchal and powerful earth goddess."[43] Thus, Tepeyac itself became a shifting relay among multiple traditions and conflicting political and social demands.

"Mericans," the first of Cisneros's stories to take up this complex icon and the site of her apparitions, offers the narrator Micaela's brief account of the hours she and her two brothers spend waiting and playing in the famous square before the shrine to la Virgen de Guadalupe in Mexico City, while their "awful grandmother" prays inside the church (17). The portrait of the square and the basilica emerges through a series of prohibitions: "we must not," "we cannot," "we have promised." Micaela's jocular, irreverent tone reduces her abuelita's sign of the cross to "kissing her thumb" and renames the repetitive prayers of the rosary "Mumbling. Mumbling. Mumbling" (17). Micaela repeatedly moves between the church where her grandmother prays and the square where her brothers play. Counterpoised to her unwillingness to join in the insistent prayers of the "awful grandmother" are her frustrated attempts to enter her brothers' constantly shifting games. These games, like the square and the church, are defined by prohibitions made primarily in gendered terms.

Outside, Micaela watches as a tourist asks in a "Spanish too big for her mouth" for "Un foto" of Micaela's older brother. When Micaela's brother offers his siblings some gum, the tourist exclaims, " 'But you speak English!' " Micaela's brother then replies nonchalantly, " 'Yeah . . . we're Mericans' "(20). Here the story undercuts the "relation of *mastery* predicated between the seer and the seen."[44] The approach of the tourists and their mistaken presumption of the children's nationality link the space of the shrine to the global commodity markets of tourism. In contrast, Micaela correctly assesses the tourists' position ("they're not from here"), supplanting the tourists' reliance on a standardized specular frame—a visual code that makes ethnicity and nationality identifiable via skin color—with a cultural acumen marked by normative gender assignments: "Ladies don't come to church dressed in pants. And everybody knows men aren't supposed to wear shorts" (20).

The tourists have come in search of an unchanging Other, a relic outside their own temporal order. So they attempt to include Micaela's brother in their construction of a quaint portrait that can be preserved and taken home. For the tourists, the young boy is as static and unchanging, as outside their own temporality, as the basilica itself. The irony of the story is that the tourists themselves become objects of curiosity and amusement. Hence, the basilica is simultaneously represented as religious shrine and tourist site, an object of veneration and of curiosity, although for the children it appears to be neither. Or, rather, it is alternately theater and playground, as well as tourist site and shrine. The juxtaposition of the presumptuous tourists and the disapproving grandmother characterizes the crossing of identities forced on the children and suggests the kind of shuttle diplomacy in which the collection itself engages. The story concludes abruptly with Micaela's musing refrain, "We're Mericans, we're Mericans, and inside the awful grandmother prays" (20). *Mericans,* of course, plays on *Americans* and *Mexicans.* Micaela opposes this hybrid identity category to the "awful grandmother," who seems to function metonymically as both the Church and Mexico.[45] But *Merican* also suggests the children's hybridized sense of space.

"Tepeyac," the story that follows "Mericans," makes that sense even more complex. As Laura Pulido points out in another context, the state has a commercial and national interest in producing certain places as objects of desire.[46] Tourist guides provide maps of potential experiences and pleasures at such sites, cooperating with the state by promising to deliver these sites unchanged and outside of time. Literature often participates in this process, of course, but "Tepeyac" reverses the work of the guidebook, suggesting that the object of desire is not the place but an unrecoverable, unnameable memory. Although "Tepeyac" follows "Mericans," the significance of their juxtaposition is complicated. The narrator of "Tepeyac" is an adult, not a child; the story is an intimate, internal journey, not an amusing snapshot or episode. Yet, like a guidebook, "Tepeyac" enumerates the highlights of a walking tour, focusing, however, on the commercial and less-picturesque aspects of the tourist site: shoe-shine men, photographers, "women frying lunch in vats of oil," people selling holy cards and balloons, and the neighborhood tortillería and tailorshop (22–23). By interweaving memories of walking to her grandfather's store and descriptions of people who make their living taking advantage of tourists and pilgrims, the narrator deprives Tepeyac of its privileged status. In some sense, she "privatizes" the shrine; more important, she suggests that, in Massey's words, places require "the notion of articulation."[47] No place exists apart from the social interactions that construct it or the discursive systems that elaborate it.

As the walking tour nears an end, the narrator begins a count, in Spanish, of the steps from the street to her grandparents' door. Then, in an extraordinary transition, she continues the count until it identifies not steps but the years that have passed since her visits to Tepeyac as a child. The story thus brings us into the "present tense" of the narrator, who has returned to find everything in the neighborhood transformed, including the earthquake-damaged basilica, which is now "crumbling and closed" (23). If tourism flourishes by alternately invoking the comfort of sameness and the anxiety of disappearance and loss, "Tepeyac" functions as a means of confronting loss and change. What is lost for the narrator, however, seems not to be the once-familiar neighborhood; her visit is not an attempt to *recover* a memory or to return to an experience. Rather, the trip is an effort to *acknowledge* the loss of a memory, to indicate its unavailability and lay it aside. The narrator notes that her grandfather was "least familiar with" her among his grandchildren, and he did not remember her. As an adult, she suggests the surprise he might have felt that she, "after all this time," is the one to "remember when everything else is forgotten, you who took with you to your stone bed something irretrievable, without a name" (23). "Tepeyac" becomes an allegory of an irretrievably lost relationship with a beloved grandfather and, by extension, with Mexico, because both relationships were truncated and fragmented.

Katherine Ríos insightfully argues that the "I" who remembers in "Tepeyac" is "the transgressive one who crossed over" the multiple borders between Mexico and "that borrowed country," between memories and expectations, and then began to write about these crossings.[48] In the slippage between steps and years, "Tepeyac" allegorizes the costs of these crossings. The story's title indicates the breadth of this loss. Tepeyac is a pre-Cortesian place name, and for the child of "Mericans" it is a meaningless fragment, a spatial referent without a history. For the adult narrator, Tepeyac is more than a remnant of the havoc wrought by imperialism. It is more than the place name left behind by a conquered, largely dismantled, and romanticized earlier civilization: it also suggests alternatives to the current hegemonic order. To allegorize it is to keep that alternative within memory's reach.

Three hundred years after the Virgin purportedly appeared at Tepeyac, the Alamo, a shrine originally dedicated to San Antonio, became a symbol of nationalism and Manifest Destiny. In 1835 Texans declared their independence from Mexico. Early the next year, the battle over the Alamo—a church with a collapsed roof surrounded by the walls of a former convent and barracks for the various Indian communities enslaved by the Spanish prior to Mexican independence—was waged. Better armed and fortified, though outnumbered, the young republicans barricaded themselves inside the Alamo but were nonetheless defeated by Mexican troops. The defeated settlers transformed their loss into highly effective propaganda, making "Remember the Alamo" a battle cry for revenge. During the 1846–1848 U.S. war against a newly decolonized Mexico, the battle cry resurfaced and was again used to justify U.S. aggression. During the next few decades, the Alamo served first as an army post and then as a supply store and whiskey house. The site itself disappeared from public memory, although the battle cry continued to circulate, encapsulating a series of dyads that fed the national imaginary: us/them, civilized/savage, Anglo/Mexican, conquest/defeat, ours/theirs, pure-bred/mongrel.[49]

It is important to note that the Alamo did not settle immediately into the hyperreal site made famous in movies and tourist brochures. At the turn of the century, a fierce battle was waged first to preserve the original buildings and later to control their memory.[50] Adina de Zavala, who led the preservation battle, wanted to remember the Alamo as a mission church, thereby recalling its role during the Spanish colonial period and signaling Mexican American history in Texas. Intent on preserving the memory of the Tejanos who fought alongside Anglos for the independence of Texas, de Zavala, the granddaughter of the first vice-president of the Republic of Texas, collected numerous maps and histories of the church and fort and lobbied for funds to purchase the Alamo for public preservation. She turned to Clara Driscoll, who donated the funds and subsequently wrested control of the buildings from de Zavala. Driscoll advocated a narrative of Texas independence that centered at the Alamo and eliminated any reference to Tejanos' participation in the independence movement or in the government of the republic. Heir to a railroad and ranching fortune that grew in part due to the economic reconfiguration of south Texas—a reconfiguration that left Tejanos economically devastated—Driscoll began the process of producing the Alamo as a tourist site and symbol of white supremacy. Her campaign to preserve the site as a symbol of Anglo masculinist heroism resulted, in Richard Flores's words, in the "bifurcation of the past, as events between 'Texans' and 'Mexicans,' and the uncoupling of the Battle of the Alamo from its social and political ground legitimate[d] the place of Anglo-Americans in the emerging class structure of South Texas."[51] Battles over the shrine's legacy continue in rituals such as the Anglo-controlled Festival of San Jacinto and the Chicano crowning of El Rey Feo.[52]

Unlike Tepeyac, which functions as a central construct in two of Cisneros's stories, the Alamo apparently serves only to situate the reader. The story's title quotes the battle cry, "Remember the Alamo," but the site itself is given only cursory attention: "Every Thursday night at the Travisty. Behind the Alamo, you can't miss it. One-man show, girl. Flamenco, salsa, tango, fandango, merengue, cumbia, cha-cha-chá. Don't forget. The Travisty. Remember the Alamo" (63). The Travisty is a gay Chicano club featuring drag shows; the narrator, Rudy Cantú, dances there as "Tristán," a name that means "very sad" and plays with "tan, tan," a common Spanish phrase for "The End." The club's name is also a pun of the surname of William Barret Travis, who apparently arrived in Texas shortly before its declaration of independence, having recently killed a man and abandoned his wife and children.[53]

According to the mythology that developed around the battle for the Alamo, at a critical moment Travis told the defenders that they were doomed to defeat, then drew a line in the sand, daring all those committed enough to cross the line and continue to fight.[54] Whether true or not, the story has come to embody Anglo masculinity and heroism. Calling the gay club "the Travisty" ironically critiques conventional masculinity as symbolized by the Alamo's constellation of war, death, courage, and violence. Cisneros reworks the site as "the place" of homosexuality, which functions as the necessary scandal of heterosexuality. The club's location "behind" the Alamo positions it in the heart of a tourist zone but outside tourism's purview. "Remember the Alamo" both quotes the battle cry and ironically twists its significance, reducing it to a directional signal while suggesting that the Alamo itself has more than one meaning.

The narration of "Remember the Alamo" is periodically fractured by lists of unexplained names that force the reader to speculate on their significance; between these chunks of names, the narrator, Rudy Cantú, moves in and out of the character Tristán, to whom he refers in the third person. Through a contrapuntal alternation between fantasy and disavowal, the story alludes to Rudy's alienation from his family, his loss of lovers, and his early sexual molestation, as well as to his ongoing experience with homophobia, shame, and illness. The speaking subject assumes two positions, and in the interstices between them we get a mini-portrait, a retablo, of the enforcement of homophobia through space. Speaking of Tristán, Rudy claims: "He's not scared of the low-rider types who come up at the Esquire Bar, that beer-stinking, piss-soaked hole, jukebox screaming Brenda Lee's 'I'm Sorry.' ¿Eres maricón? You a fag? Gives them a look like the edge of a razor across lip" (66). Built into this portrait of hate-speech is Rudy's fantasy of a response, his desire to enact violence against the speaker. This scenario demonstrates how hate-speech polices space by invoking fear, implying that it is not safe for Rudy to enter the ironically named Esquire Bar. If in his fantasy life Tristán can walk the streets of San Antonio unharassed, Rudy cannot. Uttering the word maricón—especially when coupled with the gay man's anxiety that the word might be accompanied with physical violence—clears the streets, so to speak, produces boundaries and limits, exits and entrances. Sexual spatial segregation is maintained: the Travisty counters the Esquire, or, in a binarist spatial logic, enables the Esquire's dominance.[55]

What, then, does this story have to do with the Alamo? How does it challenge the dominant narrative of the shrine and its place in public memory? "Remember the Alamo" suggests that public monuments have more than one meaning and more than one function. If they are used to organize public memories, they may also be appropriated to organize countermemories. In this sense, the Alamo is not, or is not simply, a sign of a white-supremacist, nationalist narrative but is also the ironic pointer for a contesting narrative of struggle and defiance. By using the battle cry to point to alternative social spaces, the story puts into play multiple meanings of the Alamo and hence of the nation for which it pretends to be a synecdoche but may be simply a prosthesis.

In "Little Miracles, Kept Promises," Tepeyac reappears for yet another examination, perhaps suggesting an unquenchable desire to recapture a relationship with an "original," unmediated place. After quoting a series of ex-votos, Rosario De Leon reconsiders la virgen de Guadalupe.[56] For Mexicanos and Chicanas, ex-votos traditionally commemorate a miracle or blessing received, or record promises should petitions be answered. More important, they are public expressions that form an archive of a community's needs and concerns. People have appropriated the walls of churches in this manner to tell the stories of their profoundest concerns. It is significant that Rosario's reconsideration of Tepeyac comes after a series of ex-votos, since ex-votos contributed to the mythology that developed around the Virgin of Guadalupe and were the source from which the first two published texts about the site drew their material.[57] Rosario's story is in itself a kind of ex-voto. Indeed, the resonances between these ex-votos and many of the other stories in the collection suggest that ex-votos may be a model for the structure of Cisneros's collection. Furthermore, as Rosario's ex-voto reconsiders Guadalupe's meaning, it draws attention to the spatial implications of this particular form of religious expression.

Rosario describes her initial rejection of the icon and denounces its role in enforcing the subjugation of Chicanas. Avoiding the roles of *madre sufrida* (long-suffering mother) and *la dolorosa* (the sorrowful one) entails refusing to venerate the icon that symbolizes the ideology of subjugation. She concludes that she can "empower" herself only by rewriting the narrative of "the virgin" through a rethinking of place.

> I don't know how it all fell in place. How I finally understood who you are. No longer Mary the mild, but our mother Tonantzín. Your church at Tepeyac built on the site of her temple. Sacred ground no matter whose goddess claims it.
>
> That you could have the power to rally a people when a country was born, and again during civil war, and during a farmworkers' strike in California made me think maybe there is power in my mother's patience, strength in my grandmother's endurance. (128)

Rosario resuscitates the history of Tepeyac to transform the narrative of the Virgin of Guadalupe that had all but replaced the original narrative of Tonantzín. Rosario's models of power incorporate only public struggles, which she treats as analogous to her mother's and grandmother's patience and endurance. This translation from the public to the private through the nostalgic revival of a supplanted consensus neatly mirrors the ongoing contests over the meaning of public monuments, even as it remains caught within the structure that governs their production. Thus, the public meaning inspires the production of a private" meaning.[58] If Rosario attempts to disrupt the ruling consensus (so that Tepeyac symbolizes not a conquered Mexico but a rebellious refusal to submit), she does not actually supplant it. Similarly, the gay club's ironic name can comment on prevailing interpretations of the Alamo's history, but it cannot force the Daughters of the Alamo to reconsider the version of events they offer tourists. For both these attempts at defiance depend on the dominant consensus to establish their own identity, and they also come finally to rely on a static concept of place. Yet by positioning these two monuments in relation to one another and by juxtaposing multiple conceptions of them, Cisneros's stories unmask their apparent fixity and transparency.

The contrapuntal play between the Alamo and Tepeyac makes it easier to understand places as processes, as nodes in articulated networks rather than as static locales. The ecclesiastical erasure of Guadalupe's pre-Cortesian past and the refusal of the Daughters of the Alamo to acknowledge the mission/fort's role in the organization of Spanish and Mexican communities are examples of what Walter Mignolo calls the "colonization of memory." *Woman Hollering Creek* responds to such colonization through remembering and rewriting. It enables readers to understand how, "seen from an Amerindian perspective the world, more often than not, looks like coexisting territories within the same space."[59] Tepeyac, for example, home to a millennium-old tradition, is also a tourist site and a contemporary religious shrine. These coexisting territories refer to one another, but their simultaneity is not universally acknowledged. Because places emerge out of complex systems of articulation, acknowledging that they exist as simultaneous, not successive, topographies requires fluency in several discursive systems. The value of such fluency—the ironies it makes possible, as well as the bitterness it implies—emerges neatly when Rudy Cantú says, "Remember the Alamo." Questions such as which Alamo should be remembered and how it should be remembered are built into that statement and left unanswered.

By giving Tepeyac a textual weight that is given to no other site in this collection, and by situating "Remember the Alamo" in the midst of the Tepeyac stories, Cisneros establishes an alternative mapping system that implies what Mignolo calls the "mobility of the center," thereby challenging the dominant locus of articulation.[60] One narrator, for example, refers to the United States as "el otro lado" ["the other side"], thus giving Mexico nominating power (69). If, as Brian Harley argues, maps traditionally center around their cultures' "Holy Lands" in order to establish a "subliminal geography" that gives "geopolitical force and meaning to representation," then the alternate mappings provided in these stories suggest differently conceived spaces that challenge the consensus about what public monuments such as the Alamo and the basilica "mean" and what kinds of hegemonic work they can continue to perform.[61]

The Violent Copula between Public and Private

It may belabor the obvious to point out that the monumental status of public structures reflects a social commitment to the entrenched logic of the (gendered, racialized, sexualized) public/private binary. What may be less apparent is the extent to which violence, or the threat of violence, pervades this matrix. Put another way, if monuments function to announce and preserve notions of the public and of available, shared space, they do so in tandem with a widespread anxiety about the looming violence inherent in using public spaces. Virtually built into public structures themselves is a longing for the private, for a safety that is not shared. This perception of the public as dangerous and the private as safe has extraordinary ramifications.

Feminist geographers argue that some women develop individual mental maps, charting their routes, their living spaces, and their leisure choices through a series of risk-assessment scales that emerge from their fear of sexual assault.[62] These maps reflect women's assumption that they are safest at home and most at risk in public. Such maps, however, chart the geography of crime incorrectly. The majority of violent crimes against women occur in homes and are committed by acquaintances.[63] One of the primary effects of this "mismapping" is the reproduction of public space as (apparently) available to all yet fully accessible only to some. So, while public space is constructed to invite full participation, to invite all to identify themselves as fully vested citizens, it can guarantee its status only by withholding certain rights and privileges from the majority. Public space "belongs" to men (albeit to some men more than others) because women are ostensibly at risk in it; women therefore may not claim public space as theirs to navigate freely.

Why do women fear the "wrong" spaces and the "wrong" people? Because when parents, schools and other governmental institutions, and the media incessantly warn about crime, they overwhelmingly locate it in public spaces. Indeed, virtually all the "sources of information from which women learn about sexual danger suggest it is a public sphere phenomenon."[64] From an early age, women are taught to worry about sex crimes; as a result, they develop a set of "unspoken rules about dress, behavior, lifestyle, sexuality, and female loyalty and passivity in relationships" and construct "a series of boundaries in the physical and social worlds which [women] must not cross if they wish to remain safe."[65] Young girls are taught to limit their public movements, while boys' access to space increases as they grow older.[66] As women grow older, their "mental maps of feared environments are elaborated by images gained from hearing the frightening experiences and advice of others; and from media reporting."[67] Yet another source of women's anxiety about public space is the phenomenon of sexual harassment.[68] Rachel Pain contends that "the common occurrence of sexual harassment in *public* space acts to remind women of sexual danger by routinely creating a state of insecurity and unease amongst women."[69] A habit of blame also comes into play here. The seemingly innocuous question, "What was she doing there?" blames victims for their attacks and implicitly accuses them of faulty orienteering. As Mark Seltzer puts it, the serial killer's piles of bodies have "come to function as a way of imagining and situating, albeit in violently pathologized form, the very idea of 'the public' and more exactly, the relations of bodies and persons to public spaces."[70] The media's production of the paranoid public sphere exaggerates its danger, and if it suggests that men too may be at risk, this fact does not alleviate women's concerns.[71]

In three stories, Cisneros offers a stunning analysis of the problematics of the public/private binary and the costs entailed in challenging its myriad contradictions. "One Holy Night" explores how the threat of violence to women reinscribes gendered space. If the street "properly" belongs to men, women working on corners and in front of stores are interlopers—suspect, available, and unprotected. They are held responsible when attacked because "good girls" would know better. The public/private binary also shores up domestic violence by keeping it tucked away. The story "Woman Hollering Creek," in a chilling revision of the *llorona* myth, offers an illustration of the complex role of violence within patriarchy.[72] Gill Valentine argues that the "inability of women to enjoy independence and freedom to move safely in public space is . . . one of the pressures which encourages them to seek from one man protection from all," thus reinforcing women's "confinement" in homes and creating a "cycle of fear [that] becomes one subsystem by which male dominance, patriarchy, is maintained and perpetuated."[73] Yet another effect of rendering public space as dangerous is that women become less mobile, which limits the range of their desires. It makes the category "flaneuse" inconceivable and transforms women who insist on mobility, on transgressing boundaries, into prostitutes. "Eyes of Zapata" examines the experience of a woman who defies these structures and calls into question spatial categories that attempt to control her.

"One Holy Night" brings to an abrupt halt the series of memory pieces in *Woman Hollering Creek*. From a small Mexican town, a young narrator recounts, almost in the form of a *testimonio*, the events that led up to her "Holy Night" with an older man and her subsequent exile. The nameless thirteen-year-old narrator describes meeting Boy Baby, or Chaq Uxmal Paloquín, a thirty-seven-year-old man who befriends her as she tends the family pushcart selling mangoes and cucumbers. She accompanies him one afternoon to his rented room, where he shows her his gun collection and they have sex. When the narrator reveals that she is pregnant, her grandmother vainly goes in search of the "demonio," takes the narrator out of school, burns "the pushcart and [sends her] here, miles from home, in this town of dust, with one wrinkled witch woman who rubs [her] belly with jade, and sixteen nosy cousins" (27).

The story points insistently to the spatial logic that condemns the narrator; indeed, nearly the first words out of her mouth show the extent to which she has internalized that logic: "I don't know how many girls have gone bad from selling cucumbers. I know I'm not the first." As a young girl working alone in public, she is always already sexually available and suspect, practically public property. The narrator never distances herself from that characterization, nor does she critique the spatiality that renders it plausible. She is adamant, however, in her refusal to accede to its logical extension: "I'm not saying I'm not bad. I'm not saying I'm special. But I'm not like the Allport Street girls, who stand in doorways and go with men into alleys."

That a spatial referent denotes prostitutes and that a spatial metaphor is later used to describe the narrator's mother, who "took the crooked walk too," suggest how much sexuality and normative gender assignments are understood spatially or are made manifest through references to space (27–28).

"One Holy Night" illustrates the myriad discourses that help to naturalize this spatial logic and render it invisible. One of the most interesting means of obscuring this use of spatiality is the discursive refusal to characterize the narrator's sexual encounter as rape, even though it involves a young, vulnerable, clearly naive girl and a much older man. Throughout "One Holy Night," the narrator refers to the movies, songs, and secrets that have provided her education on sexuality. In hindsight, she suggests the inadequacy of that education and the extent to which her romanticized view of a privileged heterosexuality has been demolished. At the same time, she avoids describing her experience as rape by emphasizing her own agency. She thus builds a case for her own culpability and suggests that this assault was what she desired because she was "in love" with Boy Baby. She then slides over Boy Baby's display of guns with its implicit threat of violence: "It was there, under one bald bulb, in the back room of the Esparza garage, in the single room with pink curtains, that he showed me the guns—twenty-four in all. Rifles and pistols, one rusty musket, a machine gun, and several tiny weapons with mother-of-pearl handles that looked like toys. So you'll see who I am, he said, laying them out on the bed of newspapers. So you'll understand. But I didn't want to know" (29).

Having shown the girl a menacing array of weapons, Boy Baby spins a tale of Mayan temples, tears, and insurrection, then says, "You must not tell anyone what I am going to do" (30). His injunction to secrecy further ritualizes the ensuing sexual assault because it presumes a narrative of shame. So, despite her desire to believe the contrary, the narrator's agency is located not in a choice to have sex (that is, after all, something Boy Baby "does" to her) but in a choice to keep silent. The guns function not simply to guarantee the image Boy Baby builds of himself as a revolutionary but also to warn the narrator of his potential for violence. Why else would she view the guns and wish not "to know"? Her rush not to know who Boy Baby really is contrasts starkly with her desire to know the rituals and secrets of romanticized heterosexuality.

The narratives that the family turns to also prevent recognition of the encounter as rape. Without the category of "rape," the narrator bears ultimate responsibility for her own pregnancy, and its spatial underpinnings remain opaque. An economy of blame helps to obscure the nature of the encounter and undergirds the spatial logic that facilitates it: "When Abuelita found out I was going to *dar a luz* [have a baby], she cried until her eyes were little, and blamed Uncle Lalo, and Uncle Lalo blamed this country, and Abuelita blamed the infamy of men" (32). Blame circulates among the family members, and blame circulates transnationally, with morality nostalgically located in Mexico: "But Uncle Lalo says if they had never left Mexico in the first place, shame enough would have kept a girl from doing devil things" (28). Uncle Lalo's response suggests a rhetoric of mourning and loss developed complexly around the family's earlier escape from a sentence of shame: "They were going to send me to Mexico, to San Dionisio de Tlaltepango, where I have cousins and where I was conceived and would've been born had my grandma not thought it wise to send my mother here to the United States so that neighbors in San Dionisio de Tlaltepango wouldn't ask why her belly was suddenly big" (33). By coming "here" because "there" was no longer tenable, the familiar structures of "there" are left behind; those structures are then nostalgically refigured as guarantors of a morality that can now be understood only as forfeited. Furthermore, by blaming the "infamy of men," Abuelita invokes men's traditional role as protectors of women, assigning to herself and, by extension, to all women, a certain helplessness that ensures the continuity of the violence of patriarchy and the inevitability of men exploiting physical dominance over women.

Throughout much of the story, the reader moves with the narrator, along streets with the pushcart, in front of a grocery store, into a room "that used to be a closet—pink plastic curtains on a narrow window, a dirty cot covered with newspapers, and a cardboard box filled with socks and rusty tools," back through streets into a kind of captivity, and finally to lonely isolation (29). The narrator again turns to spatial metaphors to describe her impulse to proclaim her hard-won knowledge: "I wanted to stand on top of the highest building, the top-top floor, and yell, *I know*" (30). This panoramic point of view contrasts sharply with her ever-narrowing world, and her desire to recapture it drenches the story in bitter irony. The young narrator has learned what "her place" is, and she desperately wants to transcend it. Yet she must battle instead with the lesson Esther Madriz contends all women learn as part of their socialization, that "some rights are reserved for men, such as the right to use public places."[74] Foreclosing mobility is clearly one means of limiting the range of desire.[75]

Cisneros's title story explores a different aspect of spatiality—how private violence is tacitly sanctioned by the arrangement of public space. The central figure, Cleófilas, has moved from a town in Mexico to Seguín, a small town in Texas several hours north of the border. Shortly after her marriage, Cleófilas's husband begins to beat her. When she becomes pregnant with her second child, she insists on a visit to the doctor. A nurse sees her bruises and arranges for a friend to drive Cleófilas to San Antonio so that she can escape her increasingly violent husband by taking a bus back to her father's home in Mexico.

In Seguín, Cleófilas lives in isolation, flanked by her disinterested neighbors, Soledad and Dolores (solitude and sorrow). Her husband guarantees her isolation and dependence on him by refusing to allow her to write or phone her family in Mexico. Her sense of isolation appears heightened by the spatial design of Seguín.

> This town of dust, despair. Houses farther apart perhaps, though no more privacy because of it. No leafy *zócalo* in the center of town, though the murmur of talk is clear enough all the same. No huddled whispering on the church steps each Sunday. Because here the whispering begins at sunset at the ice house instead.
>
> This town with its silly pride for a bronze pecan the size of a baby carriage in front of the city hall. TV repair shop, drugstore, hardware, dry cleaner's, chiropractor's, liquor store, bail bonds, empty storefront, and nothing, nothing, nothing of interest. Nothing one could walk to, at any rate. Because the towns here are built so that you have to depend on husbands. Or you stay home. Or you drive. If you're rich enough to own, allowed to drive, your own car.
>
> There is no place to go. Unless one counts the neighbor ladies. Soledad on one side, Dolores on the other. Or the creek. (50–51)

Cleófilas characterizes her home in Mexico in terms of relationships, however vexed, while she characterizes Seguín in terms of her own isolation and hopelessness. The Mexican town's main space for organizing sociality, the central town square (*el zócalo*), has been replaced by "a bronze pecan the size of a baby carriage." The other organizer of relationships, the church, has been replaced by the bar (the ice house). The ice house subsumes both the *zócalo* and the church steps into a commodified and alcohol-mediated sociality that largely excludes women caring for children. The other spaces in the town are also organized around commodity-exchange, shutting out those with few economic resources. Cleófilas's "map" of the city, imbued as it is with her sense of the structure of her relationship with her husband, provides few models for resistance. In mapping the city, Cleófilas effectively shows how its spatial structure reinforces the patriarchal system that leaves her bleeding and bruised. Absent from this map are the battered women's shelters, crisis care centers, or ESL schools that might help her respond to abuse without having to return to "a father with a head like a burro, and those six clumsy brothers," who don't necessarily ensure her future safety or happiness (45).

The spatial organization of Seguín combines with Cleófilas's social isolation to give her a sense that violence is closing in on her: "Was Cleófilas just exaggerating as her husband always said? It seemed the newspapers were full of such stories. This woman found on the side of the interstate. This one pushed from a moving car. This one's cadaver, this one unconscious, this one beaten blue. Her ex-husband, her husband, her lover, her father, her brother, her uncle, her friend, her co-worker. Always. The same grisly news in the pages of the dailies. She dunked a glass under the soapy water for a moment—shivered" (52). This chilling inventory of commonplace violence accompanies the commonplace activity of washing dishes, the glass submerged in water symbolizing Cleófilas's immersion in abuse and isolation. The repetitive language emphasizes the pervasiveness of violence, just as Cleófilas's map emphasizes her powerlessness to escape the next attack.

Cleófilas's eventual escape is dependent on mobility and, as Sonia Saldívar-Hull notes, female solidarity—in this case, a woman with a truck.[76] Cisneros thus reinforces the extent to which mobility is a carefully restricted privilege. Women are not allowed to move about freely. As Dolores Hayden explains, "One of the consistent ways to limit the economic and political rights of groups has been to constrain social reproduction by limiting access to space."[77] Curtailing women's mobility makes it more difficult for them to take advantage of the economic opportunities that shape spatial production and to challenge systems of social reproduction. Limiting women's movements thus not only curtails the range of their desires but also hinders their financial independence.

"Eyes of Zapata," one of the most complex stories in Cisneros's collection, portrays Inés Alfaro, a woman who encounters this prohibition against movement as well as the myriad linguistic and physical traps set to punish women who attempt to move about freely and pursue their desire to live independently. The bloody efforts of the Mexican government to put down Zapata's revolution frame the narrative. Bodies "curling and drying into leather" (95) in the sun; towns are "blistered and black" as Zapata's forces attempt to overthrow a repressive system of land management (103). Yet one of the limitations of this revolution emerges as Inés describes her mother's and her own persecution because they refuse to adhere to the codes "appropriate" for women.

Throughout the story, Inés complains about how language structures mobility. Derisive words function as directional devices, regulating the flow of desire, directing the course of behavior, and channeling power. Inés reveals the implicit violence in the murmured words that regulate mobility and structure spatiality: "*Mujeriego.* I dislike the word. Why not *hombreriega*? Why not? The word loses its luster. *Hombreriega*. Is that what I am? My mother? But in the mouth of men, the word is flint-edged and heavy, makes a drum of the body, something to maim and bruise, and sometimes kill" (105). *Mujeriego* means "skirt-chaser." Inés's question suggests that there is no equivalent category for women; their pursuit of desire is not sanctioned even by slang: *hombreriega* means "prostitute."

Ines might just as easily have asked, "Why not *callejera*?" a term analogous to mujeriego. A callejero wanders the streets; he is a flaneur, a loiterer. Even more than the word *flaneur, callejero* emphasizes the spatial aspects of desire, since *calle* means "avenue" or "street." *Callejera,* however, usually connotes a prostitute or, at best, a meddling gossip. Thus, words like *hombreriega* and *callejera* are parodies of themselves. And they parody a woman's attempt to define her own desires, to suggest that she might legitimately have access to mobility, to space, to self-defined pleasure. *Callejera* and *hombreriega* are the whispered words of regulatory gossip, once again indicating how knowledge and behavior are cataloged and governed through gossip.[78] But these words also suggest that such categories cannot of themselves curtail desire. Finally, these terms usefully draw attention to how the regulation of space reinforces the regulation of desire and pleasure, as well as the extent to which social reality, in all its minutiae, is spatialized.

Inés's query "Why not *hombreriega*?" goes unanswered, even as it echoes throughout the collection, indeed throughout Cisneros's poetry as well.[79] That it is left unanswered points to the difficulty of responding without re-constituting the grounds of inquiry; as Yolanda Broyles-Gonzalez astutely notes, "Asking new questions [requires] the designing of a new informa-tional politics."[80] To this end, *Woman Hollering Creek* makes manifest, in story after story, the extent to which the shaping of space, whether for social or economic reproduction, has an effect on identity, desire, and experience. Cisneros's nuanced and superbly crafted collection draws attention to these shaping forces and relentlessly critiques them through parody, blunt asides, and painful meditations. Like the speaker in Evangelina Vigil-Piñón's poem "Tavern Taboo," who complains, "I hate to walk by a man and be psst at / I hate to sit at a table at some mistake joint / and be psst at," the collection grinds against the gears of the informal and formal mechanisms of control that all-too-often violently reproduce the spatial status quo.[81]

5

"Against the Nostalgia for the
Whole and the One": Cherríe Moraga,
Aztlán, and the Spatiality of Memory

But how is desire possible without memory?
—EMMA PÉREZ, *The Decolonial Imaginary*

I remember once driving through Anza Borrego desert, just east of San Diego, my VW van whipping around corners, climbing. The tape deck set at full blast, every window open, bandana around my forehead. And I think, *this is México, Raza territory.* . . .That day I claimed that land in the spin of the worn-out tape, the spin of my balding tires, and the spin of my mind. And just as I wrapped around a rubber-burning curve, I saw it: "A-Z-T-L-A-N," in granite-sized letters etched into the face of the mountainside. Of course, I hadn't been the first. Some other Chicano came this way, too, saw what I saw, felt what I felt. Enough to put a name to it. *Aztlán. Tierra sagrada.*
—CHERRÍE MORAGA, *The Last Generation*

The future belongs to the impure.
—STUART HALL, "Subjects in History"

Emma Pérez continues her meditation on the relationship between desire and memory by asking, "Can the body react to intensities and flows, to touch upon its surface, without being haunted by particular pleasures that it will long for again? And again?"[1] In bringing these three concepts—desire, memory, the body—into play, Pérez complicates the notion of history as well. History becomes not just the narrative recounting of events, nor the grand accumulated past, whatever that may be, but a shifting, embodied process indelibly and intangibly affected by desires and memories.

Similarly for Cherríe Moraga, memory, desire, and the body cannot be disentangled from each other; they call and respond to one another, shaping one another's conditions of possibility. Moraga's creative, intellectual endeavors constantly attend to the processes of subjection and subject formation, but unlike many theorists, she does not omit memory and desire from her analysis. How to access memory, how to respond to it, how to possess it, where to store it, what to remember, how it shapes desire, and how desire shapes the process of remembering—these topics emerge repeatedly as central tropes, central concerns, central puzzles. Moraga focuses on these subjects not as merely historical signs but because they are essential for surviving domination and exploitation: memory fuels resistance. Moraga struggles with interpellation, with what makes subjectivity and subjection possible and at what costs; but her analysis differs, ultimately, from Louis Althusser's notion of interpellation, because it accounts for the complex legacy of memory, for its political charge, its connection to desire.[2] As she repeatedly argues, dominating systems cannot force people to forget entirely that they are dominated. Somewhere memories lie, rooted in bodies and spaces, in songs and words, signaling the terrains of power which Chicana/os navigate. Memory makes interpellation always already incomplete if not completely undone.[3]

For Moraga, memory cannot be considered apart from spatiality, even if space seems rarely to be her overt focus. The detritus of colonialism, its imperial legacy, the work of racism and homophobia and misogyny haunt the body and produce the spaces that bodies perceive, conceive, live. Moraga is indomitable in her exploration of memory's hard places, those zones of complicity where cooperation with structures of domination entail denial, repression, wounding. More than simply uncovering zones of complicity, Moraga hungers to go past them, to offer a vision worth fighting for.

As Norma Alarcón writes, given the violence of the political economy, radical, creative intellectuals "have an urgent need to overhaul our political vocabulary and grammar, to create a t(r)opography for a new world knowledge."[4] The word *t(r)opography* indicates the interanimating relationship between places (topos) and metaphor (tropology being the study of metaphors, of words used in ways that extend past their literal meanings.) *T(r)opography* also incorporates *geography,* admitting through such wordplay the crucial battle over space (for both material control and representation) inherent to the contemporary world. *T(r)opography* underscores the movement between the spatial and the figurative, emphasizing the spatial work of the imaginary and capturing the peculiar nexus between memory, space, the body, and desire that Moraga's work winds in and around.

Moraga's t(r)opography, could be said to begin with that familiar central image of "what we are fighting for," that is, Aztlán. Moraga's turn to Aztlán brings into focus Chicano nationalism's alternative cartographic practice as a contrapuntal challenge to dominant representations of space that would displace Chicana/os and dismantle our cultures. For Moraga, however, the turn to Aztlán clearly does not just function as yet another iteration of alternative cartographies. Instead, Moraga actively suggests an anticartography—one that does not conceive of space as a thing to be possessed or a set of rationalized relations to be mapped. Moraga offers a different concept of spatiality, in which land and bodies blend in both metaphysical and real senses, in which perception and living cannot be distinguished so easily. Such a conception could be said to begin with Moraga's dissection of the zones of complicity (the gendered and sexualized secrets) that structure the seemingly "domestic." For Moraga, revelation of memory's secrets holds out the possibility of wholesale transformation of the sociospatial fabric of existence, since both revolution and cooperation with domination lie within memory's reach.

Aztlán on the Run

In the poem "Passage," from *Loving in the War Years* (1983), Moraga meditates on that central trope of the Chicano Movimiento, Aztlán, the ancestral homeland of the Mexica.[5] Theoretically located in the region now called the U.S. Southwest, Aztlán was the first place of nurturance for the Mexica who eventually migrated to what is now Mexico City. "Passage" concludes the section entitled "Like a Family: Loving on the Run," a section that explores the complexity of desire and love within the context of racism and capitalism in which differences such as class and race do not disappear despite (or because of) the urgency of love and desire. The poet begins by citing a line of Aztec poetry: "on the edge of the war near the bonfire / we taste knowledge" (44). This quotation is the first in *Loving in the War Years* to turn to Nahuatl verse; it shifts the context of the entire book slightly by changing the range of resonances. It also indicates Moraga's commitment to an ongoing conversation with Chicano nationalism and influential Chicano poets such as Alurista.[6] And, not surprisingly, Moraga offers a very different method of conceptualizing such a central trope of Aztlán than that proffered by the more well-known tenets of nationalism.

The poem proper begins with the lines, "there is a very old wound in me / between my legs" (44). This wound, the poet tells us, does not come from childbirth nor from revolutions but from "a memory / of some ancient / betrayal" (44). "Betrayal" signals one of Moraga's principal concerns. Although vague here, betrayal suggests a loss predicated by gender. Later in *Loving in the War Years,* Moraga will spell out betrayals and complicities engendered by loyalty to the demands of patriarchy and nation. Linking memory and desire to woundedness, the poem shifts into a monologue with an unnamed lover as the poet explains her struggle to give in to desire, her fear of the consequences, and her hunger not for a utopia exactly but for a "desert, untouched / Sands swept without sweat / *Aztlán*" (44). In "Passage," however, Aztlán also figures as jouissance (or, more narrowly, for orgasm) and as the topos beyond betrayal. Here is the connection between place and memory and desire that Moraga seems to seek. At first, it appears that Aztlán is that desire, or perhaps that it names the origin, the homeland to which desire in Freudian terms constantly seeks to return. The poet, however, refuses to assign Aztlán a stable status, and "Passage" continues.

> Pero es un sueño. This safety
> of the desert.
> My country was not like that.
> Neither was yours. (45)

Marked through denial or dismissal ("Pero es un sueño" [But it is a dream]), through the invocation of the imaginary, Aztlán disappears as the poet returns to the legacy of betrayal, to ongoing wounding and bleeding caused by "forces / beyond our control" (45). "Passage" illustrates the allusive and elusive connections that Moraga constantly seeks out between memory (and memories, however vague), desire (however frozen), and place (however imaginary, utopic, or dystopic). Linking Aztlán to erotic desire and wounding also indicates how differently Moraga figures the imagined homeland of the Mexica than do many of her contemporaries or, indeed, her predecessors.

Ignacio Bonillas's invocation of Aztecs in 1878 suggests an early signal of Aztlán's centripetal force as an organizing narrative for Chicana/o struggles against U.S. imperial practices. Almost a hundred years after Bonillas proclaimed Mexican primacy in the Southwest, basing his claim on its status as Aztlán, Chicano activists rejuvenated the concept for similar reasons and with a similar sense of urgency. In 1969, at a Chicano youth conference, activists released "El Plan Espiritual de Aztlán," which proclaimed Aztlán a "bronze nation" and announced a set of points aimed at "repossessing" the U.S. Southwest in both economic and cultural terms. After the conference Aztlán accumulated two dominant meanings according to Luis Leal: "First, it represents the geographic region known as the Southwestern part of the United States, composed of the territory that Mexico ceded in 1848 with the Treaty of Guadalupe Hidalgo; second, and more important, Aztlán symbolized the spiritual union of the Chicanos, something that is carried within the heart, no matter where they may live or where they may find themselves."[7] Or, as Rafael Pérez-Torres puts it, Aztlán came to represent "the means of a counter discursive engagement"; yet, as an "empty signifier," Aztlán was also used to name "not that which is or has been, but that which is ever absent: nation, unity, liberation."[8]

In the years after the 1969 proclamation, Aztlán took on a life of its own, appearing on T-shirts and murals, in poetry and novels such as *Peregrinos de Aztlán* and *Heart of Aztlán*.[9] As Rosa Linda Fregoso and Angie Chabram explain, Aztlán was a well-crafted response to a specific cultural desire: "Twenty years ago, the Chicano student movement created a space where an alternative cultural production and identity could flourish. . . . [Aztlán] gave this alternative space a cohesiveness. Chicano identity was framed in Aztlán. And, Aztlán provided a basis for a return to our roots, for a return to an identity before domination and subjugation—a voyage back to pre-Columbian times."[10] Aztlán emerged as a flexible cultural symbol with a mystified history. Such flexibility proved useful to Chicano nationalism and beyond the period of the Movimiento, since it provided cohesiveness without detailing attendant properties of "belonging." Additionally, it linked Chicano identity to a temporality, an origin, prior to the Spanish and U.S. conquests, thereby partially exculpating Chicanos of any culpability in Indian genocide. At the same time, the invocation of Aztlán allowed Chicana/os to affirm a much-maligned and denied indigenous heritage, a heritage direct access to which had largely been lost. Furthermore, it provided a beloved landscape on which to project desires for a different, less-racist life.

Moraga's vision of Aztlán in the Anza Borrego desert collates the multiple meanings signaled by Fregoso and Chabram, Leal, and Pérez-Torres. She locates Aztlán—or, rather, she uses it to name her sense of connectedness to the stunning beauty of the desert before her. Aztlán offers her a sense of connection to others, just as the spinning of tires, tapes, and thoughts highlights her flickering sense of liberation. Moraga's description of herself also intimates a sly sense of self-parody, an effort, perhaps, to suggest how earnestly she felt that connection and to suggest some emotional distance from that experience. Similarly, her parody here also implicates the earnest righteousness of Aztlán as characterized by Chicano cultural nationalism. Again, there is a kind of disavowal that links this discussion of Aztlán to the earlier "Passages" and signals her broader commentary on Chicano nationalism.

In contrast, Rudolfo Anaya in his 1976 novel, *Heart of Aztlán,* elaborates on the cultural nationalist vision of Aztlán and its potential to incite a political consciousness that moves people to action. The novel traces the coming-to-consciousness of Clemente Portillo as he and his family lose their rancho and move to Barelas, a barrio in Albuquerque, New Mexico. Clemente goes to work at a nearby railroad yard, where he eventually leads a fight to supplant the corrupt union bosses and gain better working conditions. The movement fails, but not before Clemente takes a mythical journey to the "heart of Aztlán" and subsequently rallies his neighbors to recognize the greedy bosses and corrupt industrialists who have victimized them.

The novel begins as Clemente's family prepares to leave their impoverished rancho for the city where Clemente will search for wage work. Adelita, his wife, urges him to take a coffee can filled with dirt because " 'Our land is everywhere,' she said, 'we will journey across the earth, but we will never leave our land.' "[11] At the end of their first day in Barelas, in a scene seemingly predicated by "El Plan," which declares Chicano independence "with our heart in our hands and our hands in the soil," Clemente takes the can of dirt out to his new garden: "He scattered the earth of his llano over his new piece of land. He mixed the old earth of his valley into the hard city soil, and in the dark green of the night his hands dug into the earth as he sought some reassurance from the dark web of his sleeping mother."[12] He then goes inside to "caress" Adelita. Clemente's symbolic mixing of the dirt prefigures his sense of displacement and detachment in the city even as the narrative conflates Clemente's activity in the garden with foreplay.

Heart of Aztlán rigidly naturalizes gender roles in its attempt to connect a mythic Aztlán with more contemporary political activism. Aztlán is both elevated as an organizing myth and linked, as if it were a political muse, to the community's efforts to battle economic exploitation. Such a move is in keeping with Anaya's argument that the 1969 plan performed a naming ceremony in which the "Chicano community named Aztlán as its home-land" and that such naming became the "essence of the Chicano Movement" because it empowered a "renaissance" of cultural production if not political change.[13] Given Anaya's sense of Aztlán's inspirational importance, it is not surprising that, as Clemente considers whether to take over leadership of the anticorruption battle at the railroad yards, he swoons into a vision.

> And again the people called as they rushed by him.
>
> ¡Injusticia! the long lines of men bound in chains of steel called to him.
>
> ¡Miseria! frail, skeletal women cried as they gathered hungry children to their withered breasts.
>
> ¡Pobresa! the masses echoed, and the torrent was so strong it lifted him up and tossed him into the raging waters. The river at its source sang with the same message of the wind: it whispered that he was Aztlán, and when he understood that, he could reach out and touch his people. Wounds opened in his hands. He held his breath and thrust deeper into the river of the manswarm, mixing his blood with theirs, swimming against the groaning waters, diving deeper into the lake until he saw the seven springs. There at the core lay the dark, pounding heart. He had come to the source of life and time and history. He reached out and grasped with bleeding hands the living heart of the earth.
>
> Time stood still, and in that enduring moment he felt the rhythm of the heart of Aztlán beat to the measure of his own heart. . . . A joyful power coursed from the dark womb-heart of the earth into his soul and he cried out I AM AZTLÁN! [14]

Clemente's moment of primal "fucking" enables him to transcend his own body, to join with a mythic mother, and to become her while remaining himself. Such transcendence allows him to struggle past a classic align-ment between the calls for justice (associated with masculinity) and mercy (associated with femininity). His subsequent transformation into a Christ-figure prefigures his epiphanic identification with Aztlán itself. Further-more, Clemente's realization of consciousness echoes the opening passages of "El Plan": "Before the world, before all of North America, before all our brothers in the bronze continent, we are a nation, we are a union of free pueblos, we are *Aztlán*."[15]

Throughout the novel, Aztlán takes on a number of significations. It is the myth of origins deployed to grant transcendent "rights" to the land. It is also a spiritual incantation. And here, Aztlán is the "womb" into which Clemente plunges his bleeding fists. For Clemente, this sense of joining, of union and intimacy, is a necessary step to becoming the "leader of his people" and battling the railroad bosses. This erotic ritual establishes his dominance and further reinforces his sense of himself as patriarch: Cle-mente abuses his wife and rages at his daughters in one drunken stupor after another.

As a number of contemporary literary critics have observed, Aztlán col-lates a series of critiques, utopian longings, and postures that enable a multi-sited Chicano nationalist resistance to dominant labor and symbolic rela-tions.[16] *Heart of Aztlán* suggests that complex political resistance requires an organizing mythology solidly grounded in a mythic understanding of the "dark womb-heart of the earth." In just such a manner, the 1969 turn to Aztlán was a useful move, many theorists have argued, because it filled an imaginary lack that impeded organizing for political change. Genaro Padilla, for example, notes interestingly that myths such as Aztlán "do kill time. . . . In the process of transporting the individual and the community onto an ahistoric plane of consciousness, however, myth and legend must also succeed in reinvigorating the material surface of history."[17] For Padilla, the myth of Aztlán functions in contradistinction to time and thus estab-lishes a transhistorical framework from which to imagine political and eco-nomic change. For Emma Pérez, on the other hand, Aztlán is better under-stood not as a myth beyond time but rather as one intertwined with it: "Aztlán, the mythic homeland shifts and moves beneath and around us. The mythic homeland is longed for, constructed, and rewritten through collec-tive memories. Time is traversed, and a mythic past entwines with a future where a decolonized imaginary has possibilities."[18]

The question of temporality haunts characterizations of Aztlán because of temporality's centrality to nationalist imaginaries and because it underpins what could be called the moral assumptions of nationalist claims to land. It is precisely around the claims that Chicana/os made to land that the early phases of Chicano nationalism resonated with other land-based, anticolonial movements. Noting the centrality of land claims in anticolonial movements, Edward Said argues, "Now if there is anything that radically distinguishes the imagination of anti-imperialism, it is the primacy of the geographical in it. Imperialism after all is an act of geographical violence through which virtually every space in the world is explored, charted, and finally brought under control. . . . For the native, the history of his/her colonial servitude is inaugurated by the loss to an outsider of the local place, whose concrete geographical identity must thereafter be searched for and somehow restored."[19]

Aztlán exemplifies the "primacy of the geographical" in the Chicano antiimperialist imaginary. By focusing on Aztlán, Chicanos could rearticulate their own experience, not as unwelcome migrants to the United States, not as exiles from the Mexican Revolution, not as dispossessed and landless peoples, but as a community with an ancient, even autochthonous relationship to a significant geographical portion of the United States—a relationship that preceded the arrival of Columbus and that thereby granted Chicanos a status similar to that of American Indians. Additionally, the turn to Aztlán enabled Chicanas/os to analyze the United States in terms of its imperial practices and thus to connect with other land-based struggles across the globe. Aztlán fueled the redefinition of the past, modifying the past in order to change the present.

The call to claim Aztlán also provided a stunning critique of the formation of U.S. boundaries and borders. By questioning the legitimacy of the national border on moral and legal terms, the invocation of Aztlán cast doubt on reigning economic and social relations. In some sense, the turn to Aztlán inaugurated a contest over "the natural," because it challenged the naturalized boundaries of the United States by positing an even more "natural" claim to the land through references to ancestors and cultural antecedents. The desire for primacy further provided a land-based legitimacy to the newly formulated term *Chicano,* the hope being that it would strengthen political resistance and allow for the formation of a new consciousness among Chicanos, just as *Heart of Aztlán* envisions.

Part of the appeal of Aztlán lies in the stability land seems to lend; land in this formulation is understood not as shifting, not as under production, but rather as pre-given, natural, as beyond or prior to the cultural. Despite its reliance on an opaque concept of space, the proclamation of Aztlán successfully called attention to the naturalizing work of the geopolitical narrative of the United States. It claimed the moral authority of history in an effort to disrupt the construction of nationalist norms. The radicality of this effort, its uniqueness in U.S. history, explains in part its continued, if sometimes troubling, appeal. Just as the border functions as a state-sponsored aesthetic project — that is, a project through which the state aestheticizes ideological, nationalist work — so Aztlán offers a counteraesthetics by calling attention to the ideologies of nation-building.

By renominating the Southwest as Aztlán, Chicana/os not only denaturalized the U.S.-Mexico border, which had been naturalized through the continually vibrant ideology of Manifest Destiny, but also signaled an ongoing relay between subjectivity and place. Just as place can condition the possibilities for subjectivities, representations of places can affect representations of people — of available identities. Aztlán almost automatically poses a challenge to Manifest Destiny by suggesting an alternative destiny and, in challenging such an entrenched spatial narrative, reveals how spatial referents are used to naturalize identities. That is, because space is rarely thought of as produced, its capacity to be productive of something or somebody hides behind its categorization as "natural." Space sediments identities because it is considered outside of or beyond or distinct from temporality. This distinction grants space a transcendent quality and thereby reinforces "national" identities.

Yet the radicality of an anti-imperial geographic imaginary can be lost when identities are merely resedimented under a new nominative. For if the spatial renaturalizes the nation and national identities, then conceptions of both space and identity remain firmly in place. Such a dynamic troubles, for example, Said's notion of the geographic "imagination of anti-imperialism," as well as the geographic imaginary of Aztlán; not only is the spatial used to naturalize the nation, but such imaginaries are frequently caught up within an imperial conceptualization of the relationship between peoples and space.

This conceptualization becomes clear if one considers those who are excessively naturalized by being spatialized, or even unspaced. For example, colonial and postcolonial Mexico defined people, according to Ana María Alonso, in part through their relationship to place: "In colonial and post-colonial society, configurations of space were forms of dominance that fixed identities by inscribing them in the topography of day-to-day life and also localized the practices of subjects, allowing for their documentation and regulation by the state. The well-ordered polity was one in which all types of subjects had their defined and particular 'places' (lugares)."[20] More particularly "working the land," "improving the land," and so forth were ideologically charged with imprecating a relationship between people (as civilized) and a region. By working land or improving it (husbanding it, as it were), one could make a claim to that land, because such work signaled civilization while it also allowed men to claim their place as civilized.

Apaches, on the other hand, refused such a conceptualization of themselves. They chose a life of mobility over one of settlement. This choice challenged the narrative of what counts as civilized. As Alonso notes, "In the state's and the colonists' eyes, the Apache were the quintessence of wild nature and of its destructive force. And this wilderness was also a sign of unrestrained liberty, of nature's freedom from the strictures of the social, of the indomitable quality of the savage—a perpetual threat to the hierarchies of dominance of the well-ordered polity. . . . Property rights in land, including *derechos de posesión,* were a sign of work, of the activity that transformed nature, and as such were indexes of civilization. In the colonist's eyes, not only did Apache men have no property in land, but they also did not work."[21] The danger of national rhetorics around place is that they may presume a particular, naturalized, ideological link between people and place. As Alonso's analysis shows, the danger for anticolonial geographic imaginaries is that such imaginaries may inadvertently depend on a conceptualization of land and society that maintains its roots in an imperial narrative.

Such legacies can be clearly seen in Bonillas's invocation of Aztlán, which depends on a contrast with the "salvajes," the Apaches, for its moral, political force. For Bonillas, Aztlán offers a seemingly unproblematic assurance of Mexicanos' right to the land in the face of Anglo colonialist efforts to erase their historical presence—but *only* if Aztlán can be held aloft from the Apaches (who in 1880 were still troubling both Anglo and Mexicano claims to Arizona). Similarly, "El Plan Espiritual de Aztlán" argues that "Aztlán belongs to those who plant the seeds, water the fields, and gather the crops."[22] Of course, "El Plan" does not suggest as naked a contrast as Bonillas does;

rather, it both draws on a long-standing notion of civilization and twists that notion, because the workers it imagines are farm laborers, not their bosses. Nevertheless, the plan's limiting concept of who can possess the land—the plan's very reliance on the notion of possession and ownership— delimits its potential radicality as a conceptualization of the relationship between people and space. Indeed, its claims stick to an implicitly gendered logic, a masculinized sign of possession, and in this manner suggest once again the topophilia of subjectivity (the relay between possession of land, ownership, and subjectivity or citizenship): the subjects of Aztlán are subjects because they are "owners." Aztlán thus works as a double gesture, both pointing out the naturalizing work of spatial boundaries and relying on a naturalizing concept of space to produce identities, to structure subjectivities.

To simply make new claims to land is not in and of itself transformative. Indeed, the danger here is not only that such claims duplicate imperial spatial narratives but that they might also duplicate imperial racial and gender narratives as well. As Fregoso and Chabram explain, Aztlán was appealing as a means of uniting people: "In order to undo fragmentation and alienation, the Chicano student movement was recovering a past by stressing our common culture and oneness." [23] In this sense, "El Plan" and Aztlán could be said to invoke what Richard Thompson Ford calls the "nostalgia of the whole and the one, the 'pure' homogeneous community." [24] Such wholeness and unity demean difference, negate polyvocality, multilingualism, and contradiction in the name of a seeming purity. Such a conceptualization of homogeneity as wholeness, as Ford shows, has driven racial segregation in the United States for over a century. Ford further argues that this nostalgia surrounds the racialized management of space and informs the legal constructions of community, identity, and agency. The incorporation of "nostalgia of the whole and the one" into the production of Aztlán enables cultural nationalism to inadvertently sustain oppressive supporting discourses such as the violent misogyny and essentialist concepts of gender evident in Rudolfo Anaya's novel. This nostalgia relies not only on a concept of space as outside the social but also on a construction of subjectivity as whole, unified, transcendent, and bodiless, rather than contradictory, relational, temporally and spatially interconnected, and caught in a web of dislocated memories, histories, and desires.

"*Aztlán* gave language to a nameless anhelo [ache] inside me." [25] In "Queer

Aztlán: The Re-formulation of the Chicano Tribe," a long essay in *The Last Generation* (1993), Moraga's turn to Aztlán is in part a turn to language and memory in search of belonging. For what she identifies throughout her poetry, teatro, and essays is the anguish of displacement. Displacement prods Moraga into a longing for a language adequate to express her alienation. But language mirrors and enacts the imperialism that has forced her sense of exile. Her "nameless ache" attempts to create an Aztlán that both recognizes loss and is also inclusive, an Aztlán similar to, or even inspired by, Gloria Anzaldúa's concept of the borderlands.

And yet to which Aztlán does Moraga refer? The Aztlán envisioned by Bonillas, by "El Plan," by Anaya? Largely not. Still the Aztlán she welcomes is not unencumbered by these earlier utopic narratives: "*Aztlán*. I don't remember when I first heard the word, but I remember it took my heart by surprise to learn of that place—that 'sacred landscape' wholly evident en las playas, los llanos, y en las montañas of the North American Southwest" (150). But while she refers to its traditional spatial and mythical configuration, she does not keep her concept of Aztlán settled or pure or without contradiction. What Moraga's essay "Queer Aztlán" offers is ultimately a very different Aztlán than any to emerge from either the nineteenth- or twentieth-century nationalist struggles.

One of Moraga's crucial contributions to the theoretical analysis of Aztlán's "meaning" is the way she articulates it in this essay. Her discussion enables us to understand Aztlán less as a specific site or as a myth and more as naming what Raymond Williams would call a "structure of feeling."[26] Moraga suggests that Aztlán's import lies in its potential to change mundane or everyday attitudes and habits and thus to allow a different consciousness to emerge.[27] In this way, Moraga's vision closely parallels Emma Pérez's.

In *The Last Generation,* Moraga shifts Aztlán's focus from mythical origins to contemporary life: "[Aztlán] had nothing to do with the Aztecs and everything to do with Mexican birds, Mexican beaches, and Mexican babies right here in Califas" (150–51). At the same time, she maintains Aztlán's potential as a utopic site: "As we are forced to struggle for our right to love free of disease and discrimination, 'Aztlán' as our imagined homeland begins to take on renewed importance" (164). The spatiotemporal distance between Aztlán as origin (implicit in her dismissal "nothing to do with the Aztecs") and Aztlán as imaginary homeland parallels the spatiotemporal distance Moraga travels between her childhood in the San Gabriel Valley and her contemporary life as a Chicana public intellectual: "It would take me another ten years to fully traverse that ten-minute drive [from east L.A. and the Blowouts of 1969] and to bring all the parts of me—Chicana, lesbiana, half-breed, and poeta—to the revolution, wherever it was" (146). Here Moraga cites her earlier sense of psychic distance from the student activism that led to the Chicano/a protests popularly known as the Blowouts.

The Chicano nationalist turn to Aztlán as Origin suggests a nationalist teleology and relies on a narrative of authenticity and validation. As Alarcón eloquently argues, Aztlán implies "the need to 'repossess' the land, especially in cultural nationalist narratives, through scenarios of 'origins' that emerge in the selfsame territory, be it in the literary, legendary, historical, ideological, critical or theoretical level—producing in material and imaginary terms 'authentic' and 'inauthentic,' 'legal' and 'illegal' subjects."[28] "Imagined homeland," on the other hand, through its emphasis on constructedness (the creative effort to imagine), allows for the possibility of "making familia from scratch," of reformulating essential concepts, rather than merely policing boundaries. Thus, Moraga travels from an (anti)origin in cultural nationalism that rendered her alien because of her impure status to a position within an imagined homeland in which the intersections of subjectivity might not only be taken into account but be fully explored. The question for Moraga is not one of origins or possession, although she is too practical to imagine a politics that doesn't seek some form of autonomy. Rather, the question is one of creating a structure of feeling that is germane to Chicana cultural survival and growth.

What does Moraga gain by returning to Aztlán, by rejuvenating what some have seen as a tired concept? She is clearly interested in its capacity to work as a structure of feeling that would allow Chicana/os to formulate rebeldía, to resist the deprivations of the present. But for Moraga, reformulating Aztlán involves allowing room for contradictions, desire, and play; it also means formulating a concept of community and belonging (i.e., tribe) that does not maintain the structures of dominance (racism, misogyny, homophobia) encouraged by patriarchy and capitalism. That position can be seen in her linkage of Aztlán to Queer Nation, as she approvingly cites a friend's comment: " 'What we need, Cherríe, is a 'Queer Aztlán' " (147). Aztlán flourishes not as origin but as difference: "A Chicano homeland that could embrace *all* its people, including its jotería" (147). Here she appropriates Queer Nation's (mis)use of the national. Her appropriation, however, shifts from the national to Aztlán, a shift that maintains the centrality of queerness and rebukes, through this slippage, the racialized national(ism) of Queer Nation.

Difference for Moraga is not registered as simplistically metaphorical—she once again recenters indigenousness in her vision. What makes Aztlán legible, then, is its linkage to a Chicana-indigenous relationship: "For it was our Indian blood and history of resistance against both Spanish and Anglo invaders that made us the rightful inheritors of Aztlán" (154). While this invocation of "Indian blood" might be seen as merely the rehearsal of a narrative of authenticity and origin, Moraga is offering something much more complex. Rather than engaging in an ontological question, she suggests an epistemological one. She wants to move past secrecy, internalized racism, a "Chicano ambivalence about being Indians," as well as past a romanticized image of Indianness ("Aztec warrior bravado"), and toward an acknowledgment of alternative ways of understanding and conceptualizing family, community, and space (154, 156). Rather than counting blood quantums or tracing identities to specific (lost) national connections such as Apache or Navajo, she urges her readers to engage in formulating a vision of Aztlán that shirks imperial legacies through a "serious reckoning with the weaknesses in our mestizo culture, and a reaffirmation of what has preserved and sustained us" (174). In this sense, she locates one of the zones of complicity in the ambivalence and self-hatred that accompany collusion with racialized and sexualized dominance. For Moraga, queerness and Indianness inextricably link together because they have both been traditionally despised; to challenge internalized homophobia, one must also challenge internalized racism. Queer Aztlán offers a vision of belonging without Othering.

If, like Said, Moraga sees the crucial role of geography in anti-imperial struggles, she also goes further and urges a reconceptualized concept of space as produced, as process: "Land remains the common ground for all radical action. But land is more than the rocks and trees, the animal and plant life that make up the territory of Aztlán or Navajo Nation or Maya Mesoamerica. For immigrant and native alike, land is also the factories where we work, the water our children drink, and the housing project where we live. For women, lesbians, and gay men, land is that physical mass called our bodies. Throughout las Américas, all these 'lands' remain under occupation by an Anglo-centric, patriarchal, imperialist United States" (173).

Moraga's argument that "women, lesbians, and gay men" see bodies as land transforms the concept of land from its objectified status as outside culture, outside temporality, into one of process and connection, of interrelatedness. Her reconfiguration of *land* jars the term's stability in the lexicon of meaning. Land is now body; body is now housing project. All are engulfed in the production of neo-imperialism. What finally emerges for Moraga is not the nationalism of duplicated hierarchies but the challenge to language that would transform possibilities for definition. Her displacement into language is not an alienation from the concrete and material but is instead a restless play with their inextricability. Similarly, her queer land that is body, memory, desire rejects the "selective memory" that has sustained so many constructions of nationalism (156).

In this reconceptualization of land, Moraga's work finds resonance with many non-European conceptualizations of space as well as with post-Newtonian understandings.[29] This shift in such a basic locus of Western epistemology is accompanied by a shift in other concepts such as memory and desire. For Moraga, memory, turned and churning, potentially constitutes a radical politics. Memory is not a neutral source of data; the turn to memory, the attempt to create a structure of feeling through Aztlán—that is, through a challenge to spatiotemporal norms—involves understanding that the past is not fixed but malleable. Nor is the turn to memory nostalgic for Moraga; one cannot find in her poetry, plays, or essays any effort to sentimentalize the past, to wax poetic in order to cover festering secrets. Quite the opposite. Like Ford, she abhors a nostalgia for "the whole and the one." Although she does perceive the power of such a concept, her own sensibility does not allow her to embrace it. Instead, like Stuart Hall, she argues that "the future belongs to the impure."

"Especially, not even memory"

Throughout her oeuvre, Moraga places memory in an evolving vortex from which she not only suggests the significance of what is remembered but also examines the relationship between languages, space, and recollection. In so doing, Moraga undertakes a wholesale attack on the universalizing subject—Man and the epistemic violence that keeps Man in the center—served and held aloft by the underexamined categories of mother, daughter, and sister. By sorting through memories, Moraga unfolds the effect of forced contradictions and exposes the false premises that enable these contradictions to maintain their hegemony and to structure subjectivity and place.

And yet such sorting is hardly a pleasant project, as suggested by the opening lines of *Giving Up the Ghost* (1986), which are spoken by the protagonist of the play, Marisa.

> But why, cheezus, why me?
> Why'd I hafta get into a situation
> Where all my ghosts come to visit?[30]

Despite the reticence expressed here, remembering fuels Moraga's political work, even as it means a constant dance along the spine of pain and pleasure. For as one "ghost" after another visits Marisa, the narrator emphasizes the insistent character of memory, its irrepressibility.

> When they "discovered" El Templo Mayor
> beneath the walls of this city,
> they had not realized that it was she
> who discovered them.
> Nothing remains buried forever.
> Not even memory.
> Especially, not even memory. (46)

Moraga here draws on an extraordinary moment in recent Mexico City history. Without elaborating, she refers to the archaeological event in which workers tunneling to create a new subway entrance beneath the city's central square, "El Zocálo," discovered a massive Mexica temple. Its presence beneath buildings dated to the early stages of the colonial era shocked historians who had presumed all of the major Aztec temples to have been completely destroyed by the Spanish priests and armies. The excavated El Templo Mayor now sits next to the cathedral, and the two buildings exist in awkward tension.

When El Templo Mayor commanded its own excavation, when it "discovered them," it transformed Mexico City's existing sign system by defying the massive cathedral, which until then had signaled imperial destruction and cultural annihilation. Now El Templo Mayor stares down the sinking basilica and challenges it for sovereignty over the zocálo. Similarly, memories—pounded down, paved over—surge forward to disrupt the fragile sense of unitary individuality called for by Western institutions such as the state, the family, and the church.

Moraga acknowledges the massive disruption of the spatial consensus around the zocálo's meaning. In doing so, she suggests the extent to which the architectural arrangement of space helps create and even govern public memories. El Templo Mayor's presence forces a new articulation of Mexico's national memory, one that must take into account what has been lost through imperialism, what imperialism represses, and how tenuous such repression might be. If Moraga's lines suggest the practical work of architecture in structuring history, in supporting one historical narrative over another, they also allude to the metaphorical labor that spatial references perform.

In *The Last Generation,* Moraga explains that seizing these disruptive moments when memories surge forward and setting them in typescript enables a transformative political resistance: "The Chicano scribe remembers, not out of nostalgia but out of hope. She remembers in order to envision. She looks backward in order to look forward to a world founded not on greed, but on respect for the sovereignty of nature. And in this, she suffers—to know that fertility is both possible and constantly interrupted" (*Last Generation* 190). In *Loving in the War Years,* such remembering is the stay against assimilation. Ten years later, such remembering emerges in *The Last Generation* as ever more significant, as represented by the prophetic task of a Chicana scribe who must repeatedly and simultaneously turn back toward early codices and turn forward to offer up her own new codices. The danger has become ever more clearly not one of a gnawing, ugly assimilation but of *annihilation.*

In her plays and essays, Moraga imbues her remembering with a sense of haste. Yet she has not set about creating a textual museum house to preserve a stagnant, romanticized cultural order. "Our codices—dead leaves unwritten—lie smoldering in the ashes of disregard, censure, and erasure. *The Last Generation* emerges from those ashes. I write it against time, out of a sense of urgency that Chicanos are a disappearing tribe, out of a sense of this disappearance in my own familia" (*Last Generation* 2). The catastrophic "disregard, censure, and erasure" of Chicana and Chicano poetry, sculpture, philosophy, painting, dance, fiction, scholarship, and music serve a dominating cultural order. Moraga locates her artistic project against a globalization that homogenizes and packages difference for consumption. Those most likely to lose out to such homogenization, she suggests, are Chicana/os who no longer have a reservoir of cultural memories and dichos from which to draw. Moraga, like Barbara Christian, sees such a reservoir as critical for "theorizing" survival and, beyond that, for flourishing.[31]

If remembering, if keeping experiences alive, in some measure staves off cultural destruction, it nonetheless remains difficult, if only because such a process entails a word hunt, una perigrinación, for the palabras to embody the experiences. In struggling to make memory speakable, Moraga's texts expose the intricate and interanimating alliance between language and betrayal, between memory and *colón*ization. In both *Loving in the War Years* and *The Last Generation,* Moraga argues that deploying languages means facing the entrails of capitalism, patriarchy, and imperialism.

In "It's the Poverty," for example, she explores the relationship between economic hierarchies and literacy by acknowledging the degree to which educated language can be a weapon.

> I *lack imagination* you say.
> *No.* I lack language.
> The language to clarify
> my resistance to the literate
> Words are a war to me
> They threaten my family.
> To gain the word to describe the loss,
> I risk losing everything.
> I may create a monster,
> the word's length and body
> swelling up colorful and thrilling
> looming over my *mother,* characterized
> Her voice in the distance.
> *unintelligible illiterate*
> These are the monster's words. (*Loving* 62–63)

If the poet suggests that "gaining the word," that developing a means to articulate unspeakable experiences and unarticulated cultural precepts, potentially endangers her family, she does not, however, refuse to run from the monster. The poem makes the link between a kind of commodified or commodifiable literacy, a marketable skill, and the shortages endured because of unspeakable experiences: "To gain the word to describe the loss, / I risk losing everything." Such indelible, unmasked pain, marks the tenuousness of positioning, of subjectivity at the edge of colonialist education — the vacuum created by indoctrination into an ideological system (including its language) predicated on hierarchies that invalidate the poet's experiences and those of her family.

Because imperialism conquers culture by erasing languages that might threaten Euro-hegemony, the remembering Chicana scribe too frequently stumbles on the unarticulated or unarticulatable. Combing memory often entails a parallel search for the word-tools to propel the process. In "New Mexican Confession," Moraga provides a metacommentary on the relationship between imperialism, poetry, and language. By assessing the "maleness" of Whitman's poetic project, she simultaneously critiques the academic prestige that valorizes Whitman's vision of poetry's "manifest destiny," that is, its claim to be a conquering ("naming") project. She also melodically laments the loss of words needed to continue the process of restoring memories, opening heridas (wounds), and defying taboos.

> These were the words denied me in any language:
> piñón
> cañón
> arroyo
> except as names on street signs,
> growing up in california sprawl,
> boundaries formed
> by neat cement right angles. (*Last Generation* 34)

Having alluded to Whitman's list-making, his inventorying — the aesthetic embodiment of industrial capitalism — Moraga creates her own lists and suggests the gaps in Whitman's universalizing poetry. Or, rather, she points to what has been excluded from poetic language: the unlistable, the totally lost and forgotten words. The words she does highlight thereby do double duty. *Cañón* and *arroyo* don't simply name conquered spaces; they also signify the people destroyed by the terrorizing march from one coast to the other. Land developers turn to words such as *piñón*, at least in part, to romanticize and mythologize conquered spaces and thereby guarantee the death of another (threatening) culture. Making a culture appear stagnant, reified, is one sure way to hasten its destruction. Moraga's work identifies and resists this aching legacy.

And here again, she turns to the spatial to express this legacy. More than simply asserting "the primacy of the geographical" in Moraga's oppositional stance, the poem tries to articulate the unaccountable effect of a lost relationship to place; the lost language denied her also denies her access to that culture's conception of space and thus to the places themselves. What takes this lost culture's place—street signs and suburban sprawl—does not grant her a new or different access but instead signals a bounded subjectivity by stripping her of the options that cultural memory (embodied, so to speak, in language) would provide for resistance, pleasure, alternate subjectivities.

While the educational process (looming literacy) might threaten creativity (the imagination), and while Moraga, having been "educated," records the profound losses incurred by the epistemic violence of cultural hegemony, she also does not ignore the painful legacy of complicity with this project. In "Foreign Tongue," Moraga plays with the doubleness of *lengua* (tongue/language/interpreter) to suggest the complicated exchanges between sexuality, language, imperialism, and patriarchy (*Last Generation* 43). The poem offers an allusive critique of her "English-only" childhood, that is, of her mother's decision not to teach her children Spanish. The poem mourns the lost sensibility of familiarity and intimacy that would have been made possible through fluency, but at the same time suggests that the poet has nevertheless gained such fluency.

> She witholds
> the language
> not the words
> but the abandon they evoke. (43)

Abandonment can be read here as both erotic (what Moraga in another poem refers to as the "relampago [lightening] between my legs") and cultural (the cultural ties abandoned by a strategic, if unwelcomed, assimilation). At the same time, the interplay between language, words, and abandonment suggests an awareness of what knowledge enables, what it makes possible. "Foreign Tongue" also folds together the relationship between sexuality, language, and the dynamic of desire between mother and daughter, between women.

> Traidora
> que soy

to discover
la fuerza
de la lengua
por los labios
of another

not hers. (43)

The ferocity of the tongue. With an allusion to her early essay, "La Vendida," Moraga here suggests the inextricable relationship between discovery (conquest), the erasure of language, and the lips of another. The final line of the poem—"not hers"—puns on "mother's" to emphasize the distance between them. She names herself traitor for having been seduced, for embracing los labios de las mujeres, for learning multiple new lenguas, for discovering the power of the tongue and, by implication, speaking such power. That the pull toward assimilation, toward a state of permanent forgetfulness, involves a struggle "Foreign Tongue" makes clear, particularly through the implicit reference to Malinche, but also through the way the word *traidora* evokes battle.

Similarly, the poet names herself traitor for refusing servitude to men, to a cultural order that insists women

repel
el deseo
que quiere
estallar
por la boca. (43)

A bitten lip, silence, desire shoved aside. Keeping back "el deseo" results in self-mutilation, perhaps causing an implosion—anger, energy, ecstasy curbed rather than allowed to burst forth from her mouth. The speaker of this poem refuses such an action; instead she welcomes the "abandon" but with a knowledge of its costs. Such knowledge is textually highlighted with a turn of the page, the subsequent poem being titled "We Have Read a Lot and Know We Are Not Safe" (44).

Moraga calls herself traitor for turning her back on the assimilationist pie, for returning to, indeed for embracing, her "mother tongue." Disloyal to

heterosexism, a normative regime that outlaws "her kind," Moraga nonetheless yearns to "create a theatre, a poetry, a song that dares to expose that
very human weakness where we betray ourselves, our loved ones, even our
own revolution" (*Last Generation* 41). In calling for an examination entre
nosotros, Moraga both embraces the labels assigned her (*bocona, vendida, malinche, traidora*) and refutes their validity by defying the violence called forth
by refusals to uphold patriarchal and imperialist categories.

Looking backward, being haunted, acknowledging that "the road to the
future is the road from our past" involves uncovering painful herridas, betrayals, complicities (*Last Generation* 171). Writing about a major exhibition
of Chicana/o art, Moraga suggests that Chicana/o artists should turn to a
new project and move "possibly to a place of deeper inquiry into ourselves as
a people . . . *entre nosotros,* where we write, paint, dance, and draw the wound
for one another in order to build a stronger pueblo" (*Last Generation* 71).[32]
This kind of remembering—for example, the ghostly rape memory uncovered in *Giving Up the Ghost,* or the marital/homoerotic anxiety exposed in
Shadow of A Man, or the family conspiracy to maintain the closet in *Heroes
and Saints*—offers the latent possibility of either permanent paralysis or re-
juvenation. The betrayals that take place entre nosotros are often the most
buried and hidden; to reveal them may mean knocking out the hard-won
crutches of survival, but it can also mean moving past festering secrets. Or
as Yvonne Yarbro-Bejarano notes in her extraordinary study of Moraga and
radical Chicana feminist theory, "the repressed or shameful part of oneself
or one's community, when confronted and embraced, can become a major
source of empowerment for all."[33]

The memories Moraga continually returns to therefore include the
wounds caused by obedience to and defiance of the cultural injunction
to "put the man first" (*Loving* 103). For Moraga, it is this injunction, jeal-
ously guarded, that orders Chicana sexuality, that establishes it as second-
ary, largely despised, and always marked deficient. It is this injunction that
undergirds heterosexism and that marks lesbian desire as monstrous, outrageous, prohibited, and a betrayal of the cultural order. And it is this injunction, culturally encoded and signaled in multiple and insidious ways,
that Moraga refuses to maintain even though it means ripping the shroud
of romanticized motherhood that cloaks female complicity with this cultural law.

In *Loving in the War Years* Moraga argues that refusing this complicity and tackling the injunction to put the man first means gaining freedom and also breaking away from "la procesion de mujeres, sufriendo." In some sense, she replaces the old injunction with a new one: "Free the daughter to love her own daughter" (*Loving* vii). In *The Last Generation,* Moraga turns to the story of la luna, Coyolxauhqui, to indicate the dangers awaiting *la hija rebelde,* the woman who will not put the man first. This Mexica story reveals what is at stake in a "war / that never pronounced itself" and that is behind "the secret agenda of denial which has so often turned the relationships between mother and daughter, sister and sister, and compañeras into battlegrounds" (*Loving* 78, 140). What is at stake, it would seem, is the very order of the cosmos, the very determinants of earth—the sun and the moon. Challenging the patriarchal order, Moraga suggests in this reading of the Coyolxauhqui myth, threatens to overturn the rhythm of day and night, a social upheaval that would reverse the basic structure of nature. In reading this myth so astutely, Moraga also unmasks how the patriarchal system was naturalized to maintain a social order so dangerous to women.

But if being la hija rebelde is dangerous, being inspired by Coyolxauhqui holds out the promise of a revised sense of motherhood and desire, as well as the potential for new art. For at the heart of la luna's story is the refusal to comply with a patriarchal order: "In my own art, I am writing that wound. That moment when brother is born and sister mutilated by his envy. He possesses the mother, holds her captive, because she cannot refuse any of her children, even her enemy son. Here, mother and daughter are pitted against each other and daughter must kill male-defined motherhood in order to save the culture from misogyny, war, and greed. But el hijo comes to the defense of patriarchal motherhood, kills la mujer rebelde, and female power is eclipsed by the rising light of the Sun/Son" (*Last Generation* 73). The violence of this story suggests the rigid effort to naturalize an imprisoned motherhood governed by a magisterial manhood. But it also suggests that betraying this injunction to put the man first holds out the possibility of mutilation and freedom. For just as Coyolxauhqui becomes the loveliness of the moon, betraying the patriarchal cultural order holds out the possibility for a "motherhood reclaimed and sisterhood honored" (*Last Generation* 73). For what Moraga wishes abolished are the moments when sisters betray each other, comadres betray one another, daughters betray one another, in order *not* to betray "el hombre," in order to put the man first.

In turning to Coyolxauhqui, Moraga illustrates at once betrayal, the production and reproduction of patriarchy, and the romanticism that enshrines a disempowered but complicit motherhood. If the wounds caused by the re-enactment of this scene in daily life remain hidden, they do not lie dormant, Moraga suggests. They function instead to strengthen patriarchal definitions of mujer, madre, familia. That means they function to reinforce a latent distrust, as well as a seething anxiousness about the pre-scripted betrayals ahead.

Such repetitive wounding increasingly endangers Chicanas. Globalization has hardly produced "good times" for a woman of color unattached to a man. One has only, for example, to turn to the experiences of maquila workers to sense the danger. As the internationalization of both capital and the workforce continues, resisting artists like Moraga respond to the new and ever-more-widely entrenched abuses of power and economic exploitation, while simultaneously attending to the neonationalist, racist anxieties behind such conservative fronts represented by the family-values campaigns, the anti-immigrant campaigns, and the drug war/gang sweeps.

Moraga's vision of desire reclaimed from the patriarchal script extends beyond a refusal to continue to be complicit with patriarchy's demands. Instead, she writes openly of what it means to desire her mother. Moraga suggests that part of what allows these conservative fronts to flourish is the silence not only around lesbian desire but also around the dynamic of desire between mothers and daughters. Such silence enables betrayals that leave women too weak to battle the interlinked ravagings of capitalism and patriarchy. By eroticizing the domestic sphere not in heterosexual terms, but rather through a narrative of mother-daughter erotics and lesbian desire, Moraga suggests a very different way to sexualize space.

Wrenching desire away from male-centeredness entails opening the realm of "the taboo," that normative guardian—the prescriptive warning meant to serve as a form of containment or imprisonment. But this is no easy task, for as Amalia says in *Giving Up the Ghost,* "I was not afraid the gods would enact their wrath against our pueblo for the breaking of the taboo. It was merely . . . that the taboo . . . *could* be broken. And if this law nearly transcribed in blood could go . . . then, what else?" (52). The problem with such a taboo, Amalia suggests, is that it does not exist independently, but rather structures a culture more broadly. Changing it necessarily entails cultural revolution.

Moraga also brings into focus one of the results of keeping lesbian desire culturally closeted. Lesbians are forced to explain, to make rational, their desire—in a sense reinforcing the normative character of heterosexuality (because heterosexuality is "normal," it need not be "explained"). So, even in the act of resistance, of charting an oppositional methodology, the process of explaining the source (or establishing a myth of sources) of one woman's desire to make love to another woman may reinscribe oppressive containment systems, leaving the narrative of heterosexuality intact.

Moraga constructs her desire as a response to love and as a refusal to conspire with patriarchal oppression. By acknowledging the erotics of her relationship with her mother, Moraga challenges the unspeakability of the mother-daughter incest taboo. But it is not really incest to which Moraga refers; it is not a question of brutalized power dynamics. Instead, she refuses to deny the erotic component of her own love for her mother, even though her own admission of this desire is marked by its denial—although she may speak of this desire, she cannot enact it. "Grabbing my hand across the table, 'Honey, I know what it's like to be touched by a man who wants a woman. I don't feel this with your father,' squeezing me. 'Entiendes?' . . . The room falls silent then as if the walls, themselves, begged for a moment to swallow back the secret that had just leaked out from them. And it takes every muscle in me, *not* to leave my chair, *not* to climb through the silence, *not* to clamber toward her, *not* to touch her the way I know she wants to be touched" (*Loving* 11).

The rhetoric of butch-femme supplies an easy analysis of this scene: Moraga would fill the gap created by her father's lack of passion for her mother; she would take the "male" role. But in this particular case, such facile analysis simply reinscribes heterosexuality's normative regime. Rather, this confessional moment of a passion not enacted can be understood not only as a critique of heterosexuality's failure but also as part of the continuum of Moraga's own effort to sort out her experience as a "half-breed," a Chicana as well as a lesbian. For the conversations with her mother always seem freighted by both—by her disavowal of what her white father has come to represent and how that disavowal challenges her own attempts to formulate an alternate self-understanding. It also signals a daughter's desire to care for her mother, a care that cannot be entirely divorced from erotics. In such a manner, through the spatial image "across the table," Moraga attempts to shift erotics away from its puritanical position as taboo and position it again within the quotidian.

In this moment, in describing her mother's passion and her father's passionless response, Moraga indicates a significant element of her artistic project—the contrapuntal interplay between race and sexuality. Is this erotically charged moment between mother and daughter simultaneously a rejection of the erotics of whiteness? Or is it a negotiated step toward recognizing the productive activity of a racialized erotics and the inescapability of such racialization?[34] Moraga writes from the particular disjuncture between how she is identified (frequently as white) and with whom she identifies. Embracing her mother's passion enables an affirmation of "her own forgotten places" and simultaneously amplifies the sense of distance she feels from the erotics of whiteness.

Moraga's exploration of race and sexuality begins with a gap in passion: the dispelled rush "to clamber toward her." This representation of a daughter's desire for her mother, according to Norma Alarcón, "brings us face to face with the fantastic cultural silence, religious or Freudian, with regard to what the girl's position is in the Holy Family or Oedipal triad."[35] Moraga's narrative ruptures the "oedipal family romance" that forms the "underlying structure of the social and cultural . . . organization of Western societies."[36] Dominant family discourse, like the production of nationalist discourse, depends on a triadic circulation of desire that bypasses the mother–daughter relationship. In arguing for such desire's presence, its productivity, Moraga makes it possible to critique the violence, elisions, and discursive limitations of the family romance and thereby to confront "other social formations of violence."[37]

Only by violently prohibiting lesbian desire can patriarchy maintain its claim to truth, its transcendent status as natural. Repeatedly, fluidly, Moraga collates memories—folds them in on themselves and shakes them out so that repressed recollections cannot maintain silent complicity with oppression, but rather, having been revealed, can force a reconfiguration of subjectivities and relationships. Moraga's poetry, plays, and essays repeatedly stage treachery, duplicity, anguish, and enraged desire as well as devotion, humor, and loyalty. Particularly through her plays, Moraga works out the questions formulated in her essays and poetry, the roadblocks to reconfigured subjectivities, the layers of ritual that bury and mask betrayal and treachery. Moraga's integrity, her willingness to turn inward and reveal the multidimensionality of her own memories and desires, suggests her commitment to this oppositional work. Such revelations are nowhere more painfully startling than in a far-reaching passage in *Loving in the War Years*.

> I once had a very painful conversation with my mother—a conversation about moving away from her. I am the only person—male or female— among my relatives who ever left home for good without getting married first. My mother told me that she felt in some way that I was choosing my "friends" (she meant lesbian lovers) over her. She said, "No one is ever going to love you as much as I do. No one." We were both crying by then and I responded, "I know that. I know. I know how strong your love is. Why do you think I am a lesbian?"
>
> Dead silence. But I knew, I felt in the air, that it was the silence of an unspeakable recognition. Of understanding finally, what my being a lesbian meant to me. I had been "out" to my mother for years, but not like this. (138–39)

La hija rebelde exposes the erotic desire that cannot be excised. Like the "discovery" of El Templo Mayor, such a spoken memory changes forever desire's signifying system. In this context, male referents drop out and the inspiring passion of a mother's love becomes the signal for an erotic desire that refuses to be reinscribed within normative heterosexuality or to be contained by categories that usually do patriarchy's dirty work. Here, then, is the root of Moraga's turn to the politics of memory in her attempt to dig out a repressed or denied memory of desire that helps to structure systems of containment. In just such a manner she attempts to break apart the unacknowledged relations that allow patriarchy to work as a cooperative enterprise.

One could argue, then, that Corky's comments in *Giving Up the Ghost* epitomize much of Moraga's artistic effort.

> I have this rock in my hand
> it is my memory
> the weight is solid
> in my palm it cannot fly away (23)

On the one hand, the "rock in my hand" evokes the stones thrown by rioters against police and army; it evokes the rocks that break glass and shatter placid waters. At the same time, such weighty memories cannot simply flit away from Corky, who is about to recount being raped. For Corky, memory is weapon and threat both against others—against a patriarchal and homophobic system—and ultimately, unresolved, against herself. Would that it could fly away. Corky writes these words on a wall; an announced stay against interpellation, perhaps. A refusal to let memory be entirely untraceable or even unrepresentable. More to the point, Corky's words attempt to challenge the spatializing work of memory, to challenge the landscape's occlusion of experiences that would threaten those who benefit from a particular representation of it.

Temporal Geographies

Moraga further examines the spatiality of memory in her play *Heroes and Saints*, focusing on how the representation of landscape helps to structure relations of power detrimental to the people who actually construct that landscape. The play challenges representations of the idyllic and fertile California landscape and the aesthetics of violence that make such a landscape viable. It offers, in turn, (alter)native concepts of land and bodies reminiscent of Moraga's reformulation of Aztlán.

Perhaps in order to accomplish so much, *Heroes and Saints* immediately establishes a relationship with the history of agricultural labor struggle by invoking the Chicano Movimiento and the United Farm Workers' ongoing labor struggles. In notes to the play, Moraga explicitly situates *Heroes and Saints* in relation to Teatro Campesino's *Shrunken Head of Pancho Villa*, as well as to the continuing threat of pesticides. She also invokes Aztlán in the headquotes to the play by citing a crucial line from the 1969 "El Plan": "Aztlán belongs to those who plant the seeds, water the fields, and gather the crops" (87). And her dedication reads, "For Aztlán's Children" (87). In contextualizing the play in this manner, Moraga gestures toward the tradition of Chicana/Mexicano theater. At least as early as the mid-nineteen thirties, radical theater troupes such as Teatro Azteca accompanied Mexican migrant workers striking against growers, a tradition that continued with

Teatro Campesino in the 1960s.[38] In this sense, her play establishes a continuity with a long tradition of farm-labor-theater protest—a tradition she refuses to see forgotten.

Heroes and Saints focuses on the Valle family in McClaughlin, California, who battle the effects of pesticide contamination, misogyny, and AIDS. Centering on Cerezita, a teenage girl who is all head (and no body), the play explores how embattled farmworkers attempt to gain restitution for damage the pesticides have wrought. Cerezita, literally a talking head, dramatizes the birth defects that pesticide exposure causes.

Yet while Cerezita is the central focus of the play, *Heroes* also takes note of activist efforts to draw attention to their cause. At the same time, the play explores the costs of misogyny and homophobia and shows how the destruction of the environment must be related to the devastation of AIDS and the destructive wars in Central America. Moraga's conception of spatiality in this play moves past modernist, capitalist notions of space. For example, in the opening notes, Moraga comments, "The hundreds of miles of soil that surround the lives of Valley dwellers should not be confused with land. What was once land has become dirt, overworked dirt, over-irrigated dirt, injected with deadly doses of chemicals and violated by every manner of ground- and back-breaking machinery. The people that worked the dirt do not call what was once their land their enemy. They remember what land used to be and await its second coming" (91). Land, for Moraga, cannot be understood apart from relationality. Land is not an object, outside sociality, or, indeed, outside spirituality and enchantment; it is neither transparent nor opaque. In this dramatic commentary, the playwright attempts to resacralize land by rendering the concept as completely distinct from the transformation of the earth wrought by agribusiness.

She further complicates this notion of space at the conclusion of the play by suggesting an intricate link between people and space: "Put your hand inside my wound. Inside the valley of my wound, there is a people. A miracle people. In this pueblito where the valley people live, the river runs red with blood; but they are not afraid because they are used to the color red. It is the same color as the river that runs through their veins, the same color as the sun setting into the sierras, the same color of the pool of liquid they were born into. They remember this in order to understand why their fields, like the rags of the wounded, have soaked up the color and still bear no fruit"

(148). Rather than understand this narrative of connection as essentialist (although that might be possible and tempting), the play suggests something more complex here. This closing monologue, delivered shortly before the fieldworkers begin to torch the poisonous fields that surround them, attempts to metaphorically explicate how the production of the social entails the production of the spatial in a processual relationship. Taken together, these suggest that the conceptualization of space is not distinct from the conceptualization of people.

Here, then, is Moraga's theatrical "return to Aztlán"—a companion of sorts to her essay, "Queer Aztlán"; both depend on a central redefinition of land that moves it out of a capitalistic mode that treats it as a rationalized object of possession, as an object of exchange that energizes patriarchal claims to supremacy. Notably, in both passages cited here and in "Queer Aztlán," the conception of land Moraga offers cannot be considered apart from memory or language—land is epistemologically structured rather than ontologically beyond culture.

Heroes and Saints signals this understanding in part through its exploration of radical labor activism. Here are the author's notes for scene 1, act 1: "At rise in the distance, a group of children wearing calavera masks enters the grape vineyard. They carry a small, child-size cross which they erect quickly and exit, leaving its stark silhouetted image against the dawn's light. The barely distinguishable figure of a small child hangs from it. The child's hair and thin clothing flap in the wind" (92).

An unidentified group of activists, the play tells us in the next scene, have been attempting to call attention to the untimely deaths of children. They fear that the pesticide-contaminated groundwater used by the farmworkers has caused birth defects and abnormally high rates of cancer in children. By dramatically hanging the dead, deformed bodies of cancer-stricken children in the grapefields as symbolic sacrifices to the grapes of agribusiness, the activists indeed do gain attention for their cause.

In turn, the owners attempt to bring an end to such activism by patrolling the fields after the publicity challenges the owners' dominance and further enrages the townspeople. For example, in one crucial response to the publicity generated by the stunts, a bottled-water company offers to donate water to the schools so that children will not have to drink the groundwater. The school district refuses this gift, insulted that anyone would insinuate that its water was unsafe. This move infuriates the townspeople and leads to the closing act of sabotage: "Moments later, there is the crackling of fire as a sharp red-orange glow spreads over the vineyard and the Valle home" (149).

What is to be made of these crucifixions? They limn the grotesque, to be sure. Yet they also comment in an oblique manner on what José Rabasa calls the aesthetics of colonial violence: part and parcel with the production of imperialism are the narratives that in epic or other forms celebrate the vanquishers' tales of conquest and plunder. Such epics rely on a process of aestheticizing the resulting violence by drawing on the way art "civilizes horrendous acts."[39] "Civilizing" occurs in part, Rabasa argues, because of the assumption of disinterest and distance that underlies what counts as aesthetic and because the aesthetic helps to "keep the audience from empathizing with suffering" (139).[40] In other words, the aesthetic serves to keep an audience separate and distant from violent events, thereby allowing the audience to derive pleasure from the artistry of the description.[41] In this way, the representation of violence can impart delight.[42] Additionally, a sentimental aesthetic often facilitates violence even as it attempts to "call our attention to abuse."[43] Such aesthetics emphasize the vulnerability of the sufferers (usually of children and women), but also manage to keep audiences at a distance from the "materiality of pain" so that representations of violence do not challenge the colonial project.[44]

In stark contrast, the "barely distinguishable figure" of a dead child offers the possibility of an anti-aesthetic, one that inspires empathy and horror rather than pleasure and delight. By shifting to the "real"—that is, to "real" bodies rather than representations—by locating the dead children on crosses and in grapeyards, the activists arrest attention and thus communicate the materiality of pain and loss felt by the farmworkers and their community as well as by the children who suffered immensely before their deaths. As one of the leading activists tells a prying reporter, "They always dead first. If you put the children in the ground, the world forgets about them. Who's gointu see them, buried in the dirt" (94). While the speaker imagines that the "world forgets," she might have also characterized a national response as one of ignorance and willful repression. Yet, as the activists understand, the world cannot so easily forget when confronted by images of dead children in pastoral grapefields. The juxtaposition forces them to rethink the grapes, the growers, the bodies.

Of course, the activists do not forgo aesthetics since they utilize the symbology of Christianity. And they understand the performativity of their project, as indicated by how they deploy calavera masks to invoke *Día de los muertos* and the cultural traditions venerating and defying death. But theirs is a project to stop violence by invoking its effects, by displaying its effects rather than celebrating them dispassionately. Thus, the anti-aesthetics of *Heroes and Saints* shifts the terms from imaginary violence to the violence of agribusiness even as the main voice of the activists, Amparo, expresses doubt about its reception: "Que la gente . . . the peepo like tha' kina t'ing, to look at somebody else's life like that t'ing coont never happen to them" (93). Her comment locates the problematics of identification entailed in the performative and in the aesthetic. Here she suggests the pleasure that the spectacle of violence offers when its audience can distance themselves from it, can refuse to identify with the sufferers. Her hope, however, is that the TV audience will not be able to successfully remain at a distance and that their horror at the deformed bodies and the children's "hair and thin clothing flap[ping] in the wind" will motivate a broader campaign against agribusiness exploitation of its workers and the environment.

In larger terms, the specter of crosses in the vineyard and the individual crucifixions of dead children also challenge the stereotypical landscape of California. For more than a century, California has advertised its bountiful farms; photo on photo of the harvested, blooming, lush California farmlands repeatedly reinscribe this "story" of California, offering a landscape of beautiful, plentiful growing crops. Such representations of the California landscape are in keeping with the tradition of Western landscape painting, which, for more than four centuries, has sought to order sociospatial relations, as Don Mitchell suggests, "by making all that is uncomfortable or unaesthetic to the owners of property (or more generally to the bourgeoisie) invisible or 'natural.' "[45] Not surprisingly, images of California's agricultural landscape almost never include, for example, depictions of farmworker camps. Such images would trouble the efforts of landscape to impose a particular way of seeing both California and its produce, its commodities.

Heroes and Saints offers a double contestation of the California landscape. That is, the play focuses on the efforts of the Valley dwellers to challenge the image of the California landscape directly by sabotaging it not only through the crucifixions but also by burning the fields. These efforts expose the conditions of exploitation necessary for agribusiness to generate vast profits. In this manner, the workers attempt to "overcome not just conditions of inequality and the oppressive work of power, but the stabilized landscape itself. They must destabilize not just the relations of place, but the very ground upon and within which those relations are situated and structured."[46]

At the same time, the play itself challenges established perceptions of California by denaturalizing its economic dependence on conditions of exploitation and inequality. *Heroes and Saints,* in concert with labor activism, makes visible those who labor to produce the landscape, those who work the fields and gather the harvest; by making these actors visible, by taking their claims of exploitation seriously and dramatizing them, Moraga helps to "invalidate claims made by capital and the state" on workers' behalf.[47] *Heroes and Saints* illustrates an oppositional methodology on the ground, with the ground, in an effort to remake the ground by insisting on the relationship between spatiality and sociality.[48] Moraga names that connection in a stroke of insight in *Waiting in the Wings* when she refers to her body as a "temporal geography."[49] With this term she offers reconceptualized concepts of land and body that refer to each other not as binary terms but rather as an interanimating collective caught up with varying temporalities: a processual (temporal), textual (graph) worlding (geo). Through such interconnecting, Moraga, nearly twenty years after her groundbreaking publication of *This Bridge Called My Back,* moves closer to what she called "un sueño" in *Loving in the War Years,* closer to the possibility of the "safety of the desert" (*Loving* 45).

In turning or returning to Aztlán, Moraga seizes on its capacity to invoke an alternative geography, to suggest different memories and to allow competing memories room to maneuver or provide a stay against interpellation. Aztlán, like El Templo Mayor, like the dead babies hanging in the grapefields, shatters the naturalizing stance of spatiality, a stance that hides such spatiality's legacy of violence and oppression. In the nineteenth century, Ignacio Bonillas invoked an Aztec lineage in an attempt to rebuke the ongoing abstraction of space under way in Arizona; a century later, Moraga continues that effort, but, as a feminist, she anatomizes the linkages between imperialism, racism, and patriarchy. And, perhaps more than any other writer under discussion, Moraga considers the relays between consciousness, memory, desire, body, space, land. *Heroes and Saints,* for example, concludes with immolation. The burning fields articulate the workers' rejection of the grower's killing landscape. The signs of that killing are not enough to transform the system. The very ground must be remade. Yet, in this play, it is not just that the fields burn—so do institutions such as familia and concepts such as the body. What Moraga seems to suggest, then, is an immolation, a revolution of space and language, a revolution that like her phrase for bodies, "temporal geographies," makes clear the spatiality of discourse and the discursiveness of space. Such a revolutionary agenda seems all the more pressing given the transformations of spatiality under way at the behest of globalization and the U.S.-directed war on drugs.

6

"War Again, or Somesuch":

Narrating the Scale and Scope

of Narcospatiality

The development of large new trading organizations along with an accelerated consolidation of corporate power at the end of the twentieth century have drawn attention to the significance of scale for capitalist development.[1] Scholars who recognize the importance of new trading systems like the European Union and the North American Free Trade Association have increasingly turned to the study of globalization and cosmopolitanism, along with their corollaries, borders and diasporas. Yet, in keeping with the continuing invisibility of spatiality, scholars have paid little heed to scale itself; that is, few have noted the narrative structure through which spatial differentiation occurs. While many scholars may have failed to remark on scale, Chicana fiction writers have not. Chicana/o literature offers a range of meditations on scale and its role in economic and cultural change.

Although the production of space does not appear central to Mary Helen Ponce's "The Marijuana Party" or Alberto Alvaro Ríos's "The Child," both offer a means to examine the social (political, racial, and class) work of scale.[2] Both stories attend to the scale at which the policing of Chicana/o communities and the criminalization of narcotics and Latina/os occurs. And both stories predict the transformation of space at all scales that has been brought about by what one could call the hundred-year "war on drugs."[3]

"Scaling" is the name given to the process by which space is divided, organized, categorized, that is, the process of dividing the world into various regions, zones, nations, neighborhoods, communities, trading groups, and so forth.[4] By demarcating spaces, by establishing limits and thus contents, and by fixing spaces within a framework of spatial relations, or "nested hierarchies," scale narrates and thereby helps to organize and produce space. Or as Neil Smith explains, "In a literal as much as metaphorical way, scale both contains social activity, and at the same time provides an already partitioned geography within which social activity *takes place*. Scale demarcates the sites of social contest, the object as well as the resolution of contest."[5] To which Don Mitchell helpfully adds, "Scale consists of both materiality (for example, the 'levels' at which production or reproduction are, through struggle, organized) and ideology (the 'levels' at which legitimacy is, through struggle, organized). Each feeds off and informs the other."[6] Part of the difficulty, then, in considering scale is that it works through the material, the metaphorical, and the ideological simultaneously.

As a tool for capital development, scale helps "fix" a crucial contradiction in capitalism: the drive to eliminate spatial barriers while producing space. Capital eliminates or overcomes spatial barriers in order to speed up the circulation of material, people, and capital, yet this requires investing in space. As David Harvey explains, "spatial barriers can be reduced only through the production of particular spaces (railways, highways, airports, teleports, etc.)."[7] In order to accumulate, capital must expand. In its efforts to globalize, however, capital nevertheless requires relatively established, local, territorial organizations, offering "integration and coordination of technological capacities, natural goods, public and private forms of fixed capital, infrastructural configurations, the social relations of production, institutional-regulatory frameworks," and so forth.[8] These territorial organizations are only relatively fixed; in times of crisis caused by over-accumulation, they can be "torn down, reconfigured and reterritorialized"—that is, re-scaled—in order to ease the crisis and allow for a new round of accumulation.[9]

Nation-states have a stake in the management and production of scale. Consider, for example, the production of the "American West" in terms of scale. The U.S. government invested directly in its production by funding railroads, managing and funding the Indian Wars that cleared the territory, and organizing land rushes and land grants. Being on the receiving end of this management, Chicana/os and American Indians were scaled out of the process and seen as deterrents to the production of this scale. Furthermore, the production of the "West" depended on massive federal mediation in the form of wars (against Mexico in 1848 and against Indian nations throughout the nineteenth century), grants, tax-breaks, and other incentives. Through such means the "West" was produced and intertwined in a much larger federal scale.

Scale bounds social activity—from the everyday to the monumental. Thus, scale also contributes to the process of producing subjectivities and identities through spatial differentiation. Given the extent to which identities are narrated through spatial terms, or conflated with spaces (or representations of spaces), or organized around and through places, the mechanism that helps signify spatial difference requires attention. Not surprisingly, scale also plays a role in the struggle for social change. Because scale "contains," scale can be the site of struggle, the arena around which struggle is often waged. Consider, for example, the spatial work entailed in organizing against zoning laws that encourage liquor stores in some neighborhoods, but not others; or the work that emerges to battle the placement of incinerators and prisons in some neighborhoods; or the fights that emerge around whether to allow a range of construction projects, from freeways to high-rise apartments to parks. As Richard Thompson Ford eloquently argues, such battles over zoning continue to be used to maintain racial segregation, despite ostensibly race-neutral laws.[10] Such struggles take the scale of the neighborhood as their starting point, as both a basic means to organize the actors in such a struggle and as a practical end of the struggle. Thus, if scale contains struggle, it may also be said to help produce the terms of struggle.

Scales ranging from the body to the neighborhood to the nation can thus become the center of struggle. Similarly, struggles often must "jump scale" in both their claims and their reach by moving, for example, from a local worksite to the regional, if not the transnational, in order to have an effect.[11] The power of scale jumping can be seen when we remember how the United Farm Workers pushed its campaign against lettuce- and grape-growers from regional California protests to national boycotts.[12] By jumping scale, it transformed a local, regional struggle into a national, political movement.

Given scale's significance for both the definition of space and the evolution of struggle and given Chicana/o literature's ongoing analysis of spatiality, it is not surprising to find Chicana texts that theorize scale. "The Child" and "The Marijuana Party" are two important examples of fictional works that consider scale at what could be called its cutting edge (if the narcotics economy is understood in both its formal and informal guises as exemplary of post-Fordist economic change).[13] Additionally, the two stories consider scale in terms of the body, the region, the home, the neighborhood, and the transnational. By examining these various scales, the two stories reveal how the narcotics economy intertwines with the everyday. Furthermore, located as they are at a moment just prior to the acceleration of the narcotics interdiction economy (with its own jumping of scale), both stories suggest how that economy reflects global change and how intensely it has come to affect Chicanas and Chicanos.

Body Counts

Alberto Ríos's "The Child" is a richly textured meditation on the intertwining of death, language, boundaries, borders, journeys, narcotics, and bodies. Within Ríos's first collection of stories, *The Iguana Killer* (1984), "The Child" is a bit of an anomaly; while his other stories describe various childhood experiences at weddings, with friends, at birthdays, "The Child" transposes the point of view, turning nostalgic images of childhood into politically charged international encounters. Its presence reverberates throughout a collection intended for young adults inasmuch as the story suggests a latent threat to potentiality, an unseen vulnerability, and undercuts the nostalgia seemingly encouraged by its counterparts.

Stylistically, however, "The Child" is similar to the rest of *The Iguana Killer*. Throughout the collection, Ríos uses short and spare sentences. Adjectives appear rarely. Adverbs are even more rare. The condensed language helps to create a nostalgic and bemused but distant tone that frequently slides into the tragic or sorrowful. In "The Child," however, emphasis shifts from the tonal to the thematic: rather than capturing the tone of childhood, the frugal sentences convey the story's impressive set of meditations. By refusing to call attention to itself, the prose seemingly foregrounds the plot alone, but closer examination reveals a multilayered, poetic narrative, emerging out of what José David Saldívar calls a "narcorealist" imaginary.[14]

Set on a bus traveling from Hermosillo, Sonora, to Nogales (a city that stretches across the border between Sonora and Arizona), "The Child" focuses on two widows. While on their way to a funeral, the two women pass the long hours of the bus trip by repeatedly inquiring about the health of a sick child anxiously attended by a male passenger who says he is taking the sick boy to the United States for medical care. Midway through the trip, the bus stops so that its passengers can eat lunch. Having enjoyed their lunch but continuing to worry about the sick boy on the bus, the women take him a glass of water. When the two get back on the bus, they notice that the child's companion, whom they have presumed to be his father, has disappeared. They also discover that the little boy is not terribly sick; he is dead. The story closes as one of the women tells her friend, over the phone, across the borderline, that the child had been dead for a long time; his body had been opened and excavated, filled with bags of opium, sewn shut, and reclothed in an elaborate attempt to smuggle drugs into the United States.

Ríos's customarily spare prose relays the extraordinarily dramatic plot almost as if prose itself was beside the point. Yet this disjuncture between baroque plot and arid prose contrapuntally structures a set of tensions opened up by "The Child," including those between the body and mind (signaled through a consideration of body language versus spoken language), between embodiment and death, and between the horror of violence and its banality. By exploring such tensions, "The Child" uncovers the multiscalar sociospatial changes that have emerged alongside and as a result of what, since the story's publication, has come to be called the war on drugs.

MINDING / FINDING THE BODY

"The Child" should not be simply called a meditation on death or even a fictionalized account of the effects of the narcotics economy, although it is both. Instead, given the intricate narrative revelation first of the child's deadness and second of his posthumous gutting and stuffing, "The Child" can better be analyzed in terms of its consideration of embodiment, of bodies and spaces. Discussions of death, maladies, illness, and funerals punctuate the narrative and draw attention to questions of embodiment. Such discussions, perhaps particularly those about the women's typical clothing and their status as widows, draw attention to cultural attitudes toward death. The two women "wore black, more out of habit than out of mourning for their husbands, both of whom had been dead for more than ten years. . . . On their heads they wore black veils and on their legs black stockings with lines up the back" (12). If their clothes work to enshrine the family romance, they also work as a visible and constant reminder of death. Additionally, their clothes resignify public space by commenting on the "liveness" of the public, of crowds, through negation. Their long journey, a bus ride of several hours to a funeral, further underscores the cultural rituals that surround death and highlights the importance with which death is treated, which thereby heightens the contrast between the ritualized concern for funeralized bodies and the drug-filled dead body with which the women unknowingly ride.

As the bus ride begins, the child's "illness" draws the widows' attention to him. Throughout the first half of the trip, Mrs. García, in particular, pays attention to the boy, peppering the man who cares for him with questions and advice. She urges him to give the boy *"yerba buena* tea" and asks if he has tried adding "honey and lemon? Maybe with a little bit of tequila" (15). Interspersed with her questions are references to her own medical problems: "Chills can be very terrible, especially if you have arthritis. I have this bracelet for arthritis and it helps. . . . Dr. Valenzuela. Do you know him? Sometimes it helps the pain I get in my left shoulder, too. And a lot of liquids. Don't they always say that?" (15). She also refers frequently to the funeral to which they are heading and tells the man that her friend "died of cancers" (16). Mrs. García's questions and comments highlight the care given the body and, in constructing the child as merely sick, reinforce the shock of the discovery that he is dead. In this context, her questions also illustrate how physical maladies become ironic signs of life, just as they become a coded means to discuss embodiment.

The revelation that the child is not sick but dead furthers the story's consideration of embodiment. The discovery follows a lunch in which the two women discuss what secret the restaurant possesses for making such good quesadillas, as well as the quesadillas' potential for provoking heartburn if consumed too fast. The meal, with its implications of vitality and prosperity, precedes the discovery of death. In a simple act of kindness, Mrs. García then takes the child some water, worrying that he might be thirsty in the heat.

> "Ah, this child is cold. His chills must be like ice," said Mrs. García. Her eyebrows.
> "Here, let me see." Mrs. Sandoval's hands.
> "Wait," said Mrs. García. She moved the blanket so as to rearrange it and stared at the white child. Vanilla ice cream. "Oh, oh my God!" she screamed, and moved like she had put her hands into the flames of a stove, like when she first learned to make tortillas. She was a young girl

then. She moved back with the same kind of strength. Mrs. Sandoval caught her as she fell, fainted.

"*¡Dios mío!* Jesus? Help, ah, this child is dead, he is dead!" screamed Mrs. Sandoval in much the same voice as Mrs. García had screamed. Very high. (19)

The body, when covered and merely observed, is sick; when uncovered and touched, it is dead. In searching for a reaction, Mrs. García moves violently to what might have been her first contact with mortality, her first memory of searing pain and the possibility of death. The discovery that the child is actually dead propels Mrs. García into a kind of primal memory of being socialized as female. The sensation of vanilla ice and her body's urgent revulsion signals both an early memory and an unwelcome identification with the dead child, just as the image of burnt skin underscores the text's consideration of the relationship between the body and memory; the body remembers and such body memories jump time and space. Furthermore, the image of a young girl pulling away from the flames while her first tortillas get singed reinforces the precariousness of the body, the body's instinct to protect itself, and thereby reinforces the obscurity of the "Vanilla ice cream" body lying on the seat before her.

As Susan Bordo notes, "Through routine, habitual activity, our bodies learn what is 'inner' and what is 'outer,' which gestures are forbidden and which required; how violable or inviolable are the boundaries of our body, how much space may be claimed, and so on."[15] With the condensed imagery of the passage above, Ríos offers a similar insight. The images tunnel back in time, moving Mrs. García from the present to the past through her body. The cold body reminds her of the hot flame, returning her to a lesson, turning tortillas, that would become a habit, but that would also teach her about bodily violability and boundaries. Her contact with the vanilla ice body unravels these early lessons, throwing into confusion their structuring binaries of inside and outside, hot and cold, alive and dead.

This brief narrative interlude, the recovery of a distant memory, also acts to delay the unfolding of the revelation that the boy is dead. The revelation is announced not by Mrs. García but by her friend Mrs. Sandoval. Catching her fainting friend and left with the task that would transform the bus into "an elevator full of voices" (19), she declares the child dead. Again the narrative reinforces the bodily aspect of the discovery—this time by emphasizing not bodily memory but the high-pitched, "screaming," "very high" voice of shock.

Short sentences such as "Her eyebrows" and "Mrs. Sandoval's hands" move the narrative away from the cold child to eyebrows and hands of the living, so capable of expression—yet here telling the reader nothing, except to recall the immeasurable contracts between the dead and alive. The intrusion of body parts—"eyebrows" and "hands," those tools crucial for physical expression, for "speaking" in a slightly different register from the voice "very high"—ties the revelation to the text's consideration of the relationship between body and language. Such an intrusion also interrupts the flow of the story, delays the revelation, to focus on body parts, synecdoches for the very alive bodies standing before the dead one. The shift from one woman's eyebrow to the other's hands also seems to merge the two women, a merger the story itself promotes from the first sentence, which notes that "the two ladies shared a single face," to the last, which points out that the women react "in much the same voice"(12, 19). Such blending of bodies signals the question of boundaries and borders that the text and the "fact" of the child perturb.

The story's title comments ironically on what turns out to be an excavated body, a body that is a container, an elaborate and expensive effort to foil the border guards. The treatment of the child's body stands in stark contrast with the treatment of the body of Mrs. Sandoval's brother—the object of a funeral and wake, of mourning and ritual. The revelation that the child is not merely an abandoned corpse but a container, a burro, ruptures notions of a seamless bodily integrity. Rarely is the body figured as cask, as stuffed and mounted, as a performance prop. Here "the body" is reassigned meaning, forced to perform posthumously; denied the rituals that enshrine the body and comfort mourners, the child is transformed into a utilitarian item. The body as container not only indicates the desperate (and innovative) measures narcotics traffickers will take to move cargo but also reveals the necessary fictions of bodily inviolability.[16]

The wake and funeral that Mrs. Sandoval attends when she arrives in Nogales further elaborates the contrapuntal relationship between the anonymous child and her brother's enshrined and honored body. The child's death is irrevocably linked to Mrs. Sandoval's brother's death, making both intimate and oddly familiar. Mrs. Sandoval responds by trying to weave the child's death into the narrative of her own life: "She prayed the rosary almost all the way to Nogales. What tragedies, her brother and then this child, this innocent child. She would wear black for the rest of her life, she decided. Her life would not last so long. This was the least she could do" (21).

Her thoughts move from the funeral to which she is going, to the dead child whose "Vanilla ice cream" body confounds her initial sympathetic construction of him as sick, and finally to her own body. In deciding to "wear black for the rest of her life," she transforms her body into a visual altar and moves it beyond being a symbol of mourning for her deceased husband. It is as if she would see her body as a utilitarian object, almost like the child-container (whose utility seems beyond comprehension). She recodes herself, in effect, as a kind of portable gravestone, a signifier of tragedy, and also as a visual harbinger of her own impending death. Even more perhaps than the death of Mrs. Sandoval's brother, the dead boy signals her own mortality. At the same time, her choice to permanently wear black flags the transformation of the borderlands brought about by narcotics trafficking and interdiction. Here she suggests that her own "local" tragedy (her widowhood) folds into the ongoing crisis of death and mutilation engendered by the war on drugs.

By challenging the body's boundaries, by turning it into a shell or container, the image of the dead, stuffed child makes a complex statement about scale, particularly since many conceptualizations of scale begin with "the body."[17] That is, the rupture of the body calls into question assumptions about the intransigence or stability of scale. As a structuring background, as merely a description of spatial difference, scale seems largely fixed. But if the body, the basis of scale, is not a fixed unit of measure, can the region or the national similarly have a fictive status? Similarly, the shock of discovery — as well as its reverberation through the bus, the phone, the reader — increases the scale at which the narcotics economy has an effect, establishing, one might say, a new constellation of horror and fear.[18] This relay of shock, as it jumps scale, metaphorically suggests the nested and interdependent structure of relationships across and among various scales. Finally, the discovery of the child's deadness invokes the disorientation that results when the transnational scale converges with the seemingly homogenous local scale, thereby indicating the multiscalar complexity of the borderlands.

The child as container or burro works metaphorically in other ways, too, symbolizing, for example, the once-frequent claim that Mexico was merely a transit zone for narcotics and Mexicans merely couriers, untouched by the problems of addiction.[19] Additionally, the narrative decision to use a child points elliptically to the damage done to Mexico's future by narcotics prohibition and the informal economy it promotes. It also symbolizes the continuing incorporation of child labor into the global economy and implies the brutalization of children that such insertion entails. Furthermore, the revelation of the child's deadness throws into relief tacit rules and assumptions about bodies and spaces, suggests the unspoken cultural rules of spatial propriety—that certain kinds of bodies "appropriately" inhabit or fill certain kinds of spaces.[20] By breaking these rules, the dead body on the bus forces the articulation of such cultural rules and their role in the production of space. That it is the body of a child, not an adult, implies the extent to which notions of appropriate bodies in appropriate spaces govern the narrative construction of childhood as well. The story also gestures to the deaths of drug couriers who, for example, swallow balloons of heroin for the purposes of smuggling it, only to have the balloons burst and cause instant death by massive overdose. All of these are signaled by the pivotal scene of two widows hovering over a once very vulnerable, but now vanilla ice child.

SHORTHAND

In "The Child," bodily movements offer a kind of shorthand—not a supplement to the verbal, but a substitute available through familiarity. The story's second sentence highlights this theme, the narrator noting "the wordless singing of tears" before the bus departs the station. The work the body does to communicate becomes a major chord in the story. Sighs, nods, shrugs function as "the other words" (13). The narrative implies that such bodily movements bear a reassuring form of authenticity or transparency that spoken language cannot because words are "not always understandable" (14). Similarly, the capacity to speak with one's body signals not just familiarity but a humanity that can be trusted. For example, when a policeman speaks, "It all came from his mouth, like a sergeant"; only later, when the policeman nods his head rather than speaking does the narrator note with relief, "He was a man after all" (20). When the two women are about to separate from each other, Mrs. García asks her friend's permission "with all her body" (20). And, in observing how uncomfortably a large man sits in a bus seat, "Mrs. Garcia's head said no, God, from side to side, it's too much to bear" (17).

Furthermore, body parts punctuate the narrative even as they work to carry the weight of communication. Some sentences, such as "Her eyebrows," break the flow of narrative action while other references, such as "And yes with his head," reinforce a narrative comment but disrupt the notion of language as merely or especially verbal (19). Such images of the physicality of language contrast with the silent body at the center of the story. Similarly, Ríos's consideration of the speaking body, his effort to distinguish verbal communication from bodily communication, is accompanied by references to bodily discomfort (aches and pains) and to bodily dissolution (cancers), indicating, at the very least, the challenges of communicating sensation and pain.[21]

The complex relationship between body and language is underscored when the story's meditation on "the other language" merges with the narrative pull toward the revelation that the child is both dead and transformed through a kind of horrific narcotaxidermy. Before the reader learns of such taxidermy, the narrative pauses to reveal first how the news is relayed: "Mrs. Sandoval spoke. She spoke the words of Mrs. García, who had spoken the words of the Sergeant, who had spoken the words of the doctor. More truthfully, she carried the words" (21).

What is the difference between speaking the words and carrying them? What is gained by such a distinction? The phrase "she carried the words" reinforces the story's link between the body and language. Words, like bodies, can be carried. Carrying the words attempts to keep the story *outside* the body and reinforces the horror of the revelation to follow—and the terror of internalizing it. By carrying the words, the narrative attempts to reassert the integrity of the body, its seamless boundaries. This brief comment also suggests that stories are mediated, that through repetition and spokenness, by becoming embodied, stories may be transformed. But by carrying the words rather than speaking them, Mrs. Sandoval attempts to avoid interacting with the story that she subsequently repeats: "The child was dead. It had been dead for a long time. This is true. But it had also been operated on. The boy's insides had been cleaned out and replaced with bags of opium. They had tested to be certain. Then the boy was sewn up again, put into clothes. Sometimes this happens. This was not the first" (21). By carrying the words rather than speaking the words, Mrs. Sandoval almost ceremonially keeps the story outside of herself, as she surely must have wished the opium had been kept outside of the child's body. She also, perhaps, becomes a pallbearer so that by carrying the words she also gives the child the more formal rituals of death. Such carrying further suggests that the story itself offers a ritual funeral for the child who "was not the first."

Bodies vehemently speak of the tragedy. People react to the news by, "moving their faces in a thousand ways" (21). On hearing that the child has literally been transformed into a drug capsule, Mrs. Sandoval is rendered not exactly speechless, but faced with the inadequacy of language to express her horror, she moves her head from side to side, a physical response that combines with the expression "my God" in an effort to shake off the horror of the words she has carried: "Oh my God, *Dios mío, Dios mío* was all Mrs. Sandoval kept saying, maybe with words, saying just like Mrs. García. Their heads moved from side to side, but not fast enough" (21). It is as if the two women could never move their heads fast enough to ceremonially wipe away their new knowledge. The news that what appears to be a sick child is really a kind of mirage casts aside assumptions about the body as knowable, as a stable point on which to ground knowledge, as unchanging. Where the women's gesture-language relies on body-reading skills, the dead body throws their skills into crisis, making them untenable.

This meditation and revelation crescendo together, emphasizing the horror of the excavated child and the incapacity of language, verbal or body, to adequately express it or change it. Here the power of language slips away through its inadequacy, suggesting perhaps the quandary raised by the metaphysical division of body and mind, physical and verbal; or revealing the arrogant assumption that language can be all-encompassing; or exposing the pretensions of body language to be transparent. For what may happen in the shift from "he's dead" to heads moving "but not fast enough" is the arousal of the inexplicable terror that comes from identification with "the child." What may also terrify is the rending of the comforting notion of bodily integrity symbolized by the apparently seamless use of words. If bodies are not what they appear, words may not be trusted either. Finally, the recourse to bodily movement reassures the characters of their own bodily vitality, faced as they are by the abandoned and gutted body.

At the same time, this meditation on "the other language" serves as a metacommentary on the story in particular and narrative fiction in general. For if the characters are suspicious of words, what can be said of fiction and its dependence on the (seeming) stability of words to function comfortably within meaning? That is, "The Child" may be not a meditation on language particularly but a consideration of the impossibility of adequately fiction-alizing such an atrocity in the first place. Or, approached differently, this struggle between body and verbal language comments on the seemingly rigid distinctions between materiality and metaphor. For the text seems to suggest that the material (body language) may be more trustworthy, more reliably stable than the metaphorical (verbal language). And yet the revelation of the child confounds such stability, casting into doubt the reliability of such assumptions.

TRANSPOSING THE COMMON AND HORRIBLE

Published at an earlier, retrospectively innocent stage of the most recent phase of the century-long narcotics interdiction campaign, "The Child" points out the depth to which the drug economy has transformed the quotidian practices of the borderlands.[22] While the movement of drugs in the excavated body of a child is hardly banal or quotidian, the transport of drugs on a bus, with a traveler, is quite common and highlights the degree to which the drug economy takes advantage of the everyday *and* the degree to which the war on drugs has resulted in an increased police surveillance of everyone's everyday activities.

By relying on seemingly simplistic prose to tell this story, Ríos highlights both the banality and horror of violence where the typical and the common function alongside the horrible and baroque. The narrative loses no opportunity to underscore how common the bus trip is, how typical the characters: the bus arrives every Wednesday and Sunday; it always stops at the restaurants El Sopilote and El Yaqui along the way; everyone always gets quesadillas at El Yaqui ("Rumor had made them larger than any of the other choices, had put more letters in their name" [18]); the bus is more crowded on Sundays than Wednesdays; people read the same magazines, and the same *kind* of magazine, over and over again.

Similarly, "the widows Sandoval and García" are portrayed almost as archetypes. The two main characters, as was once typical of Mexican widows, carry rosaries and wear black, and mantillas, and shawls as the visible signifiers of their cultural status. They also "shared a single face, held together by an invisible net, made evident by the marks it left on their skins," and they dress "in the manner of most of the other ladies their age who were at the bus station just then" (12). The description of the two women emphasizes the degree to which they mirror each other in clothes and attitude, which both reinforces their conventionality and signals a status that would merit them a certain amount of *respeto* (respect, reverence). That they serve, in a sense, as each other's double further underscores their status as archetypes, as being just like "the other ladies their age," as common or typical. The story's emphasis on the two women's intimacy reinforces the familiar and common, which largely rely on such intimacy.

"The Child" begins as the two women await a bus to take them to the funeral of Mrs. Sandoval's brother. Their ride from Guaymas through Hermosillo to Nogales takes them through the major cities of Mexico's northern state of Sonora, which borders Arizona, thus tracing a common circuit of navigation for families in that region. Rather than a movement from periphery to center, as immigrant journeys are often spatially imagined, the women's trip illustrates a movement more typical for families in the borderlands with cousins, brothers, sisters, and children scattered throughout ranches and cities on either side of "the line." This circuit also reinforces the banality of the story. In portraying the bus ride's typicality, "The Child" sets up the horror of its closing revelation, which makes the trip anything but typical. The vanilla ice body transforms the quotidian into the terrifying, shaking loose the familiar from its moorings in the repetitive and taken-for-granted.

This attention to the familiar or the usual contrasts with the "uncommonly quiet" bus. Indeed, almost immediately on boarding the bus Mrs. García notes the unusual silence of the passengers and concludes, "One would think the Republic was at war again, or somesuch"(13–14). With this clipped comment, "The Child" artfully tracks not just a historical or merely spatial transformation but a psychic one as well. Mrs. García's sense that "the Republic was at war again" indicates the magnitude of the change. Notably, it is the almost uncanny quiet of the bus—the change in sociality, the modulated, nearly invisible shift in public behavior—not the gutted body, that prompts her sense of a shift momentous on the scale of a war. Mrs. García's phrasing, "war again, or somesuch," is particularly suggestive. *Again* indicates iteration, the return of the catastrophic and even terrible. *Or somesuch* modifies war's commonality by shifting emphasis from iteration to the problem of naming a slight but noticeable shift in a precisely calibrated sociality. At the same time, however, *somesuch* suggests a quotidian state of affairs that resists precise naming. The reference to the Mexican Revolution—a ten-year battle that resulted in massive social upheaval—indicates the scale of change

Mrs. García detects.[23] Her immediate swerve away from this thought also denies the vast sociospatial changes being wrought by the narcotics industry at every scale by shifting it back into the generic. In this way, "The Child" prophetically captures a transformation that is now far more visible, given nearly twenty years of border militarization. It has indeed been "war again, or somesuch."

NARCOGLOCAL

It is through the rupture of the familiar that consideration of the multi-scalar effect of the war on drugs can be most clearly seen in "The Child." The excavated body indicates the effect of the narcotics trade at the scale of the body. Additionally, the story depicts the narcotics industry's effect at the scale of the local (the bus) and the community (the widows' families), as well as, or especially, at the scale of the region—that is, at the scale of the borderlands. "The Child" demonstrates how the international is drawn into the regional through narcotics, how the narcotics economy has helped to modify the region, making the experience of everyday travel, everyday concern for others, and everyday habits of thought vulnerable to the terrible and the bizarre. Indeed, it even predicts the magnitude of such change and what Venezuelan sociologist Rosa del Olmo aptly calls the concomitant development of the geopolitical control model through narcotics interdiction.[24]

That the borderlands have been transformed by the war on drugs can hardly be denied. As historians, news reporters, and sociologists have noted, la frontera has not only received increased attention from the U.S. government, but it has also experienced increased violence. The Mexican Army is a growing presence throughout Jalisco, Sonora, and Baja California, just as the border patrol in conjunction with the U.S. Army increasingly appears throughout Texas, New Mexico, Arizona, and California. Corruption ensnares the entire judicial apparatus—from police to prosecutors to judges to jailers—on both sides of the border.[25] Simultaneously, the war on drugs has led to multiple economic transformations of the region. Local economies suddenly flourish after years of decline, then just as suddenly experience slowdowns. New businesses appear, existing businesses record rapidly increasing profits, then all is deserted.[26] Not only do local residents encounter closer surveillance by both governments, but they must also navigate new and changing tensions in their personal relationships, jobs, and family networks.

Popular culture similarly reflects this transformation through film and music. Narco-corridos, for example, track these changes, offering critiques particularly of the United States, but attacking the Mexican police and army as well.[27] These songs also indicate the spatial transformation of la frontera by exploring and commenting on increased policing, the violence that impinges on people's mobility, the health-care clinics that the informal narcotics economy has provided, and the prisons and jail cells that the formal economy has built. Thus, far more than merely tracking the experiences of the corridos' heroes, narco-corridos detail the sociospatial changes wrought by the "war again, or somesuch."

"The Child," too, presents a surprisingly "glocal" vision of the war on drugs, revealing how the global is enmeshed in the local and hinting at the narcotics industry's economic complexity, a complexity that cannot be easily described in Fordist or Keynesian terms. This impossibility is hardly surprising given the transformation of capitalism over the last half century. Indeed, what Neil Brenner observes about contemporary capitalist change can easily be said about the narcotics economy as well: "If North Atlantic Fordism congealed around the national spatial scale, the emerging post-Fordist socio-spatial configuration is grounded on new articulations among subnational and supranational scales within an increasingly globalized world-system. The current round of globalization entails less an obliteration of the national spatial scale than its rearticulation with the subnational and supranational spatial configurations on which it is superimposed."[28]

If the narcotics economy, in both its formal and informal manifestations, functions at both the sub- and supranational, then "The Child" usefully illustrates this multiscaled operation. In presenting a highly localized story of a bus trip transformed by a particularly violent reconfiguration of a body, it draws the "local" nature of the trip into the international and even global context of the narcotics industry. The vanilla ice body and the speechless widows symbolize the vulnerability of everyone to the complex socioeconomic changes that such a shift in spatial grammar entails. And if the story does not track the precise economies of narcotics, it does indicate their psychological valences, suggesting how intricately intertwined the war on drugs is with the life of la frontera and how inadequate existing structures of representation are for those forced to contend with that war.

"There's Marijuana in My Bedroom!"

Mary Helen Ponce's "The Marijuana Party" provides an extraordinary counterpoint to "The Child." A short story with an altogether different tone and emphasis, published more than ten years after "The Child" appeared, "The Marijuana Party" plays with the banal, satirizes the concept of drug use as masculine adventure, and parodies the transformation of "the barrio" into a new zone of surveillance. Where Ríos's story gently meditates on the relationship between body and language, challenging the concept of the body by recasting its boundaries and invoking a speechless terror about the body's transformation into container, Ponce's story takes up the discourse of sobriety, subtly suggesting the links between "industry" and "sobriety" and anatomizing how various desires arise through the daily tedium of production and consumption. Finally, the story reconfigures the production of "home" for Chicanas by transforming it from a site of labor and reproduction to an ironic enclosure for the clandestine pursuit of desire.

"The Marijuana Party" follows the morning activities of Petra, who "feverishly works" around her home while her children attend school and her husband is at work. In the midst of planning her work for the day, Petra realizes that it is her fortieth birthday, "that ominous cut-off date that will make her middle-aged." Fuming over how to celebrate the nearly forgotten day, Petra concludes, "I want to do something dangerous, *prohibited*. 'Far out,' as my kids would say." As she continues working, cleaning and cooking, she comes across a half-smoked marijuana cigarette in her bedroom. The discovery makes her feel "giddy" and, grinning, she says to herself, "Well, what do you know? There's marijuana in my bedroom!" The illicit substance seems to transform the room and heightens its status as an erotic zone. She recalls that her nephew had left it on the patio the week before and decides that she'll "get high" to celebrate her birthday. Calling her friends Tottie and Amalia to come join her, she tells them, "I have a little surprise." Petra thus further heightens the prohibited tone of her plan by shrouding it in secrecy, implying that secrecy ignites desire (141–42).

Throughout the story the narrator takes care to convey the tedium of

Petra's day and the intensity of her labor. Such industriousness creates a desire to defy, just as the culturally sanctioned occupations of wife, mother, and homemaker arouse a desire to exceed such roles. Danger and safety, prohibition and approval constitute one another and, to a certain extent, constitute Petra. Thus, the narrative introduces the discourse of sobriety (of industry and production) and shows how such a discourse creates its own opposition. Petra's anxiety about what turning forty may mean almost predicates her desire to defy it as well, suggesting that the discourse of aging functions in cooperation with the discourse of sobriety to regulate and monitor both production and excess.

As the three women talk about Petra's afternoon plans, Amalia informs Petra that she has joined the PTA's drug-abuse committee. Petra's teasing response "You get more important by the minute" undercuts Amalia's self-righteousness but also suggests the extent to which the claim to civic/personal/community importance is tied to activities that augment institutional power through various surveillance mechanisms. Additionally, Petra's sarcasm undermines the value of a primary cultural avenue for the creation of a national consensus on narcotics laws and for the normalization of community groups as local organs of surveillance and crisis management. Amalia's participation in the drug-abuse committee helps to enshrine the sense of middle-class morality being under siege. Petra's refusal to condone such moral panic emerges through her parody of Amalia's participation.

After Amalia and Tottie arrive, the three comadres share wine and appetizers while Amalia lectures on the dangers of drugs. Petra responds by teasing the two about her secret, then ushering them "to the rear of the house, and towards the bed on which atop a flowered bedspread lies a lone cigarette, matches and an ashtray. '*Miren, aquí está el* surprise,' giggles Petra, drawing the curtains close together" (146). Petra's switch to Spanish introduces the revelation, with the phrase "el surprise" highlighting and upending the surprise itself by linguistically showcasing the word itself, but at the same time disjoining it from the rest of the sentence, giving it humorous emphasis and playing with linguistic difference.

The scene offers a stunning parody of popular culture's portrayal of the seduction to addiction. From almost the inception of campaigns to criminalize narcotics use, the media, in concert with public policy, has offered a standard narrative of addiction. Typically, a marauding man of color, occasionally described as a "hot tamale peddler," seduces a virginal white

woman into a life of drug addiction and sex work by offering her marijuana, cocaine, or opium. Through a series of substitutions, "The Marijuana
Party" mimics popular films' perennial scenario of the descent into addiction. The "lone cigarette" replaces the virginal white woman, and the forty-
year-old and giggling Petra stands in for the seductive man of color.[29] The
scene depends for its humor on its readers' familiarity with the narratives
of danger, promiscuity, and fallen morality that surround narcotics usage.
Here Petra's theatrical presentation of the little bit of marijuana left behind
by her nephew elevates the "roach" into a grand jewel displayed proudly as
a kind of gateway for women undergoing midlife crises.

Extending the metaphor of the lover's scenario, the two women quar-
rel with Petra, misunderstanding her intent, and she replies, "I'm trying to
make life interesting, my friends. So quit griping!" It takes a moment for
them to figure out what Petra is offering, and when they do, Amalia protests,
"Dammit, Petra, is this some kind of a game?" Petra responds, "The game of
life, Amalia!" Amalia continues to complain and declares, "Next you'll be
showing porno movies." To which Petra replies, "How did you guess?" (146–
47). The marijuana cigarette, lying before them on the bed as if it were a
lover, predicates Amalia's anxiety about another realm of prohibition, pornography. At the same time, Amalia's declaration brings to the surface the
erotics of their encounter but immediately displaces it onto the visual spectacle of pornography. Amalia almost automatically sees "sex" when she sees
"drugs." One seeming excess invokes another.

Furthermore, the jokes about pornography and the narrative's suggestion
that Petra and Tottie frequently watch porn together imply something else
as well. The two women's joint pleasure in pornography indicates their own
eagerness to explore sexuality, to take pleasure in the potentiality of their
bodies, and indeed to pursue the education of their own desires. Additionally, their consumption of porn offers them a means to defy the strictures
of their social locations as Chicana wives and mothers, women whose sexuality and desires are safely contained within the realm of the family. And,
finally, their turn from pornography back to marijuana implies the relay
between desire and consumption—a relay largely considered *prohibido*.

Petra's desire to "make life interesting" and to consider it a game reflects how, in the midst of the repetitive gestures of everyday life—cleaning, caring for children, cooking—political aspirations arise and threaten
to challenge or debunk dominant relations of production. Petra's effort to

get outside of the everyday by doing something "prohibited" or "far out" or "interesting" also threatens to challenge the narrative of domestic legitimacy. In wanting to smoke a joint, she defies the Fordist discourses of sobriety that define what a "good wife" should do. By planning to show porn movies, she gives agency to her desires, identifies herself as desiring, and thus steps out of the strictly defined boundaries of Chicana sexuality.

As the three mujeres take turns smoking the joint, Amalia notices that a police car is slowly driving past the house. She panics, not surprisingly, since her involvement with the institutional efforts to police youth makes her the most paranoid participant in the birthday celebration. " 'Wrong address,' whispers Petra. 'They always have the wrong address' " (150). This remark is the only point in the story when she whispers anything. So what is implied by saying that the police "always have the wrong address"? Beyond being just an exaggeration, this assertion emphasizes the notion of address as property and suggests that the police's charge, en praxis, is to protect property and capital.[30] Petra's complaint that they always have the wrong address implies that the Los Angeles Police Department does not have a sense of what the "right" addresses might be and casts into doubt its policing priorities. Petra's comment, however, is a whispered and impacted statement, one set within the boundaries of her own sense of defiance and desire for excitement. The cruising patrol car also guarantees that she is achieving what she desired at the start of her day—to do something "prohibited."

Once Amalia becomes high, she attempts to justify the sensation by pointing out that "if I'm gonna be on the Drug Abuse committee I should know at first hand the dangers of. . . ." This comment is met with an immediate critique, " 'What dangers? Honestly!' Tottie fondles her pearl necklace and smiles at Amalia." Here the women's interaction threatens to erupt into an openly erotic encounter. But that is forestalled by a series of interruptions. In the midst of their conflicted reverie, they are interrupted first by Petra's daughter and then by her neighbor. The neighbor comes over to tell Petra that she has called the police because the neighborhood kids have been "lounging on my fence, smoking pot! I tell you!" and that she has heard that they should be on the "lookout" for a red-haired dealer driving a blue car. Petra returns to her now giddy friends and reports the conversation, to which Tottie replies, "Greta? The lady next door, knows a dealer? My God! That must be how she cleared her arthritis!" (152–54).

While the women joke, dismissing Greta's anxiety, her news showcases another aspect of narcotics interdiction: the complex interactions between communities of color and the police that have arisen along with the drug economy. People's fear of narcotics, a fear created in part through government campaigns against drugs, compels them to turn to the police, just as Petra's hissing note about the police's penchant for wrong addresses indicates it is an ambivalent choice at best. Framing this interaction, however, is a comment by Petra's mailman who notes with relief that his children are too old to succumb to the troubles of narcotics: "Say, *comadre,* did I tell you I spotted some kids down the block smoking pot? It's getting closer to home, that's what I told my old lady. It's getting closer to home. I'm sure glad my kids. . . ." (149). His comment that "It's getting closer to home" is doubly ironic given that in that very home, while he eats Petra's pumpkin bread, Tottie and Amalia are getting high. Yet his comment haunts this story in a certain sense because it also indicates the real and vital dangers of the narcotics economy, which Ponce here seems only to satirize. Furthermore, his concern is not simply a dutiful middle-class propriety but reflects anxiety about the intrusion of a multibillion-dollar, supranational industry into the neighborhood. Similarly, Greta's frustration and anger result not in the removal of the neighborhood boys or the drug dealer but in the descent of the police and a sharpening of the angles of surveillance.[31]

The subsequent scene reflects what Jimmie Reeves and Richard Campbell refer to as the "narrowing of the margins of illegality" that the drug wars have engendered.[32] The three women are interrupted for a third time, by a policeman who knocks at the door almost as soon as Greta departs.

> "Good afternoon, ma'am. I'm Sergeant Cooper with the Neighborhood Watch. We're canvassing the neighborhood to alert them to . . . say, are you burning trash?"
>
> "No, Captain! I mean Sergeant. Well, come to think of it, I put some old newspapers in the fireplace and . . ."
>
> "Hummmm—mind if I take a look around?"
>
> "Around where?"
>
> "Well, uhhh, I'm here to alert folks on New High Street about the rise in drug abuse among high school kids. The LAPD is asking folks to call if . . . Ummmm, you sure you're not burning leaves? It's against the law, you know. Incinerators were banned in 1958, or thereabouts."
>
> "What were you saying about drugs?"
>
> "Only that we want all concerned citizens to be on the watch for a

blue car driven by a blond-haired man. He comes around during lunch-
time . . . He's hustling school kids. Here, call the number on this card.
We're determined to find . . ."

"So am I!"

"Well, thank you very much for . . . say, mind if I take a look around?
I could almost swear I smell . . ."

"Officer, I just remembered something. About ten minutes ago I saw
a blue car cruising by. The driver had red hair, but he sure looked suspicious!"

"Yeah?"

"And Captain! My neighbor told me some hoodlums smoke pot behind her house. Over there . . . the white house with the pine tree."

Petra waits while the policeman darts across the lawn towards Greta's,
then re-enters the house. (154–55)

The humor of this interaction resides in Petra's skill in turning the policeman's attempts to search her home in on themselves. Her play with his title
serves at once to reinforce the paramilitary character of the police and to
undermine his authority by alternately elevating his rank and then deflat-
ing it. Appearing flighty gives her an interesting linguistic advantage and
enables her to deflect his efforts to enter her home without a warrant. Petra
also uses her neighbor's information to distract the policeman, so that he
turns his attention to the more prototypical drug user—high-school "hoodlums"—and away from the women who clearly do not fit that prototype.

Ponce's story also reworks the "typical" drug dealer. "The Marijuana
Party" characterizes the neighborhood dealer as Anglo, rather than as the
stereotypical man of color. Yet if the story upends one stereotype, it relies
on another. That "the dealer" enters the neighborhood from the "outside"
duplicates the rhetoric surrounding the spatiality of narcotics. Since the ini-
tiation of political policies about narcotics, the rhetoric of inside/outside
has defined the contours of the drug economy.[33] In the spatial imaginary
of drug narratives, dealers are outsiders, invaders who in some sense infect
a "pure," drug-free population. Thus, such narratives depend on a nostalgic construction of an inside space, a zone of respectability, characterized as
under siege. But Petra manages to satirize that narrative, turning it to her
own ends in an effort to distract the police officer's attention. Her passion-
ate claim that she too is looking for the drug dealer heightens the irony of
their interaction and codes her as zealous guardian of the "inside." Unmoved

by the antidrug rhetoric about "protecting our children," Petra both affirms the policeman's claim to institutional authority and undercuts it through the double significations of her responses.

By recasting "middle-aged housewives" into the prototypical masculinist role of experimental drug adventurer and porno film voyeur, "The Marijuana Party" also highlights the extent to which drug discourses are overdetermined by gender expectations. In cultural production especially, drug experimentation is gendered masculine, brave and defiant. Drug addiction is gendered feminine, hysterical and dependent. Through the story's parody of this gendering, its cultural work and legacy become a little clearer. In other words, the story works on the presumption that its readers will be familiar with the gendered terms of drug use and pornography. In disrupting these terms, it denaturalizes such entrenched linkages.

The story concludes as Petra proposes that they watch "porno movies" and Amalia objects because she has "just joined Catholic Mothers Against Pornography" (155). Petra dismisses her but nevertheless urges her to return next Friday for another joint-smoking session if she "can line up a sitter." Petra also tells Tottie to "bring the Lysol spray and lots of bobby pins," while she herself will "be on the lookout for a blue car" (156). Petra's dismissal of Amalia is a dismissal of claims to middle-class respectability. By participating in a series of state-sponsored groups, Amalia endorses a construction of Chicana middle-class identity as organized in part around surveillance practices. Petra's dismissal of these organizations and the causes to which they attach themselves partly disrupts the consensus on which those groups depend.

Indeed, Ponce's satire of the PTA correctly locates this organization as one of the principal vehicles for the proliferation of stereotypes of Mexicans as drug dealers. Early in the federal anti-marijuana campaign, government officials enlisted white women's clubs and PTA groups to fight against marijuana use and encouraged the promulgation of marijuana's stereotypical association with Mexicans.[34] Amalia's membership on the drug abuse committee alludes to the long history of such parental organizations created to protect youth from the dangers of drug abuse. These organizations formulate a narrative that, under the guise of parental concern, imply that the nation "America" is in danger because "her youth" might succumb to the powers of narcotics. Nationalism thereby becomes enmeshed with parenting in an ever-widening attempt to manage behavior.

By highlighting bourgeois investment in regulation, Ponce also critiques the strategies of Othering on which it depends. By linking Petra's pleasure in the prohibited to Amalia's pleasure in policing activities, "The Marijuana Party" suggests a continuum between prohibition and indulgence, where the interdicted or taboo renders its object variously desirable through negation. And, like Ríos, Ponce pointedly turns to the politics of scale. If Ríos suggests the multiscalar effects of the narcotics economy in both its formal and informal guises, Ponce explores the significance of scale to the management of space.

The intertwined conversations about the PTA, for example, not only link narcotics interdiction to the long history of parental moral activism but also delineate one of the primary scales at which narcotics interdiction has taken place. The prohibition of narcotics has been managed in part through the micropractices of local civic organizations that operate alongside the macropractices of national foreign diplomacy. By making narcotics interdiction significant at the scale of the family and the community, the federal campaign reinscribes a national family romance in which the interests of the family and the nation appear to be identical. The satirical effects of "The Marijuana Party," however, hold up this family romance to its own unromantic aspect as a disciplinary machine profoundly loyal to the commands of the nation.

"The Marijuana Party" differs from "The Child" in its treatment of gender. Ponce's story forces into focus the performativity of gender roles, whereas Ríos's story tends to naturalize them. But Ponce's satirical treatment of common drug tropes provides an even more significant difference between the two. Specifically, "The Marijuana Party" offers a feminist critique of domesticity through its parody not only of defiant "housewives" but also through its critique of state-promoted groups that further enshrine the family romance. The story also takes on Chicano cultural expectations of female responsibility. If, as Rosa Linda Fregoso explains, "Chicanas can occupy only one position, either as the self-renounced female, *la madre abnegada* (suffering mother), the passive virgin, or the embodiment of female treachery and sexual promiscuity, respectively sublimated into the either/or binary of *'virgin de guadalupe/la malinche'* in Chicano nationalist discourse," then Ponce's story abruptly tackles such discourse, revealing the flattened stratification such binary narratives insist on.[35] Tottie, Petra, and Amalia (despite herself) resist such stratification through their exploration of prohibitions specifically linked to desire. Tottie and Petra's parody of Amalia's club activities also implicate the state's efforts to further promote the reproductive domesticity necessary to patriarchal discourse. Both Tottie and Petra's refusal to take Amalia's activities seriously and Petra's dismissal of the policeman's project challenge the discursive mechanisms that would render them, as women, eccentric subjects. Through such a series of shifts and splits, "The Marijuana Party" intervenes in the naturalized rhetoric surrounding narcotics, the nation, and the family.

Scaling the Drug Wars

The two stories establish different relationships to the narratives of crisis that pervade the twentieth-century debate over narcotics, narratives typified by Richard Nixon's declaration, "If we cannot destroy the drug menace in America, then it will surely in time destroy us."[36] Nixon's charge has been repeated in various ways by each of his successors, even as it set in motion the contemporary manifestation of the narcotics economy with its activities of coercion and heightened police surveillance of the broad range of everyday activities.

Both stories depict a reality that is more ambivalent and complex than Nixon's rhetoric would indicate, although neither story attempts to dissociate "the real" from the stereotypical. While these stories could be understood to contribute to stereotypes, they are ultimately more sophisticated than that. Given the representational history of narcotics, especially the denigration of Mexicans by associating them with the demonized trade in marijuana, both stories deserve more careful consideration. U.S. news reports dating back to 1914 link marijuana with Mexicans and madness, marijuana being blamed for arousing "[Mexicans'] worst passions, lust and blood shedding."[37] Such reports also regularly claimed that marijuana use produced a "murderous delirium" and led to incurable insanity.[38] In one account that circulated during the first half of the twentieth century, a Mexican mother and her children were thought to be near death after inadvertently eating marijuana: "Neighbors hearing outbursts of crazed laughter, rushed to find the entire family insane."[39] In other words, from its introduction into mainline U.S. consciousness, marijuana has been inextricably associated with Mexicans and madness. Its common 1930s appellation, "loco weed," further embedded that association in the national imaginary.

As the federal government's campaign to prohibit marijuana picked up speed in the mid-thirties, newspapers and magazines published reports that claimed "schoolchildren" were being given a drug "which maddens the senses and emaciates the body" by "Spanish Americans" or "hot tamale peddlers."[40] World War II–era anti-marijuana campaigns also capitalized on stereotypical representations of pachucos to reinforce the association.[41] Such linkages became all the more significant as the U.S. government began to identify marijuana as the gateway drug; as Harry Anslinger put it, "Young hoodlums . . . all started by smoking marijuana cigarettes."[42] With this claim, the already entrenched association between marijuana and Mexicans (and Mexico) took a more insidious trajectory. More than racializing or spatializing marijuana, this assertion created a dangerous shift in public perception: marijuana was no longer understood as just a symptomatic problem but as a menace to the nation's foundation. It thereby implicated Mexican Americans as posing a threat to the nation's future.

Racialization of the drug trade was not (and is not) limited to marijuana, of course.[43] It proved useful for criminalizing opium and cocaine as well. Not only did this process render white male involvement in the narcotics industry invisible (a move Ponce's story seeks to overturn in a small way), but it also helped to hypercriminalize men of color and, by extension, communities of color. In tackling the deeply enmeshed relationship between narcotics and Mexicans, Ríos and Ponce dissociate their characters from the narcotics imaginary promulgated by the U.S. government for more than a century, striving to make possible a more complex and analytically sophisticated imaginary.

Additionally, Ríos and Ponce both point to the connection between the narcotics economy and the politics of spatial management. A primary tactic for regulating the movement and use of narcotics has traditionally been to police and control space. Indeed, the blueprint for zoning regulations emerged in the United States not because philanthropists wished to safeguard the lives of people living in crowded tenements but because politicians wanted to protect property values. Such efforts were particularly blatant in California, where elected officials devised zoning codes in order to condense the scale of Chinese immigrant's economic activity, especially their establishment of laundries, stores, homes, and opium dens.[44] As a real-estate attorney noted in 1931, "It may sound foreign to our general ideas of the background of zoning yet racial hatred played no small part in bringing to the front some of the early districting ordinances which were sustained by the United States Supreme Court, thus giving us our first important zoning decisions."[45] Urban historians have also noted that zoning laws were created largely to manage difference, establishing clearly defined homogenous regions that both protected the accumulation of capital and regulated social and cultural capital. Creating "sociospatial differentiation," Raphael Fischler notes, "benefited the upper classes by enabling them to reinforce and reproduce social distinction across generations."[46] In some sense, the relay between zoning, race, and narcotics indicates that the U.S. government's authority to police space depends in part on its capacity to create and enforce spatial narratives about racialized bodies and racialized zones.

Ponce's story illustrates how the narcotics economy uses multiple scales and how it helps reinforce those scales' hierarchical relationship to one another. For example, in its scornful parody of Amalia's immersion in various surveillance organizations, "The Marijuana Party" illustrates how the national scale is localized and, as Soja explains, "profoundly empowered in terms of its effects on daily life."[47] Similarly, the story depicts how family and neighborhood produce each other as scales enmeshed in the regional or metropolitan as well as the national and international. In other words, Ponce's characters conceptualized themselves in part through reference to an array of scales. In her story, it is the movement of the narcotics economy (both drugs and policing) into the neighborhood that illuminates the process, with policing helping to create a sense of neighborhood, just as Petra's and the mailman's responses to narcotics, to dealers, reinforce the construct of the neighborhood.

"The Marijuana Party" might well be read as a prognosticator of how scale would become a central tool in the war on drugs in the 1980s and 1990s. By focusing on a purported threat to the neighborhood, by parodying the assumptions people make about who uses drugs and where, the story exemplifies the battles over property and identity that would come to preoccupy narcopolitics. For example, the scale of schoolyard and neighborhood became the focus of political debates over narcotics enforcement in the 1990s, resulting in the hypercriminalization of narcotics use in certain areas. In this manner, the family (romance) as the local unit of nation continued to hold discursive sway because it was in the name of the endangered family that such spatialized activity could be hypercriminalized.

Just as zoning has its roots in efforts to institutionalize segregation, it continues to promote segregation.[48] Richard Thompson Ford argues that although restrictive covenants and other racialized zoning measures have been declared unconstitutional or illegal, zoning ordinances continue to be one of the principal tools in the racialized regulation of space.[49] Because "zoning is an exercise of the police power," it has also become a crucial tool in the war against drugs.[50] Communities, for example, followed the federal government in establishing highly criminalized zones, that is, zones in which an offense carries doubled and tripled penalties.[51] Schoolyard statutes, as they are called, create "high visibility drug enforcement zones," and intensify penalties for crimes committed within these zones. These laws further reinforce the differential treatment of space that serves to naturalize de facto discrimination. At the same time, as Ford and others note, the orchestration of place by state powers also encourages place-based political activism and community identity.

"The Marijuana Party," in particular, illustrates how people navigate the processes of spatial production made natural through the repetitive effect of zoning ordinances. The characters, for example, recognize their neighborhood as a community potentially threatened by the informal narcotics economy—a threat that is both spatial and familial; they also recognize the ambivalent threat that the police pose ("they always have the wrong address"). The scaling of space that defines their region as available to police mistakes also prompts Petra to rebuke the police officer.

Thus, both stories construct narratives of inside and outside that imply a local community portentously invaded by the extralocal narcotics economy. The extralocal reinforces the scale of the neighborhood and further naturalizes it. Beyond the "locality" of the bus, "The Child" also charts a local borderland by offering a map of a long-standing regional network (Hermosillo to Nogales via Guaymas). It implies that the man and "child" have been on the bus since it left Mexico City. The comfortably stable Sonoran region is destabilized not by local drug traffic but by the extralocal narcotics industry. Similarly, "The Marijuana Party" narrates a tightly knit barrio where mailmen stop for coffee and neighbors warn each other of potential problems. The dealer and the cop are constructed as outsiders, as extralocal. Likewise, Amalia's many committees valorize the local and local surveillance organs as necessary to the protection of the community and as light-houses (of sorts) that alert the local to threats from the outside. Schoolyard statutes similarly rely on the constitution of the local as under siege.

Narcotics interdiction rhetoric takes advantage of the endangered locality narrative to urge federal and international policing and surveillance, to in effect jump the scale of spatial control. In the name of the local, local power and autonomy are dissolved in order to construct a geopolitical control zone. U.S. policy has also held that in the name of the local (in this case, the nation) it may police and direct the activities of the world at large (the outside that is the source of threat). As Rosa del Olmo points out, "The Rea-gan administration's insistence on looking abroad for the solution to U.S. drug consumption has allowed for the legitimization of U.S. intervention—diplomatic; financial and even military—in other countries."[52] It has also allowed the hyperpolicing of certain local zones within the nation itself.

Thus, in the name of the local, vast extralocal and hyperlocal spatial con-trol is obtained. An oppositional movement that would seek to reverse the extent of U.S. policing authority, to delegitimate the racialized differen-tiation of space established in the name of narcotics interdiction, and that would attempt to mitigate the violence intrinsic to the drug industry must be cognizant of the contradictory narratives of scale. Ponce and Ríos have attempted to do just that, for if the drug economies have created their own geographies, stories like "The Marijuana Party" and "The Child" help to un-make them or at least help to point out their construction and techniques of legitimization through the uses of scale.

"The Child" also suggests the scale politics undergirding the narcotics economy. If it shows through the dissolution of the body's boundaries the permeability and constructedness of scale, it also offers yet another illus-tration of the glocal work of the narcotics economy. Where Ponce's story offers a window on the debate over the scale at which surveillance may take place, Ríos's story indicates the intermeshing of narcotics at every scale. Narcotics movement, production, and interdiction are global phenomena, managed by networks, and are, as Soja notes about glocalization more gen-erally, "constantly being localized in various ways and with different in-tensities at every scale."[53] In "The Child," the scale of the nation-state dis-appears into the scale of the region (la frontera), just as the scale of the body disappears into the scale of the bus. The story thereby exemplifies one of the primary components of globalization—its dissolution and reconstruction of all spatial scales. "The Child" suggests, at least ten years before the popularization of global narratives, that the national scale at which U.S. hegemony has been naturalized is up for grabs and that new sub- and supranational territorial configurations are emerging, not least of which is the new NAFTA/narcospatiality of the frontera.

Taken together, "The Child" and "The Marijuana Party" indicate in part the array of responses the narcotics industry engenders: from horror to parody, from critique of police practices to doubts about language's capacities, from the arousal of desire to stifling violence. Representations of the narcotics economy tend to focus on the drama of policing and drug-dealing, but these two stories shift the focus toward quotidian practices and responses as well as toward the dramatic intrusions that the narcotics industry somehow repeatedly enacts. Moreover, what the two stories provide is more than just a sense of such multiscalar effects signaled by layers of intrusions (dealers, police, bodies and so forth): they also provide models of how to examine the emergence of the "glocal," of the intermeshing of the supranational with the subnational in yet another manifestation of the "changing same."[54] And, finally, the two stories suggest some of the ways in which Chicana/o culture has registered so massive a transformation, both spatial and psychological, a transformation that has continued for more than twenty years. That these insights come not from the studied pens of urban theorists but from the creative analyses of Chicanas and Chicanos indicates the breadth of knowledge available within Chicana literature and culture and the extent to which other kinds of specialists might have much to learn from people so keenly aware of the production of space.

Conclusion:

Spelunking through the Interstices

At the beginning of the twenty-first century, Latinas and Latinos are very much in the U.S. news. Newspapers across the country have been reporting results of the 2000 Census, which show a dramatic increase in Latinos and Latinas, especially Mexicans and Chicana/os, in nearly every state in the nation, particularly in urban centers not traditionally considered Latina/o hubs (Detroit, Atlanta, Indianapolis), as well as in rural areas across the Midwest and South.[1] The growing Latino presence can be attributed to both improved census methods and immigration/migration. Not surprisingly, given the decade-long anti-immigration campaigns, the 2000 Census has led to anxious commentary on how a Latina/o presence will change the nation.[2]

Inevitably the rise of what Raúl Villa astutely calls the "Mexopolis" has also lead analysts to envision, whether anxiously or warmly, a horizon of change for national political and cultural realms.[3] That horizon has to some extent, of course, already been passed, a crossing missed by commentators well-schooled in ignoring populations and cultures made invisible by the continuing hegemony of the black/white binary within the national narrative.[4] Such claims of transformation (both utopic and anxiously myopic) must also be assessed alongside major Latina/o political defeats at the beginning of the twenty-first century. These include Antonio Villaregosa's loss of the Los Angeles mayoral race, as well as the losses of mayoral candidates Fernando Ferrer and Herman Badillo in New York City.[5] As these losses suggest, major political or cultural change will come neither cheaply nor easily as long as the spatial demographic shifts under way remain in the service of a capitalist system dependent on Latina/o surplus labor.

The recalcitrance of this system, of its post-Keynesian militarism, of NAFTA/narcospatiality makes the revolutionary spatial theories of the writers discussed herein all the more significant and deserving of wider recognition. For if they offer new concepts of place, land, bodies and alternative cartographies and spatial epistemologies, they do so in terms not outside of temporality but very much attuned to the deprivations of both the past and the present. Their spatial imaginaries offer critique, that ineffable desire for change, as well as examples of people thriving, resisting, and making space. Yet the work of critical geography has largely emerged without reference to the spatial epistemologies of Chicana literature. That is indeed unfortunate, since so many of its spatial claims and discoveries had been anticipated, theorized, and illustrated by Chicanas.

This rich spatial sensibility is wonderfully visualized by Delilah Montoya's "Tijerina Tantrum." Montoya's collage refers to a revolutionary attempt to write a new anticolonial geography stretching from New Mexico to Puerto Rico.[6] Between 1963 and 1969, Reies López Tijerina and a group called La Alianza organized a series of protests calling for the return of ejido land that the U.S. government had seized. Part of this land, once used as shared grazing areas by Chicana/o farmers in northern New Mexico, had been turned into the Kit Carson National Forest.[7] What made the loss of the ejido lands particularly galling was that the government designated these once communally held lands off-limits to small ranchers and farmers, although they remained available to agribusiness and mining companies. For a period of six years, La Alianza occupied national forest campgrounds, challenging the sovereignty of the U.S. government and its local representatives, the Forest Service. During one occupation campaign, La Alianza elected a governing board similar to earlier *ayuntamientos,* a local form of democracy designed to govern shared resources. At the height of their struggles, La Alianza established ties to radical Puerto Rican and American Indian activists who were similarly attempting to decolonize lands held by the U.S. government. When the New Mexico state police moved in to break up the protests, La Alianza retaliated by arresting two forest rangers and trying them for trespassing and acting as public nuisances. The government did not get the joke. It imprisoned Tijerina, intimidated the members of La Alianza, and drained them of their resources by repeatedly taking the group to court.

Montoya's collage commemorates the twentieth anniversary of the last Tijerina revolt. The photos of the resistance campaigns function as icons of a spatiohistorical charge, of the attempt to write a new geography that, as Moraga calls for, would radically redefine concepts at the heart of capitalism's infrastructure—property, body, land. Each photo tells a piece of the story; taken together, they emphasize the government's fire-power against unarmed protesters. The red ink that laces the photos together evokes the deadly legacy of U.S. imperialism in New Mexico, while the montage's title, "Tijerina Tantrum," describes the federal attitude toward a heartfelt and, for a period, international insurrection movement. *Tantrum* suggests the patronizing attitude of the government toward the actions of people defiantly attempting to have an effect on the production of space.

The central photos provide an extraordinary contrast with the historical, documentary pictures. Various shots, perhaps of a woman, reveal a dancing body; yet this body is fragmented, cut in pieces, as it moves now toward, now away from the camera, almost cinematically invoking musical rhythms. The pleasure of the dancer vaguely defies the coercive threat of violence that literally surrounds her. If this dance ritualizes the protests in an allusion to dance's historical role in claiming land, it also contrasts vividly with the tanks, gunfire, and marching protesters in the surrounding photos, suggesting that pleasure and identity are immersed in and framed by histories of struggle against the militarism of the state. It further suggests the centrality of the body to the making of space, a centrality denied by the process of abstraction that capitalism depends on.

"Tijerina Tantrum" reasserts the spatiality of race, sexuality, and gender in a class war over land use, over the creation of space at all scales. Like the literature discussed here, the collage plays with history and desire, property and ownership, and asks the viewer to consider these arenas from multiple angles without a unified theme, without a unified, meaning monopolizing, narrative. "Tijerina Tantrum" visualizes the ongoing Chicana/o struggles to shape space and exemplifies a spatial imaginary that understands the relations of power and pleasure implicit in spatial production.

Having begun this work at the border, I somehow feel it necessary to end at what Héctor Aguilar Camín calls "la frontera nómada," the nomadic or wandering borderlands. Such a start and such a return indicate the centrality of the border, of my experience growing up so near it. Grasping the mechanics of the border, I've discovered, involves iterative and recursive trips to it. This recursive return also, perhaps, reflects my own experience of crossing and feeling crossed, of growing up in a family that felt simultaneously ambivalent, anxious, and proud of its indigenous, Mexican, and Irish heritages and its 200-year contradictory history at the border. And maybe it reflects my own sense of being a border, often (mis)recognized or illegible as a Chicana by people to whom patriarchal surnames remain the most authentic and authenticating of signs, and thus being forced to spelunk through the interstices of mainline narratives of identity. The (re)turn to the border also, of course, reflects the border's centrality to the field of Chicana/o critical analysis just as it mirrors the ongoing concern of border meanings in an era of continuing global economic synchronization. And certainly my interest in offering different analytical approaches to border studies also stems from my desire to challenge the ongoing efforts of the U.S. government to further militarize borders of all sorts and to demonize those who cross them. The border, of course, brings together the temporal and the spatial, the metaphorical and the material at multiple, imbricated, and sliding scales, a mezclada that Chicana spatial theorists, including the writers I have considered here, challenge and mine as they construct the terrains of a radical mestiza praxis. Finally, I offer a recursive conclusion, turning to the ever-fungible border because I agree with and hope that, as Gina Valdés writes, "pero por cada frontera/existe también un puente."[8]

Notes

Introduction

1 See "National Register of Historic Places Inventory-Nomination Form: El Paso and Southwestern Railroad Passenger Depot." March 13, 1986, pp. 3–4. For additional details, see Robert Jeffrey, "The History of Douglas, Arizona" (master's thesis, University of Arizona, 1951); and Robert Glass Cleland, *A History of Phelps Dodge, 1834–1950* (New York: Alfred Knopf, 1952).

2 Louis Sahagun, "Border Town Tires of its Corrupt Aura," *Los Angeles Times,* 28 December 1996, sec. A, p. 12.

3 For a discussion of the growth of prisons across the United States see Ruth Wilson Gilmore, "Globalization and U.S. Prison Growth: From Military Keynesianism to Post-Keynesian Militarism," *Race and Class* 40, no. 3 (1998/99): 171–88; Christian Parenti, *Lockdown America: Police and Prisons in the Age of Crisis* (London: Verso, 2000); Marc Mauer, *Race to Incarcerate* (New York: New Press, 1999).

4 See, for example, Mark Sullivan, "Drug Money Fills Vacuum in Strapped Border Towns," *San Diego Union-Tribune,* 30 November 1990, sec. A, p. 1; Paul Brinkely-Rogers, "Town on Arizona Border Thrives as It Goes to Pot," *Houston Chronicle,* 17 November 1991, sec. A, p. 5.

5 Craig Offman, "The 10 Most Corrupt Cities in America," *George* (March 1998): 90–102. More recently Douglas has again been in the news not simply because its longtime police chief was arrested for narcotics-related corruption but also because its vigilante-ranchers have been threatening migrant workers. See Carol Morello, "Living in Fear on the Border," *USA Today,* 21 July 1999, sec. A, p. 1.

6 Mary Poovey offers a helpful discussion of the rise of "abstract space" alongside Adam Smith's theories of capitalism (*Making a Social Body: British Cultural Formation, 1830–1864* [Chicago: University of Chicago Press, 1995]).

7 For extremely useful discussions of abstract space see Henri Lefebvre, *The Production of Space,* trans. Donald Nicholson-Smith (Cambridge, Mass.: Blackwell, 1991); Edward Dimendberg, "Henri Lefebvre on Abstract Space," in *The Production of Public Space,* ed. Andrew Light and Jonathan

Smith (Lanham, Md.: Rowman and Littlefield, 1998), 17–48; Neil Smith, "Antinomies of Space and Nature in Henri Lefebvre's *The Production of Space*," in *The Production of Public Space*, 49–70. For a provocative discussion of Lefebvre that shifts the focus from abstract space (and attendant periodization) to space as perceived, conceived, and lived—what he calls the "trialectics of space"—see Edward Soja, *Thirdspace: Journeys to Los Angeles and Other Real-and-Imagined Places* (Cambridge, Mass.: Blackwell, 1996).

8 For a brief discussion of the copper company's influence across the region see Carl Rathburn, "Keeping the Police Along the Mexican Border," *Harper's Weekly* (1903): 1632–34.

9 Neil Brenner, "Globalization as Reterritorialization: The Re-Scaling of Urban Governance in the European Union," *Urban Studies* 36, no. 3 (1999): 431–51.

10 Ruth Wilson Gilmore, "Globalization and U.S. Prison Growth."

11 Patricia Preciado Martin, *Songs My Mother Sang to Me* (Tucson: University of Arizona Press, 1992), 23.

12 Edward Soja, "The Socio-Spatial Dialectic," *Annals of the Association of American Geographers* 70 (June 1989): 210. Quoted in Edward Dimendberg, "Henri Lefebvre on Abstract Space," 20.

13 Ruth Wilson Gilmore, "From Military Keynesianism to Post-Keynesian Militarism: Finance Capital, Land, Labor, and Opposition in the Rising California Prison State" (Ph.D. diss., Rutgers University, 1998).

14 A note here on terminology. I have subtitled this project *Chicana Literature and the Urgency of Space* in part because my focus is on Chicana literary contributions. As readers will note, however, I do discuss a few texts by Chicano or Mexicano authors. By calling attention to my focus on Chicana literature, I am not attempting to hide a Chicano presence, but in some sense to comment on the typical practice of titling studies that include both men and women in studies of Chicano fiction. If Chicano can be "inclusive" even for texts published in the year 2000, why can't Chicana? Throughout the text itself, however, I use the more conventional a/o when I wish to specify both men and women.

15 Doreen Massey, *Space, Place, and Gender* (Minneapolis: University of Minnesota, 1994), 8.

16 Ibid., 120.

17 Neil Smith and Cindi Katz, "Grounding Metaphor: Towards a Spatialized Politics," in *Place and the Politics of Identity*, ed. Michael Keith and Steve Pile (London: Routledge, 1993), 67–83.

18 Here I am drawing on Henri Lefebvre's theories but attempting to avoid his clunky terminology. Lefebvre argues that space entails its production in three interanimating ways—not precisely three spaces, but rather three

processes. First, for Lefebvre, spatial practices or "spaces of production" may be understood as the production of social relations, divisions of labor, the practical necessities of life (for example, shelter, however temporary) (*Production of Space,* 31–33). The second category is "representation of space," the concepts developed by engineers, artists, planners, and those who claim to direct the proper or appropriate uses of space; these concepts include technologies for understanding space, like Euclidean geometry and theories of relativity. Such representations, Lefebvre argues, include a "system of verbal (and therefore intellectually worked out) signs" (39). The third arena, "spaces of representation," might be called "the lived temporality of space" (Dimendberg, "Henri Lefebvre on Abstract Space," 21). These processes interact in what Soja calls the trialectics of space (*Thirdspace*).

19 Norma Alarcón, "Tropology of Hunger: The 'Miseducation' of Richard Rodriguez," in *The Ethnic Canon: Histories, Institutions, and Interventions,* ed. David Palumbo-Liu (Minneapolis: University of Minnesota Press, 1995), 151.

20 For a discussion of the relationship between conquest and Cartesian concepts of subjectivity see Enrique Dussel, *The Invention of the Americas: Eclipse of the "Other" and the Myth of Modernity,* trans. Michael Barber (New York: Continuum, 1995). Dussel argues quite persuasively that "the I-conquistador forms the protohistory of Cartesian ego cogito and constitutes its own subjectivity as will-to-power" in part because the "modern ego was born in its self-constitution over against regions it dominated" (36, 43). My use of *topophilia* here differs from the notion made popular by the humanist geographer Yi-fu Tuan who uses the concept to describe the affect for particular places (Yi-fu Tuan, *Topophilia: A Study of Environmental Perception, Attitudes, and Values* [Englewood Cliffs, N.J.: Prentice-Hall, 1974]).

21 Rosaura Sánchez, *Telling Identities: The Californio Testimonios* (Minneapolis: University of Minnesota Press, 1995), 1.

22 María Amparo Ruiz de Burton, *Who Would Have Thought It?* ed. Rosaura Sánchez and Beatrice Pita (1872; reprint, Houston: Arte Público Press, 1995). María Amparo Ruiz de Burton, *The Squatter and the Don,* ed. Rosaura Sánchez and Beatrice Pita (1885; reprint, Houston: Arte Público Press, 1992).

23 For further discussion of naturalism and capitalism see George Henderson's wonderful study, *California and the Fictions of Capital* (New York: Oxford University Press, 1999).

24 Rafael Pérez-Torres, *Movements in Chicano Poetry: Against Myths, Against Margins* (New York: Cambridge University Press, 1995), 19, 274.

25 Chela Sandoval, *Methodology of the Oppressed* (Minneapolis: University of Minnesota Press, 2000), 182.

26 Sonia Saldívar-Hull, *Feminism on the Border: Chicana Gender Politics and Literature* (Berkeley: University of California Press, 2000), 11.

27 Karen Mary Davalos, *Exhibiting Mestizaje: Mexican (American) Museums in the Diaspora* (Albuquerque: University of New Mexico Press, 2001), 192.

28 J. Hillis Miller, *Topographies* (Stanford, Calif.: Stanford University Press, 1995), 9.

29 Joseph Frank, *The Idea of Spatial Form* (New Brunswick, N.J.: Rutgers University Press, 1991).

30 These include José David Saldívar, *Border Matters: Remapping American Cultural Studies* (Berkeley: University of California Press, 1997); Raul Villa, *Barrio-Logos: Space and Place in Urban Chicano Literature and Culture* (Austin: University of Texas Press, 2000); Krista Comer, *Landscapes of the New West: Gender and Geography in Contemporary Women's Writing* (Chapel Hill: University of North Carolina Press, 1999); Carl Rotella, *October Cities: The Redevelopment of Urban Literature* (Berkeley: University of California Press, 1998); Miguel López, *Chicano Timespace: The Poetry and Politics of Ricardo Sánchez* (College Station: Texas A&M Press, 2001). Miller might not have stated his case so boldly—indeed, he implies that he was the first since Frank to theorize space and literature—had he considered the vital spatial-literary studies which appeared before his. I am thinking of Melvin Dixon's eloquent and provocative study, *Ride Out the Wilderness: Geography and Identity in Afro-American Literature* (Urbana: University of Illinois Press, 1987); Kristin Ross's *The Emergence of Social Space: Rimbaud and the Paris Commune* (Minneapolis: University of Minnesota Press, 1988); Juan Bruce-Novoa's *RetroSpace: Collected Essays on Chicano Literature, Theory, and History* (Houston: Arte Público Press, 1990); and Tey Diana Rebolledo's, *Women Singing in the Snow: A Cultural Analysis of Chicana Literature* (Tucson: University of Arizona Press, 1995). Rebolledo offers the best survey of the turn to spatial themes in Chicana literature, focusing on space as received and conceived, rather than produced. Both Rotella and Villa tend to distinguish between what Rotella calls "cities of feeling" and "cities of fact," but Rotella is explicit in his rejection of poststructuralist approaches to space, while Villa offers a densely nuanced, sometimes Foucauldian reading of Chicano cultural production in terms of spatial production that illuminates both arenas. Dixon considers how African American writers turned to language to create figural landscapes that offered an alternative theater for both black culture and identity. His analysis of the performative work of language covers some of the same ground that preoccupies Miller, who is also interested in how writers turn to topographical tropes to express what they cannot through other means. Krista Comer's feminist analyses considers not only the productive effects of space, but women's attempts to manipulate those effects,

to turn the landscape into what she astutely calls a "wildcard." Comer may also be more closely aligned with Saldívar, Ross, and Sánchez—all of whom draw upon Henri Lefebvre's insights to discuss how space as medium and mediator of sociality has an effect on and is affected by cultural production.

1 Razing Arizona

1 Patricia Preciado Martin, "The Journey," in *Infinite Divisions: An Anthology of Chicana Literature,* ed. Tey Diana Rebolledo and Eliana S. Rivero. (Tucson: University of Arizona Press, 1993), 167–71. Originally published in 1980 in *La Confluencia* 3: 3–4.
2 Ibid., 169.
3 Ibid.
4 Ibid., 170.
5 *Arizona Daily Star,* 21 March 1880.
6 I don't want to imply a lack of response on the part of Tucsonenses to these racialized narratives. This chapter will argue quite the contrary, but my focus will be a short period of the nineteenth century. So I want to note that throughout the twentieth century, Chicana/os in Arizona contested these ongoing narrative productions. See for example Manuel Murrieta Saldívar, *Mi letra no es en ingles: La resistencia cultural sonorense en la poesía de "El Tucsonense" 1915-1957* (Hermosillo: Instituto Sonorense de Cultura y Gobierno del Estado de Sonora, 1991). See also Angela Barrera, "To Heal Humanity: Teresa Urrea's Lifelong Threat and Posthumous Legacy" (master's thesis, Indian University, 1999).
7 Here I am following Don Mitchell, who urges us to study how "the link between landscape and representation structures the conditions under which people work and reproduce their labor power" (*The Lie of the Land: Migrant Workers and the California Landscape* [Minneapolis: University of Minnesota Press, 1996], 2). Focusing on landscape's structuring capacities—that is, attending to representations and their effect—is important because, according to Mitchell, "The look of the land plays a key role in determining the shape that a political economy takes" (17). So, in addition to the labor required to shape a place, to mine its minerals, build dams and railroads, carve tunnels and develop towns, there is the work of representing the fruits of such labor as natural, such that laborers are rendered invisible and evidence of contests over the future forms of the land eliminated.
8 For detailed history of Arizona that includes an analysis of the creation of apartheid-like conditions, see Joseph Park, "The History of Mexican Labor in Arizona during the Territorial Period" (master's thesis, University of Ari-

zona, 1961); Thomas Sheridan, *Los Tucsonenses: The Mexican Community in Tucson, 1854–1941* (Tucson: University of Arizona Press, 1986); and Miguel Tinker Salas, *In the Shadow of the Eagles: Sonora and the Transformation of the Border during the Porfiriato* (Berkeley: University of California Press, 1997). See also Hiram Hodge, *Arizona as It Is: Or, the Coming Country* (New York: Hurd and Houghton, 1877); Hubert Howe Bancroft, *The History of Arizona and New Mexico, 1530–1888* (1889; reprint, Albuquerque: Horn and Wallace, 1962); and Thomas Farish, *History of Arizona* (Phoenix, Ariz.: Filmer Bros. Electrotype Co., 1915).

9   For details of events leading to the Gadsden Purchase see Edward Wallace, *The Great Reconnaissance: Soldiers, Artists, and Scientists on the Frontier, 1841–1861* (Boston: Little, Brown, and Company, 1955); Oscar J. Mártinez, *Troublesome Border* (Tucson: University of Arizona Press, 1988); Thomas Sheridan, *Arizona: A History* (Tucson: University of Arizona Press, 1995); Frederic A. Coffey, "Some General Aspects of the Gadsden Treaty," *New Mexico Historical Review* 8, no. 3 (July 1933): 145–64; and Louis Bernard Schmidt, "Manifest Opportunity and the Gadsden Purchase," *Arizona and the West* 3, no. 3 (autumn 1961): 245–64. For an extensive history of border-management policies, see Joseph Nevins, *Operation Gatekeeper: The Rise of the "Illegal Alien" and the Making of the U.S.-Mexico Boundary* (New York: Routledge, 2002).

10 Senate Executive Doc 119, 32nd Cong., 1st sess., 1852, S. Exec. Doc. 119, vol 14, 277–78. See entry dated 20 December 1850.

11 For details of these efforts see Park, "History of Mexican Labor in Arizona"; Bancroft, *History of Arizona and New Mexico;* and Rodolfo Acuña, *Occupied America,* 3rd ed. (New York: Harper and Row, 1989).

12 Schmidt, "Manifest Opportunity," 225.

13 The Treaty of Guadalupe Hidalgo ceded the portion of Sonora north of the Gila River. This region was largely settled by Navajos, Hopis, Maricopas, Pimas, and other Indian nations. Mexicanos had charted the region but had not settled there. The region south of the Gila River (including Tucson, Arizona) had been more fully explored, developed, and settled by Mexicanos. For this reason, Sonorenses protested the loss of southern Arizona under the terms of the Gadsden Purchase more than the loss of northern Arizona under the terms of the Treaty of Guadalupe Hidalgo. When the Gadsden Purchase was completed, the new territory was folded into the existing Territory of New Mexico. It is helpful to recall that until the Organic Act of 1863 was passed, the Territory of New Mexico included what are now the states of New Mexico *and* Arizona. The Organic Act divided the territory in half, creating the Territory of Arizona as distinct from the Territory of New Mexico. Today the two states have the same boundaries as they did after the 1863 act.

14 Remarks of Mr. Solomon G. Haven of New York on "The Bill to Enable the President to Fulfill the Third Article on the Treaty Between the United States and the Mexican Republic known as the Ten Million Mexicans Treaty Bill." House of Representatives. 27 June 1854. (Bancroft Library, Washington: John T. and Lem. Towers, 1854): 8.

15 Bancroft, *History of Arizona and New Mexico,* 594.

16 Quoted in Schmidt, "Manifest Opportunity," 262.

17 In these dispatches to the *Los Angeles Times* written during the final phase of the war against the Apaches, Lummis described only a small portion of Arizona—the eastern region of the Gadsden Purchase—but he repeatedly suggests that his representation characterizes the entire state. These dispatches are collected in Turbesé Lummis Fisk, ed., *General Crook and the Apache Wars* (Flagstaff: Northland Press, 1966), 5, 18. For further discussion of Lummis' production of the Southwest see Martin Padgett, "Travel, Exoticism, and Writing the Region: Charles Fletcher Lummis and the 'Creation' of the Southwest," *Journal of the Southwest* 37, no. 3 (autumn 1995): 421–49.

18 Joe Park contends, "Company agents warned their eastern directors that Mexican workers, while plentiful, were often untrustworthy and treacherous. Handbooks and guides, while publicizing the opportunities for settlement in Arizona, also advised settlers and travelers to be prepared against marauding bands of 'Snorians' who were as dangerous as the Apache, if not even worse, when encountered in isolated areas" ("History of Mexican Labor in Arizona," 2).

19 My discussion here is indebted to Gearóid Ó Tuathail, *Critical Geopolitics: The Politics of Writing Global Space* (Minnesota: University of Minnesota Press, 1996).

20 Helena Viramontes, *Under the Feet of Jesus* (New York: Dutton Press, 1995), 20.

21 William H. Emory, *Notes of a Military Reconnaissance, from Fort Leavenworth, in Missouri to San Diego, in California* (New York: H. Long and Brothers, 1848).

22 John Russell Bartlett, *Personal Narrative of Explorations and Incidents in Texas, New Mexico, California, Sonora, and Chihuahua, Connected with the United States and Mexican Boundary Commission During the Years 1850, '51, '52, and '53* (New York: D. Appleton, 1854).

23 William H. Emory, *Report on the United States and Mexican Boundary Survey Made under the Direction of the Secretary of the Interior,* 2 vols. (Washington: A. O. P. Nicholson, 1857).

24 For a discussion of these travel writers see my essay " 'Full of Empty': Creating the Southwest as 'Terra Incognito' " in *Nineteenth-Century Geographies,* ed. Helena Michie and Ronald Thomas (Trenton, NJ: Rutgers University Press, forthcoming). For an example of a particularly vituperative traveler

see J. Ross Browne, *Adventures in the Apache Country: A Tour Through Arizona and Sonora, with Notes on the Silver Regions of Nevada* (New York: Harper and Brothers, 1869). Browne's travel essays were originally published in *Harper's* in the early 1860s. See also Raphael Pumpelly, *Across America and Asia: Notes of a Five Years' Journey around the World and of Residence in Arizona, Japan, and China* (New York: Leypoldt and Holt, 1870); John C. Cremory, *Life among the Apaches* (San Francisco: A. Roman and Company, 1868); and Samuel Woodworth Cozzens, *The Marvellous Country; Or, Three Years in Arizona and New Mexico, the Apaches' Home Comprising Description of this Wonderful Country, Its Immense Mineral Wealth, Its Magnificent Mountain Scenery, the Ruins of Ancient Towns and Cities found therein, with a Complete History of the Apache Tribe, and a Description of the Author's Guide, Cochise, the Great Apache War Chief. The Whole Interspersed with Strange Events and Adventures* (1874: reprint, Minneapolis: Ross and Haines, 1967).

25 Sheridan, for example, relies on Bourke.

26 John G. Bourke, *On the Border with Crook* (New York: Charles Scribner's Sons, 1891), 1.

27 Ibid., 450.

28 José David Saldívar has also commented on Bourke's imperialist nostalgia; see his *Border Matters: Remapping American Cultural Studies* (Berkeley: University of California Press, 1997).

29 Renato Rosaldo, "Imperialist Nostalgia," *Representations* 26 (spring 1989): 107.

30 Bourke, *On the Border,* 451.

31 For an exemplary discussion of why the discursive mode became crucial to wealthy Californios rendered poverty stricken, see Rosaura Sánchez, *Telling Identities: The California Testimonios* (Minneapolis: University of Minnesota Press, 1995).

32 The Manuel Gamio Papers, held in the Bancroft Library, offer stunning accounts of these activist efforts in Arizona. My thanks to Curtis Marez for pointing them out to me.

33 Bourke, *On the Border,* 84.

34 Ibid., 85.

35 Richard Griswold del Castillo, "Tucsonenses and Angelenos: A Socio-Economic Study of Two Mexican-American Barrios, 1860–1880," *Journal of the West* 18, no. 1 (1979): 58–66. See also Arnoldo DeLeon and Kenneth Stewart, "A Tale of Three Cities: A Comparative Analysis of the Socio-Economic Conditions of Mexican-Americans in Los Angeles, Tucson, and San Antonio, 1850–1900," *Journal of the West* 24, no. 2 (1985): 64–74.

36 Bourke, *On the Border,* 85.

37 Ibid., 86.

38 Ibid., 86.

39 Federico José María Ronstadt, *Borderman: Memoirs of Federico José María Ron-stadt,* ed. Edward F. Ronstadt (Albuquerque: University of New Mexico Press, 1993), 4.

40 Sylvester Mowry, *Memoir of the Proposed Territory of Arizona* (Washington: Henry Polkinhorn Printer, 1857), 10.

41 See 9 Jan. 1881; 16 Jan. 1881; 23 Jan. 1881; 13 Feb. 1881, and 27 Feb. 1881, *El Fronterizo.*

42 *El Fronterizo,* 13 February 1881. All translations are mine unless otherwise noted.

43 Joe Park details the extent to which filibusterers or filibusteros (also trans-lated as freebooters) attempted to conquer all of the state of Sonora. He further shows the passive complicity of the U.S. government during this period. Numerous essays in the Spanish-language newspapers of the time also tracked filibusteros—a term once used for Antillian pirates. See, for ex-ample, "Proyectos filibusteros," *El Fronterizo,* 14 Augusto de 1880; and "Pro-yectos Anexionistas," *El Fronterizo,* 25 Enero de 1880 and 18 Enero de 1880.

44 Santa Cruz de Hughes's testimonio is archived within the Bancroft Collec-tion at the Bancroft Library, University of California, Berkeley. A slightly different account was published in a section entitled "As Told by the Pio-neers," in the *Arizona Historical Review* 6, no. 2 (April 1935): 66–74. This version does not include the account of the troop departure.

45 Although Page provides a translation of her testimonio, along with some editorial notes, I have elected to retranslate it.

46 Santa Cruz de Hughes, "The Mexican Troops Departure from Tucson," 3.

47 Ibid, 3–4.

48 Ibid, 5–6. Ellen Trover in the *Chronology and Documentary Handbook of the State of Arizona* (Dobbs Ferry, N.Y.: Oceana Publications, 1972) identifies the first Spanish exploration as early as 1526. Missions were established as early as 1696 and Mexican occupation was continuous from that point on (1).

49 Santa Cruz de Hughes, "Mexican Troops' Departure," 4.

50 For a discussion of relationships between the central Mexican government and its northern territories see David Weber, *The Mexican Frontier, 1821–1846: The American Southwest under Mexico* (Albuquerque: University of New Mexico Press, 1982).

51 "Reminiscences of Carmen Lucero as Interpreted by Miss Maggie Brady to Mrs. George F. Kitt, 1928," Carmen Lucero Hayden File, Arizona Historical Society, Tucson, Arizona.

52 Patricia Seed, *Ceremonies of Possession in Europe's Conquest of the New World, 1492–1640* (Cambridge: Cambridge University Press, 1995).

53 Santa Cruz de Hughes, "Mexican Troops' Departure," 4–5.

54 Ibid., 4.

55 Ignacio Bonillas, "Fragmentos del discurso cívico," *El Fronterizo,* Domingo, 29 Septiembre de 1878. Bonillas was not alone in attributing the multistoried ruins to the Aztecs. William Bell argued for a similar origin in his *New Tracks in North America: A Journal of Travel and Adventure Whilst Engaged in the Survey for a Southern Railroad to the Pacific Ocean, 1867–68,* vol. 1 (London: Chapman and Hall, 1869). Bell, of course, does not discuss the political ramifications with anything like the clarity of Bonillas.

56 Bancroft, for example, mentions the possibility of future battles over land grants. *El Fronterizo* and other papers extensively covered court cases over land grants. See also Ray Mattison, "The Tangled Web: The Controversy Over the Tumacacori and Baca Land Grants," *Journal of Arizona History* 8 (1967): 70–91.

57 For an exemplary discussion of the use of Aztlán in the Chicano Movimiento see Daniel Cooper Alarcón, *The Aztec Palimpset: Mexico in the Modern Imagination* (Tucson: University of Arizona Press, 1997). See also Rafael Pérez-Torres's richly provocative analysis of the work Aztlán does, in "Refiguring Aztlán," *Aztlán* 22, no. 2 (1997): 15–41.

58 Ramón A. Gutiérrez, "Aztlán, Montezuma, and New Mexico: The Political Uses of American Indian Mythology," in *Aztlán: Essays on the Chicano Homeland,* eds. Rudolfo Anaya and Francisco Lomelí (Albuquerque: University of New Mexico Press, 1989), 186.

59 See the *Congressional Globe,* 38th Cong., 2d sess., 3 February 1865.

60 Pérez-Torres, "Refiguring Aztlán," 22.

61 Ibid., 28.

62 It would perhaps be another hundred years before Chicana feminist critiques of Aztlán in the work of Alarcón, Moraga, and Anzaldúa—to name only a few—would begin to shift the terms of spatial-social matrix beyond the terrain of a liberal masculinist imaginary. These discursive revisions of a spatial-social imaginary by Chicana feminists are considered in chapters Three, Four, and Five.

63 "El Tucson," *El Fronterizo,* 13 October 1878.

64 According to Thomas Sheridan, Carillo Gardens become an important counterpublic space where Mexicanos could congregate without harassment (*Los Tucsonenses,* 51–52).

65 "Reminiscences of Mrs. Carmen Lucero."

66 Henri Lefebvre, *The Production of Space,* trans. Donald Nicholson-Smith. (Oxford: Blackwell, 1991), 383.

67 "El Tucson," *El Fronterizo,* 13 October 1878.

68 Fernando Coronil, "Transcultural and the Politics of Theory: Countering the Center, Cuban Counterpoint," introduction to Fernando Ortiz,

Cuban Counterpoint: Tobacco and Sugar, trans. Harriet De Onís (Durham, N.C.: Duke University Press, 1995), ix–lvi.

69 "De la discusion nace la luz," *Las Dos Repúblicas,* 22 Julio de 1877.

70 I am referring here to the deportation of Yaquis to the hennequin plantations of the Yucatán, as well as to other efforts by the Sonoran elite to colonize Yaqui territory. See Evelyn Hu-DeHart, *Yaqui Resistance and Survival: The Struggle for Land and Autonomy, 1821–1910* (Madison: University of Wisconsin Press, 1984).

71 "De la discussion nace la luz," *Las Dos Repúblicas,* 22 Julio de 1877.

72 "Sombras de amor," *Las Dos Repúblicas,* 22 Julio de 1877.

73 Armando Miguélez, *Antologica historica del cuento literario chicano (1877–1950)* (Ph.D. diss., Arizona State University, 1981), 56.

74 Authorship here is of some import if only because the political ramifications of this story differentiate it from the many romantic poems published in these early newspapers. Many of the poems published under female names all-too-frequently reinscribe traditional patriarchal gender roles, preaching devotion to faith, family, and husband in ways that would support the nationalism of the papers' publishers. Yet closer analysis, as is necessary, may reveal a far more subtle critique in these poems than my cursory examination found.

75 A. Gabriel Meléndez, *So All Is Not Lost: The Poetics of Print in Nuevomexicano Communities, 1834–1958* (Albuquerque: University of New Mexico Press, 1997), 170.

76 Barbara Johnson, *The Feminist Difference* (Cambridge, Mass.: Harvard University Press, 1998), 13.

77 See Senator Wheeler's remarks and the last debates over territorial status in the *Congressional Globe,* 37th Cong., 2d sess., 8 May 1862: 2023–29. See also further debates, 37th Cong., 3rd Sess., 19 February 1863: 1101–2; and debates on 20 February 1863: 1125–28. See also Bancroft, *The History of Arizona and New Mexico,* 506–19.

78 See Manuel P. Servín and Robert Spude, "Historical Conditions of Early Mexican Labor in the United States: Arizona—A Neglected Story," *Journal of Mexican American History* 5 (1975): 43–56. See also A. Yvette Huginnie, "A New Hero Comes to Town: The Anglo Mining Engineer and 'Mexican Labor' as Contested Terrain in Southeastern Arizona, 1880–1920," *New Mexico Historical Review* 69 (October 1994): 323–44. See also Huginnie's "Strikitos: Race, Class, and Work in the Arizona Copper Industry, 1870–1920" (Ph.D. diss, Yale University, 1991).

79 Here I am drawing on José David Saldívar's *Border Matters,* 173–75.

80 For an account of the role of gardens in Tucson, one that understands the complex layers of a "two-fold conquest," see Raquel Rubio-Goldsmith,

"Civilization, Barbarism, and Norteña Gardens," in *Making Worlds: Gender, Metaphor, Materiality,* ed. Susan Aiken, Ann Brigham, Sallie Marston, Penny Waterstone (Tucson: University of Arizona Press, 1998), 274–87.

2 *Double-Crossing la Frontera Nómada*

1 For a reproduction of "Self-Portrait on the Border Line Between Mexico and the United States," see Hayden Herrera, *Frida Kahlo: The Paintings* (New York: Harper Collins, 1991), 93.
2 Ramón Eduardo Ruíz, *The People of Sonora and Yankee Capitalists* (Tucson: University of Arizona Press, 1988).
3 Neil Brenner, "Global, Fragmented, Hierarchical: Henri Lefebvre's Geographies of Globalization," *Public Culture* 10, no. 1 (1997): 136.
4 That this concept has not disappeared is amply illustrated by former Mexico City Mayor Cuahutemoc Cárdenas' own claim: "Esa rebelión mostró a todo el país que el siglo XX mexicano se termina sin que se haya superado la situación de exclusión y desamparo en que han vivido todo el siglo los pueblos indígenas," afirmó. "El siglo XXI hereda la cuestión indígena que cinco siglos anteriores no resolvieron. No habrá democracia ni justicia ni modernidad en Mexico si el nuevo siglo no la resuelve desde sus primeros momentos" ["The Chiapas rebellion demonstrates to the entire country that the twentieth century is ending without our having overcome the conditions of abandonment and exclusion that the indigenous peoples have experiences for the entire century," he stated. "The twenty-first century inherits the question that five previous centuries have not resolved. Mexico will not have democracy nor justice nor modernity if in the new century it does not resolve this issue from the very first moments of the century"] (David Brooks, "La cuestíon indígena, asignatura pendiente para el siglo XXI, señala Cárdenas en EU," *La Jornada,* 7 Mayo 1998, p. 1).
5 *Border* functions, then, as a spatial term. In contradistinction to *post,* which more commonly functions as a temporal term with a spatial valence that goes unnoted, *border*'s spatial valence usefully elides its temporal counterpart.
6 See Ken Ellingwood, "Border Policy Violates Rights, Groups Charge," *Los Angeles Times,* 11 February 1999, sec. A, p. 3.
7 Henri Lefebvre, *The Production of Space,* trans. Donald Nicholson-Smith (Oxford: Blackwell, 1991), 220.
8 Ibid., 222.
9 Tom Morganthau, "Closing the Door?" *Newsweek* (25 June 1984): 18.

10 Mark Fineman and Craig Pyes, "Texas Border Ranchers Decry Drug Smug-glers," *Los Angeles Times,* 7 July 1996, sec. A, p. 11.

11 Carl Gutiérrez-Jones, "Desiring B/orders," *diacritics* 25, no. 1 (1995): 103.

12 Julia Kristeva, *Powers of Horror: An Essay on Abjection,* trans. Leon Roudiez (New York: Columbia University Press, 1982), 5, 12.

13 For a brief critique of the border as metaphor, see my article "The Fun-gibility of Borders," in *Nepantla: Views from South* 1, no. 1 (spring 2000): 171–90.

14 Gina Valdés, *There Are No Madmen Here* (San Diego: Maize Press, 1981).

15 Mario García, "La Frontera: The Border as Symbol and Reality in Mexican-American Thought," *Mexican Studies/Estudios Mexicanos* 1, no. 2 (summer 1985): 216.

16 See Phillip Mellinger, *Race and Labor in Western Copper* (Tucson: University of Arizona Press, 1995); Neil Foley, *The White Scourge: Mexicans, Blacks, and Poor Whites in Texas Cotton Culture* (Berkeley: University of California Press, 1997); David Montejano, *Anglos and Mexicans in the Making of Texas* (Austin: University of Texas Press, 1987).

17 Gina Valdés, "Where You From?" *La Linea Quebrada* (1987): 23.

18 Irene Costera Meijer and Baukje Prins, "How Bodies Come to Matter: An Interview with Judith Butler," *Signs: Journal of Women in Culture and Society* 23, no. 2 (1998): 275–87.

19 For additional discussions of the prevalence of the term *border,* see José David Saldívar, *Border Matters: Remapping American Cultural Studies* (Berke-ley: University of California Press, 1997); and Scott Michaelsen and David Johnson, eds., *Border Theory: The Limits of Cultural Politics* (Minneapolis: University of Minnesota Press, 1997).

20 For a thoughtful critique of Taco Bell's campaign in relationship to the for-mation of migration and a discussion of the importance of repetition to border formation, see Jonathan Xavier Inda, "Migrants, Borders, Nations" (Ph.D. diss., University of California, 1996), 67–69.

21 Montserrat Fontes, *Dream of the Centaur* (New York: Norton, 1996). Toni Morrison, "The Site of Memory," in *Out There: Marginalization and Con-temporary Cultures,* ed. Russell Ferguson et al. (New York: New Museum of Contemporary Art, 1990), 299–305.

22 Morrison, "Site of Memory," 302.

23 Fontes, *Dream of the Centaur,* 338.

24 Joan DeJean, "No Man's Land: The Novel's First Geography," *Yale French Studies* 73 (1987): 179.

25 Gutiérrez-Jones, "Desiring B/orders," 105.

26 For further discussion see Miguel Tinker Salas, *In the Shadow of the Eagles:*

Sonora and the Transformation of the Border during the Porfiriato (Berkeley: University of California Press, 1997), 109.

27 For an excellent introduction to this history see Oscar J. Martínez, *Troublesome Border* (Tucson: University of Arizona Press, 1988).

28 Luis Zorilla, *Historia de las relaciones entre México y los Estados Unidos de América 1880–1958,* vol. 1 (Mexico City: Editorial Porrúa, 1965), 377.

29 Martínez, *Troublesome Border,* 47.

30 See Tinker Salas, *In the Shadow* for discussion of the increasing utility of a well-policed border to U.S. capitalists late in the Porfiriato.

31 Ibid., 86–88.

32 See Frederick Kaiser, "The U.S. Customs Service: History, Reorganization, and Congressional Jurisdiction," Congressional Research Service Report No. 78–128 (Gov), 6 June 1978, p. 10.

33 Tinker Salas, *In the Shadow,* 99.

34 See Charles R. Ames, "Along the Mexican Border—Then and Now," *Journal of Arizona History* 18, no. 4 (1977): 431–46.

35 Tinker Salas, *In the Shadow,* 168.

36 Eugene Chamberlin Keith, "Mexican Colonization versus American Interests in Lower California," *Pacific Historical Review* 20, no. 1 (Feb. 1951): 43–55.

37 "Report of the Governor of Arizona to the Secretary of the Interior" (Washington: Government Printing Office, 1893).

38 "To Establish a Border Patrol," House Subcommittee of the Committee on the Judiciary, 69th Cong, 1st sess., 12 and 19 April 1926, 18.

39 See the following discussions on these operations. John Dillin, "Clinton Promise to Curb Illegal Immigration Recalls Eisenhower's Border Crackdowns," *Christian Science Monitor,* 25 August 1993, p. 6; William E. Clayton Jr., "'Our Border Can Be Controlled,' Says Analysis of Two Crackdowns," *Houston Chronicle,* 1 June 1995, sec. A, p. 15; James Bornemeier, "El Paso Plan Deters Illegal Immigrants: Border: A Federal Study Finds Operation Hold-the-Line Effective, but Researchers Say It Causes Staffing and Morale Problems for Agents," *Los Angeles Times,* 27 July 1994, sec. A, p. 3; Rene Sánchez, "Violence, Questions Grow in U.S. Crackdown on Border Crossers," *Washington Post,* 3 October 1998, sec. A, p. 3; Sebastian Rotella, "Debate Rages on Border Crackdown in Wake of U.S.-Mexico Agreement: Immigration: Pact Will Lead to New Steps, Including Repatriation of Illegal Crossers to Mexican Interior. Meanwhile, Value of Operation Gatekeeper Is Questioned," *Los Angeles Times,* 21 February 1995, sec. A, p. 3; Sebastian Rotella, "Border Patrol Push Diverts Flow; Immigration: Operation Gatekeeper in San Diego Forces Illegal Crossers into Easier-to-Police Areas. But Smuggling, Desperation Grow," *Los Angeles Times,* 17 October

1994, sec. A, p. 3; Roberto Sánchez, "U.S. Boosts Arizona Border Patrol: 100 More Agents Set for Beleaguered Area," *Phoenix Gazette,* 18 October 1994, sec. B, p. 1; Marcus Stern, "U.S. Blockade Halts El Paso Migrant Flow," *San Diego Union-Tribune,* 27 September 1993, sec. A, p. 1.

40 DeJean, "No Man's Land," 177.

41 Martínez, *Troublesome Border,* 40. *Memorandum Prepared for the Committee on Claims with Reference to S. 15,* 76th Cong., 1st sess., 1939; *Reports of the Committee of Investigation: Sent in 1873 by the Mexican Government to the Frontier of Texas* (New York: Baker and Goodwon, 1875).

42 Ames, 435–40.

43 Tim Wells and William Triplett, *Drug Wars: An Oral History from the Trenches* (New York: William Morrow, 1992), 138.

44 H. G. Reza, "U.S. to Build Fence across Border at Tecate," *Los Angeles Times,* 25 Nov. 1992, sec. A, p. 3.

45 Nora Zamichow, "Marines Fight Drug Smugglers in Texas with Flying Drones," *Los Angeles Times,* 8 March 1990, sec. A, p. 3.

46 Michael Isikoff, "Smugglers Shifting Tactics as Balloon Patrols Border," *Washington Post,* 6 November 1988, sec. A, p. 1.

47 Jodi Wilgoren, "Electronic Wall Going Up along the Borders," *Los Angeles Times,* 17 March 1998, sec. A, p. 5.

48 See Bruno Rolak, "General Miles' Mirrors," *Journal of American History* 16, no.2 (1975): 145–60.

49 Sam Howe Verhovek, "Mexican Border Fence Friendlier than a Wall," *New York Times,* 8 December 1997, sec. A, p. 1.

50 Ibid.

51 Ibid.

52 Ken Ellingwood, "Border Springs Leaks in Imperial County," *Los Angeles Times,* 10 May 1998, sec. A, p. 22.

53 James Sterngold, "Desert Stations to Help Migrants," *New York Times,* 28 July 2001, sec. A, p. 9.

54 The border has been institutionalized through other means as well. Early in the twentieth century, Congress passed increasingly restrictive immigration legislation; they required prospective immigrants to take a literacy test, pay entry taxes, and "Head-taxes." And, in general, conditions at local customs houses for immigrants were less than ideal. As Francisco Balderrama and Raymond Rodríguez explain, "Immigrants were repeatedly forced to wait long, tedious hours before being serviced. It was not unusual for them to wait patiently all day long only to be told that they must return again the following day and endure the same arduous procedure. During the process, all immigrants, men, women, and children, were herded

into crowded examination pens. As many as five hundred to six hundred persons were detained there for endless hours without benefit of drinking founts or toilet facilities. Mexican immigrants viewed the mass public baths and clothing disinfections as indignities" (*Decade of Betrayal: Mexican Repatriation in the 1930s* [Albuquerque: University of New Mexico Press, 1995]). In other words, formal entrance to the United States required a kind of bodily transformation. These requirements enabled an us/them narrative that forced border patrol and customs agents into the position of protecting an "us" whose definitions grew more restrictive and paranoid throughout the twentieth century. And even if public baths are no longer the norm, the ongoing institutionalization of the border continues to reinforce the border as a zone of terror.

55 Norma Elia Cantú. *Canícula: Snapshots of a Girlhood en la Frontera* (Albuquerque: University of New Mexico Press, 1995).

56 In *Decade of Betrayal*, Francisco Balderrama and Raymond Rodríguez estimate that over one million people were repatriated during the Depression. While many were not forced at gunpoint to relinquish their status as U.S. citizens and return to Mexico, the social climate pressured them nonetheless. Articles in popular periodicals such as the *Saturday Evening Post* urged Mexicans to repatriate and urged Anglos to encourage such action. Balderrama and Rodríguez cite, for example, Detroit social workers who demanded that Mexican American citizens repatriate themselves because they were receiving some form of governmental aid (84). As they note: "Threats of physical violence induced many Mexicans to abandon jobs and long-established domiciles. More than two hundred Mexican tenant farmers in Mississippi were forced to pull up stakes and solicit repatriation assistance from the consulate in New Orleans. In Terra Haute, Indiana, Mexican railroad workers were forced to 'give up their jobs' when a mob of hundreds of men and women marched on their work camp and demanded that they quit immediately" (99). David Guitierrez cites a Brawley California newspaper editorial that evinced similar sentiments: "There seems plenty of relief work for the aliens—but for the American pioneer, who battled scorpions, sidewinders, rattlesnakes, the boiling sun of the desert . . . there seems to be nothing but the scrap heap. The sooner the slogan 'America for Americans' is adopted, the sooner will Americans be given the preference in all kinds of work—instead of aliens" (*Walls and Mirrors: Mexican Americans, Mexican Immigrants, and the Politics of Ethnicity* [Berkeley: University of California Press, 1995], 72).

57 Cantú, *Canícula*, 5.

58 Cantú's use of "sojourner" here suggests the presence of an intertext—

Maxine Hong Kingston's *Woman Warrior* and *China Men.* "Al otro lado" stands in for "the Gold Mountain" in a text that is similarly concerned with tracing the relationships between photography, memory, and public history.

59 Fremont B. Deering, *The Border Boys across the Frontier* (New York: A. L. Burt, 1911), 36.

60 Gerald Breckenridge, *The Radio Boys on the Mexican Border* (New York: A. L. Burt Co., 1922).

61 For a wonderful discussion of little-known aspects of gender, the revolution, and the border see Luz María Hernández Sáenz, "Smuggling for the Revolution: Illegal Traffic of Arms on the Arizona-Sonora Border, 1912–1914," *Arizona and the West* 28 (winter 1986): 357–77. See also Hector Aguilar Camín, *La frontera nómada: Sonora y la Revolución Mexicana* (México: Siglo Veintiuno Editores, 1977).

62 Amy Kaplan, "Romancing the Empire: The Embodiment of American Masculinity in the Popular Historical Novel of the 1890s," *American Literary History* 2, no. 4 (1991): 659–90.

63 Deering, *Border Boys,* 60. The narrator of Sterner St. Paul Meek's *Pagan: A Border Patrol Horse* also suggests that superior tracking skills can be attributed to "an inheritance from his Indian forebears" (New York: Alfred Knopf, 1951).

64 Deering, *Border Boys,* 60; and Breckenridge, *Radio Boys,* 228, respectively.

65 Deering, *Border Boys,* 119.

66 Breckenridge, *Radio Boys,* 211.

67 Alex Saragoza, "The Border in American and Mexican Cinema," *Aztlán* 21, nos. 1 and 2 (1992–1996):155–90.

68 Arturo Islas, *Migrant Souls* (New York: Avon Books, 1990).

69 Renato Rosaldo, "Forward," *Stanford Law Review* 48 (May 1996): 1039.

70 As Lisa Lowe argues: "Education is a primary site through which the narratives of national group identity are established and reproduced, dramatizing that the construction of others—as *enemies*—is a fundamental logic in the constitution of national identity. Second, it is suggestive about the process through which the students' conformity to those narratives is demanded and regulated: the historical narrative about victors and enemies elicits an identification of the male student with that victorious national body, and in the process of identification, the student consents to his incorporation as a subject of the American state" (*Immigrant Acts: On Asian American Cultural Politics* [Durham, N.C.: Duke University Press, 1996], 56).

71 As Maria Herrera-Sobek discusses in her thoughtful and informative analysis of a number of corridos that focus on the dangers of border crossing,

"The songs 'Yo soy mexicano, señores,' and 'La tumba del mohado' describe the border as a tomb" ("Toward the Promised Land: La Frontera as Myth and Reality in Ballad and Song," *Aztlán* 21, nos. 1 and 2 (1992–1996): 227–56.

72 Lowe, *Immigrant Acts,* 126.

73 Norma Klahn, "Writing the Border: The Languages and Limits of Representation," *Journal of Latin American Cultural Studies* 3, no. 1/2 (1994): 30.

74 For an early example of expectations that border patrol agents produce revenue, see the House Subcommittee of the Committee on the Judiciary testimony regarding a bill to augment the border patrol and consolidate the functions of the customs and immigration services: "The revenues were eight times as great as the cost of maintaining the patrol which brought in these revenues. Figure for yourselves, gentlemen, the advantages to the Government, from a revenue producing angle alone, of establishing an effective patrol." See Jackson's testimony in the "To Establish a Border Patrol" House hearings (18).

75 See Arturo Islas, "On the Bridge, At the Border: Migrants and Immigrants," Ernesto Galarza Commemorative Lecture (Stanford, Calif.: Stanford Center for Research, 1990).

76 "To Establish a Border Patrol," 17.

77 Ibid.

78 Ibid., 17–18.

3   Intermarginalia

1 Gloria Anzaldúa, *Borderlands/La frontera: The New Mestiza* (San Francisco: Aunt Lute Press, 1987).

2 Ibid., 148–52.

3 Yvonne Yarbro-Bejarano, "Gloria Anzaldúa's *Borderlands/La frontera:* Cultural Studies, 'Difference,' and the Non-Unitary Subject," *Cultural Critique* 17, no. 4 (fall 1994): 5–28.

4 *Oxford English Dictionary,* 3d edition (Oxford, UK: Oxford University Press, 2002): online.

5 Anzaldúa, *Borderlands/La frontera,* 148.

6 Ibid.

7 Ibid., 150.

8 Ibid.

9 Ibid., 152.

10 Ibid.

11 Chela Sandoval, "Feminism and Racism: A Report on the 1981 National

Women's Studies Association Conference," in *Making Face Making Soul/ Haciendo caras,* ed. Gloria Anzaldúa (San Francisco: Aunt Lute Press, 1990), 66.

12   Lucha Corpi, *Cactus Blood* (Houston: Arte Público Press, 1995); Tish Hinojosa, *Frontejas* (Cambridge: Mass.: Rounder Records CD 3132, 1995); Cherríe Moraga, *Heroes and Saints and Other Plays* (Albuquerque, N.M.: West End Press, 1994).

13   Terri de la Peña, *Margins* (Seattle: Seal Press, 1992).

14   Sallie Marston, "Who Are 'The People'?: Gender, Citizenship, and the Making of the American Nation," *Environment and Planning D: Society and Space* 8, no. 4 (1991): 451.

15   Alison Blunt and Gillian Rose, introduction to *Writing Women and Space: Colonial and Postcolonial Geographies,* ed. Alison Blunt and Gillian Rose (New York: Guilford Press, 1994), 5.

16   See for example, Daphne Spain, *Gendered Spaces* (Chapel Hill: University of North Carolina Press, 1992); Leslie Kane Weisman, *Discrimination by Design: A Feminist Critique of the Man-Made Environment* (Urbana: University of Illinois, 1992); Gillian Rose, *Feminism and Geography: The Limits of Geographical Knowledge* (Minneapolis: University of Minnesota Press, 1993); Doreen Massey, *Space, Place, and Gender* (Minneapolis: University of Minnesota Press, 1994); Linda McDowell, *Gender, Identity, and Place: Understanding Feminist Geographies* (Minneapolis: University of Minnesota Press, 1999).

17   Anthony Vidler, "Bodies in Space/Subjects in the City: Psychopathologies of Modern Urbanism," *Differences* 5, no. 3 (1993): 37.

18   Ibid., 34.

19   Ibid., 36.

20   Ibid., 35.

21   Kath Weston offers an important critique of the urban/rural trope that spatializes the gay imaginary so that "the city represents a beacon of tolerance and gay community, the country a locus of persecution and gay absence" ("Get Thee to a Big City: Sexual Imaginary and the Great Gay Migration," *GLQ* 2 [1995]: 282).

22   See Marc Stein, *City of Sisterly and Brotherly Loves: Lesbian and Gay Philadelphia, 1945–1972* (Chicago: University of Chicago Press, 2000).

23   Lawrence Knopp, "Sexuality and the Spatial Dynamics of Capitalism," *Environment and Planning D: Society and Space* 10, no. 6 (1992): 665.

24   Ibid., 666.

25   Yolanda Retter, "Lesbian Spaces in Los Angeles, 1970–90," in *Queers in Space: Communities/Public Places/Sites of Resistance,* ed. Gordon Brent Ingram, Anne-Marie Bouthillette, and Yolanda Retter (Seattle: Bay Press, 1997), 325–37.

26 Eve Kosofsky Sedgwick, *Epistemology of the Closet* (Berkeley: University of California Press, 1990), 109–14.

27 Hazel Carby, " 'On the Threshold of Woman's Era': Lynching, Empire, and Sexuality in Black Feminist Theory," in *"Race," Writing, and Difference,* ed. Henry Louis Gates Jr. (Chicago: University of Chicago Press, 1986), 314.

28 Carl Guitiérrez-Jones offers a provocative and helpful analysis of the relationship between consensus and coercion (*Rethinking the Borderlands: Between Chicano Culture and Legal Discourse* [Berkeley: University of California Press, 1995]).

29 François Lionnet, "Geographies of Pain: Captive Bodies and Violent Acts in the Fictions of Myriam Warner-Vieyra, Gayle Jones, and Bessie Head," *Callaloo* 16, no. 1 (1993): 132–52.

30 De la Peña's choice to utilize the Santa Monica–Venice area as the novel's setting, partly reflects her own background. Her mother is a Mexican immigrant and her father was a descendent of Spanish families that arrived in Santa Monica in the 1820s to take up their land grant. De la Peña continues to live in Santa Monica.

31 Raúl Villa, "Ghosts in the Growth Machine: Critical Spatial Consciousness in Los Angeles Chicano Writing," *Social Text* 17, no. 1 (1999): 111–31.

32 None of the major histories of Chicana/os in Los Angeles County say much of anything about a Chicano presence in Santa Monica.

33 De la Peña's father worked as a chauffeur for various "Hollywood personalities."

34 The sign that announces the freeway is occasionally vandalized—someone pours red paint all over the green-and-white billboard to emphasize the imperialism behind its name.

35 For a helpful account of Chicano battles over the construction of freeways in other parts of Los Angeles, see Erica Avila, "The Folklore of the Freeway: Space, Culture, and Identity in Postwar Los Angeles," *Aztlán* 23, no.1 (1998): 14–31. See also Raúl Villa for an account of an earlier novelistic critique of freeway construction and social devastation ("Marvelous Recreations: Utopian Spatial Critique in *The Road to Tamazunchale,*" *Aztlán* 23, no. 1 [1998]: 77–93).

36 My discussion of a Chicano presence in Santa Monica is indebted to conversations with de la Peña in the spring of 1992.

37 Edward Soja, *Postmodern Geographies* (London: Verso, 1989), 210.

38 Ibid., 184.

39 Ibid., 186.

40 Cheryl I. Harris, "Whiteness as Property," *Harvard Law Review* 106 (1993): 1709–91.

41 Soja, *Postmodern Geographies,* 120.

42 For evidence of such relationships turn to the acknowledgment pages in the recent works of any number of writers including Sandra Cisneros, Lucha Corpi, Terri de la Peña, Helena Viramontes, and Norma Cantú.

43 Rafael Pérez-Torres, *Movements in Chicano Poetry: Against Myths, Against Margins* (New York: Cambridge University Press, 1995), 161.

44 Alicia Gaspar de Alba explores queer Chicana writing in the context of academic marginalization in "*Tortillerismo:* Work by Chicana Lesbians," *Signs* 18, no. 4 (1993): 956–63.

45 For example, a text such as *Chicana Lesbians: The Girls Our Mothers Warned Us About,* edited by Carla Trujillo, was largely produced through an extensive network of women connected to universities (Berkeley, Calif.: Third Woman Press, 1991). Perhaps this would be a good spot to point out that my own relationship to *Margins* is complicated. I met de la Peña in graduate school at UCLA shortly after I had come out, and her novel held many resonances for me.

46 Trujillo, introduction to *Chicana Lesbians,* ix.

47 Yvonne Yarbro-Bejarano, "Sexuality and Chicana/o Studies: Toward a Theoretical Paradigm for the Twenty-First Century," *Cultural Studies* 13, no. 2 (1999): 336.

48 Ibid.

49 José Muñoz, *Disidentifications* (Minneapolis: University of Minnesota Press, 1998).

50 Norma Alarcón, "Chicana Feminism: In the Tracks of 'The' Native Woman," *Cultural Studies* 4, no. 3 (1990): 248.

51 Angie Chabram-Dernersesian, "I Throw Punches for My Race, but I Don't Want to Be a Man: Writing Us—Chica-nos (Girl, Us)/Chicanas—into the Movement Script," in *Cultural Studies,* ed. Lawrence Grossberg, Cary Nelson, and Paula Treichler (New York: Routledge, 1992), 83.

52 Alarcón, "Chicana Feminism," 249–50.

53 Convents are not always merely the site of containment or hegemonic oppression. As Raquel Rubio-Goldsmith explains, some convents can also be the site of complicated resistance to cultural and political domination. See her "Shipwrecked in the Desert: A Short History of the Mexican Sisters of the House of the Providence in Douglas, Arizona, 1927–1949," in *Women on the U.S.-Mexican Border,* ed. Vicki Ruíz and Susan Tiano (Boston: Allen and Unwin, 1987), 177–96.

54 Michel Foucault, *History of Sexuality,* trans. Robert Hurley (New York: Pantheon, 1990): 66.

55 Ibid., 20.

56 In an interview, de la Peña explained that after reading *Margins* her mother took the novel to a visiting priest who was, ironically, giving a "Mission," a week long series of evening lectures and services for local Santa Monica parishioners. She asked the priest to read the novel because she was worried about its contents. The plot itself is not the least bit autobiographical. De la Peña's mother nonetheless wanted the church to sanction her daughter's critique of it.

57 Here I am following Emma Pérez's influential call for "sitios y lenguas" (spaces and languages) that might enable broader expressions of desire and creativity beyond the material/discursive boundaries erected by racialized heteronormativity. That Pérez's call has had such resonance for Chicana feminists in particular suggests not simply the concept's insightful importance but also the extent to which Chicanas have articulated the power relations inherent to spatial production. See her "Sexuality and Discourse: Notes from a Chicana Survivor," in *Chicana Lesbians: The Girls Our Mothers Warned Us About,* ed. Carla Trujillo (Berkeley, Calif.: Third Woman Press: 1991), 159–84.

58 Michel Foucault, "Of Other Spaces," trans. Jay Miskowiec, *Diacritics* 16 (1986): 25.

59 Ibid.

60 Carla Trujillo, "Chicana Lesbians: Fear and Loathing in the Chicano Community," in *Chicana Critical Issues,* ed. Norma Alarcón (Berkeley, Calif.: Third Woman Press, 1993), 186.

61 Judith Butler, "Imitation and Gender Insubordination," in *Inside/Out: Lesbian Theories, Gay Theories,* ed. Diana Fuss (New York: Routledge Press, 1991): 20.

62 Norma Alarcón, "Making 'Familia' from Scratch: Split Subjectivities in the Work of Helena María Viramontes and Cherríe Moraga," in *Chicana Creativity and Criticism: Charting New Frontiers in American Literature,* ed. María Herrera-Sobek and Helena Viramontes (Houston: Arte Público Press, 1988), 148.

63 Alarcón, "Chicana Feminism," 253.

64 Trujillo, "Chicana Lesbians," 187.

65 Renato Rosaldo, "Cultural Citizenship, Inequality, and Multiculturalism," in *Latino Cultural Citizenship: Claiming Identity, Space, and Rights,* ed. William Flores and Rina Benmayor (Boston: Beacon Press, 1997), 29.

66 Ibid., 35.

4 Sandra Cisneros's Contrapuntal *"Geography of Scars"*

1 Sandra Cisneros, *Woman Hollering Creek and Other Stories* (New York: Random House, 1991), 84. All citations from this story collection will be given parenthetically in the text.

2 Don Mitchell elaborates on this point to argue that "landscape is both a work and an erasure of work" (*The Lie of the Land: Migrant Workers and the California Landscape* [Minneapolis: University of Minnesota Press, 1996], 6). Mitchell further suggests that the production of landscape is in part an attempt to remove a scene from contemporaneity and thereby render it static and untouched by the political economy.

3 Johannes Fabian argues in *Time and the Other: How Anthropology Makes Its Object* that temporal modalities are often used to reinforce a series of hierarchies (New York: Columbia University Press, 1983). Western European anthropologists, for example, presume a hierarchy of progress toward something like "civilization" (contemporaneous with European society). This conception uses time as a means to naturalize moral hierarchies. Those communities not considered "Western-European" lag behind Europe in the progressive race toward civilized culture. In this sense, calling the landscape of "Bread" charming suggests that it is being shifted out of contemporaneity and into a realm either of nostalgia or under-development. In either case, the privileged position (coevalness) lies with the fluid temporality of the observer.

4 Cindi Katz, "Growing Girls/Closing Circles," in *Full Circles: Geographies of Women over the Life Course,* ed. Cindi Katz and Janice Monk (New York: Routledge, 1993), 88.

5 As Caren Kaplan puts it, "When a 'place on a map' can be seen to be a 'place in history' as well, the terms of critical practice have made a significant shift" (*Questions of Travel: Postmodern Discourses of Displacement* [Durham, N.C.: Duke University Press, 1996], 25).

6 Doreen Massey, *Space, Place, and Gender* (Minneapolis: University of Minnesota Press, 1994), 2.

7 Ibid., 154, 155.

8 Edward Soja, *Thirdspace: Journeys to Los Angeles and Other Real-and-Imagined Places* (Cambridge, Mass.: Blackwell, 1996), 46.

9 Gillian Rose, *Feminism and Geography: The Limits of Geographical Knowledge* (Minneapolis: University of Minnesota Press, 1993), 37.

10 Edward Soja, *Postmodern Geographies* (London: Verso, 1989), 6.

11 It is not surprising that Sandra Cisneros has written a text so deeply aware of spatiality. In an early essay she explains that she wrote *The House on Mango*

Street (1985) in part as a response to Gaston Bachelard's *The Poetics of Space.* She found herself resisting the tendency to romanticize space evinced by her fellow graduate students at the Iowa Writers Program; she also found herself highly conscious of the effects of her own life on her perceptions of space; see her "Ghosts and Voices: Writing from Obsession," *Americas Review* 15 (spring 1987): 69–72.

12 Massey, *Space, Place, and Gender,* 180; and Michel de Certeau, *The Practice of Everyday Life,* trans. Steven Rendall (Berkeley: University of California Press, 1984), respectively.

13 Ross Chambers, "Messing Around: Gayness and Loiterature in Alan Hollinghurst's *The Swimming-Pool Library,*" in *Textuality and Sexuality: Reading Theories and Practices,* ed. Judith Still and Michael Worten (Manchester, Eng.: Manchester University Press, 1993), 207. I have also found helpful Chambers's "Pointless Stories, Storyless Points: Roland Barthes between 'Soirées de Paris' and 'Incidents,'" *L'Esprit Créateur* 34 (summer 1994): 12–30; and "Mediations and the Escalator Principle," *Modern Fiction Studies* 40 (winter 1994): 765–806. Chambers formulates loiterature as an extension of Michel de Certeau's theories of perspective and narrative, which emerge from his discussion of the flaneur. The playful concept of loiterature is useful not only because it expands de Certeau's concept of storytelling as ruse, but also because it brings to the fore literature's ongoing engagement with spatiality. Chambers's use of the flaneur offers an important narrative paradigm for initially exploring Cisneros's collection, but its connection to a masculinist bourgeois trajectory may limit its valences. Contemporary geographers have also found the concept of the flaneur appealing, and there are many analyses of the figure of the flaneur. Among the most useful is Elizabeth Wilson's "The Invisible Flaneur," in *Postmodern Cities and Spaces,* ed. Sophie Watson and Katherine Gibson (Oxford: Blackwell, 1995), 59–79.

14 Chambers, "Messing Around," 208.

15 Phillip Brian Harper, *Framing the Margins* (New York: Oxford University Press, 1994), 11.

16 In my discussion of contrapuntal techniques, I am drawing on Fernando Ortiz's landmark text *Cuban Counterpoint: Tobacco and Sugar,* trans. Harriet De Onís (Durham, N.C.: Duke University Press, 1995); and Edward Said, *Culture and Imperialism* (New York: Vintage, 1994).

17 Kristin Ross, *The Emergence of Social Space: Rimbaud and the Paris Commune* (Minneapolis: University of Minnesota Press, 1988), 8.

18 This narrative style has something in common with the testimonio, a genre that Sonia Saldívar-Hull argues has been important for contemporary Chicana writers; see her *Feminism on the Border: Chicana Gender Politics and Literature* (Berkeley: University of California Press, 2000). Thus, the text can

be understood, like the testimonio, as "a practice, a part of the struggle for hegemony" (George Yudice, "Testimonio and Postmodernism," in *The Real Thing: Testimonial Discourse and Latin America,* ed. George Gugelberger [Durham, N.C.: Duke University Press, 1996], 57). I do not claim that these stories are testimonios or that testimonios provide the generic paradigm for them, but rather that the stories often resonate with the voices and concerns of testimonios.

19 Cisneros has directed performances of "Little Miracles, Kept Promises" in San Antonio, Texas.

20 Lisa Lowe, *Immigrant Acts: On Asian American Cultural Politics* (Durham, N.C.: Duke University Press, 1996), 116.

21 Francine Masiello, "Melodrama, Sex, and Nation in Latin America's *Fin de Siglo,*" *Modern Language Quarterly* 57, no. 2 (June 1996): 270.

22 For an informed discussion of language in the collection, see Harryette Mullen, " 'A Silence between Us Like a Language': The Untranslatability of Experience in Sandra Cisneros's *Woman Hollering Creek,*" *MELUS* 21 (summer 1996): 3–20.

23 Kristin Ross, *Fast Cars, Clean Bodies: Decolonization and the Reordering of French Culture* (Cambridge, Mass.: MIT Press, 1995), 35.

24 Philip Fisher, *Hard Facts: Setting and Form in the American Novel* (New York: Oxford University Press, 1985), 9.

25 Edward Said, *Culture and Imperialism,* xiii.

26 See David Harvey, *Justice, Nature, and the Geography of Difference* (Cambridge, Mass.: Blackwell, 1996), 231.

27 Henri Lefebvre, *The Production of Space,* trans. Donald Nicholson-Smith (Oxford: Blackwell, 1991), 383.

28 Bill Brown, "Science Fiction, the World's Fair, and the Prosthetics of Empire, 1910–1915," in *Cultures of U.S. Imperialism,* ed. Amy Kaplan and Donald E. Pease (Durham, N.C.: Duke University Press, 1993), 129.

29 Sahagún, quoted in Jacques Lafaye, *Quetzalcoatl and Guadalupe: The Formation of Mexican National Consciousness, 1531–1813,* trans. Benjamin Keen (Chicago: University of Chicago Press, 1975), 215.

30 See Ana Castillo, introduction to *Goddess of the Americas/La Diosa de las Americas: Writings on the Virgin of Guadalupe,* ed. Ana Castillo (New York: Riverhead Books, 1996), xix.

31 In his highly influential work, Jacques Lafaye argues that there is a great deal of evidence that missionaries initially installed at Tepeyac an image of the Virgin of Guadalupe of Estremadura, Spain, known as the "Dark Lady of Villuercas" and credited with helping to defeat the Moors in 1492. This "Spanish Virgin" was apparently the favorite icon of Cortes as well as other conquistadores; her placement would have been both a reflection of Cor-

tesian power and a practice within the long Catholic tradition of converting a local populace by subsuming their religious tradition into Catholicism. According to Lafaye, the Virgin of Guadalupe at Tepeyac quickly developed a local history and missionaries erased nearly all ties to Estremadura, in part because they wanted to keep the alms in Mexico rather than turn them over to Spain. Thus, her feast was switched from September to December and a new image was proffered. See Lafaye, *Quetzalcoatl and Guadalupe,* 211–53.

I take the extremely helpful phrase "pre-Cortesian" from Rafael Pérez-Torres, *Movements in Chicano Poetry: Against Myths, Against Margins* (New York: Cambridge University Press, 1995), 19. The phrase serves to emphasize the more destructive arrival of Hernan Cortes rather than that of Columbus, while also calling attention to the imposition of Cartesian epistemologies.

32 Ibid., 288.

33 Woodrow Borah, "Queen of Mexico and Empress of the Americas: La Guadalupana of Tepeyac," *Mexican Studies/Estudios Mexicanos* 12 (summer 1996): 331.

34 Ibid., 338.

35 See Margarita Zires, "Los mitos de la Virgen de Guadalupe: Su proceso de construcción y reinterpretación en el Mexico pasado y contemporáneo," *Mexican Studies/Estudios Mexicanos* 10, no. 1 (summer 1994): 292.

36 As Lafaye explains, "Miguel Sánchez went so far as to claim that the image of Guadalupe was 'the first creole woman, a native of this land' " (*Quetzalcoatl and Guadalupe,* 250). See also Zires, "Los mitos de la Virgen de Guadalupe," 293.

37 Miguel Sánchez, quoted in Zires, "Los mitos de la Virgen de Guadalupe," 296.

38 See Sylvia Santaballa, "Nican Motecpana: Nahuatl Miracles of the Virgin of Guadalupe," *Latin American Indian Literature Journal* 11, no. 1 (spring 1995): 52.

39 See Borah, "Queen of Mexico," 338; and Santaballa, "Nican Motecpana," 53.

40 Castillo, *Goddess of the Americas,* xvi.

41 See Zires, "Los mitos de la Virgen de Guadalupe," 286. See also Maria Herrera-Sobek, *The Mexican Corrido: A Feminist Analysis* (Bloomington: Indiana University Press, 1990), 42.

42 See Rafael Pérez-Torres, *Movements in Chicano Poetry,* for a discussion of a post-Cortes(ian) structure of epistemology and history.

43 Norma Alarcón, "Traddutora, Traditora: A Paradigmatic Figure of Chicana Feminism," *Cultural Critique* 13 (fall 1989): 60.

44 Mary Louise Pratt, *Imperial Eyes: Travel Writing and Transculturation* (London: Routledge, 1992), 204.

45 Compare this pun to Tato Laviera's notion of "AmeRíca," a play on *Puerto*

Rico and *America* that also challenges nationalist identity constructions. See his *AmeRícan* (Houston: Arte Público, 1985).

46   See Laura Pulido, *Environmentalism and Economic Justice: Two Chicano Struggles in the Southwest* (Tucson: University of Arizona Press, 1996), 20–45. Pulido writes about the state of New Mexico's construction of an enchanted indigenous heritage and local activists' ability to take advantage of that fetishization. This construction is also, of course, a way to elide the production of atomic weapons in that region and the history of Chicano and Pueblo resistance to it.

47   Massey, *Space, Place, and Gender,* 8.

48   Katherine Rios, "'And You Know What I Have to Say Isn't Always Pleasant': Translating the Unspoken Word in Cisneros's *Woman Hollering Creek,*" in *Chicana (W)rites: On Word and Film,* ed. María Herrera-Sobek and Helena Viramontes (Berkeley, Calif.: Third Woman Press, 1995), 202; and Cisneros, *Woman Hollering Creek,* 23, respectively.

49   For useful discussions of the Alamo in popular culture, see the essays collected in Susan Prendergast Schoelwer, ed., *Alamo Images: Changing Perceptions of a Texas Experience* (Dallas: Southern Methodist University Press, 1985).

50   The history throughout this paragraph is taken from Richard Flores, "Private Visions, Public Culture: The Making of the Alamo," *Cultural Anthropology* 10 (February 1995): 99–115.

51   Ibid., 111.

52   See Holly Brear, *Inherit the Alamo: Myth and Ritual at an American Shrine* (Austin: University of Texas Press, 1995), 18–22.

53   Sonia Saldívar-Hull first pointed out to me the ironic punning of Travis's name.

54   See Rodolfo Acuña, *Occupied America,* 3d ed. (New York: Harper and Row, 1989), 8–9.

55   Edward Soja and Barbara Hooper explain that modernist binarisms such as capital/labor, self/other, individual/collective effectively naturalize the uneven development on which capital depends ("The Spaces that Difference Makes," in *Place and the Politics of Identity,* ed. Michael Keith and Steven Pile [London: Routledge, 1993], 183–205).

56   For a useful introduction to ex-votos, see Jorge Durand and Douglas Massey, *Miracles on the Border: Retablos of the Mexican Migrants to the United States* (Tucson: University of Arizona Press, 1995).

57   The museum of the Basilica of Guadalupe, for example, includes an early ex-voto that shows a procession of children begging the Virgin of Guadalupe to relieve them from the 1544 plague of Cocolixtli, while other paintings illustrate the apparitions (ibid., 13–14).

58 It should be noted that the United Farm Workers' use of the Virgin of Guadalupe was not without its detractors. In a brief but useful discussion, Pulido points out that the use of the Virgin worked as a "form of praxis and reinforced culture as difference," but this tactic also became the "subject of scorn"; one supporter, for example, withdrew her financial backing of the farm workers because of their use of religious icons (Pulido, *Environmentalism and Economic Justice*, 202).

59 Walter Mignolo, *The Darker Side of the Renaissance* (Ann Arbor: University of Michigan Press, 1995), 127, 246.

60 Ibid., 219.

61 Brian Harley, "Deconstructing the Map," in *Writing Worlds: Discourse, Text, and Metaphor in the Representation of Landscape*, ed. Trevor J. Barnes and James S. Duncan (London: Routledge, 1992), 236.

62 My discussion of women's fear of public space draws from the following works: Rachel Pain, "Space, Sexual Violence, and Social Control: Integrating Geographical and Feminist Analyses of Women's Fear of Crime," *Progress in Human Geography* 15 (December 1991): 415–31; Yvette Flores Ortiz, "La Mujer y La Violencia: A Culturally Based Model for the Understanding and Treatment of Domestic Violence in Chicana/Latina Communities," in *Chicana Critical Issues*, ed. Norma Alarcón et al. (Berkeley, Calif.: Third Woman Press, 1993), 169–82; and Gill Valentine, "The Geography of Women's Fear," *Area* 21 (December 1989): 385–90.

63 In *Nothing Bad Happens to Good Girls*, Esther Madriz explains that while "victimization rates are lower among women and the elderly than among men and the young," women and the elderly, across racial lines, fear crime more than men ([Berkeley: University of California Press, 1997], 11). Additionally, "in spite of all the messages suggesting that women are safer at home, women murder victims are more than ten times as likely as men to have been victims of intimate violence. In 1992 about 75 percent of violent crimes committed by lone offenders and 45 percent of those committed by multiple offenders were perpetuated by someone known to the victim" (17). Representations of women and crime are also at odds with statistical indicators: "Women are more likely to be victims of property crimes, muggings, and domestic violence, yet the media continually depict women as predominantly victims of sexual attacks. This image reinforces the idea that what is most important about women is their sexuality" (85).

64 Pain, "Space, Sexual Violence, and Social Control," 421.

65 Ibid., 423.

66 Katz, "Growing Girls/Closing Circles," 90–93.

67 Valentine, "Geography of Women's Fear," 386.

68 See Madriz, *Nothing Bad Happens*, 61.

69 Pain, "Space, Sexual Violence, and Social Control," 417.

70 Mark Seltzer, "Serial Killers (II): The Pathological Public Sphere," *Critical Inquiry* 22, no. 1 (fall 1995): 129.

71 While physical violence threatens women as a class, it does not affect women uniformly. White women, regardless of their sexuality, are much safer in public spaces than they may imagine, while women of color, regardless of their sexuality, face additional, more complex spatial risks. Some lesbians experience frequent verbal assaults in addition to physical threats and violence. The geographies of racism and homophobia intersect with crime to force women to navigate space differently from one another. Women are valued variously, according to such categories, and these differences are reflected both in statistics and in official responses to violence against women (see Madriz, *Nothing Bad Happens,* 12). Effective means of preventing violence vary drastically among women, and the majority of public resources targeted at prevention have been designed and distributed with heterosexual white women in mind (see Yvette Flores Ortiz, "La Mujer y La Violencia," 168; G. Chezia Carraway, "Violence against Women of Color," *Stanford Law Review* 43 (July 1991): 1303–50; Milyoung Cho, "Waking Up from a Domestic Nightmare," *Third Force* 2 (May/June 1994): 25–29; Kimberle Crenshaw, "Mapping the Margins: Intersectionality, Identity Politics, and Violence against Women of Color," *Stanford Law Review* 43 (July 1991): 1241–99.

72 For an important analysis of this revision, see Saldívar-Hull's *Feminism on the Border.* For other discussions of the reworking of the llorona myth, see Tey Diana Rebolledo, *Women Singing in the Snow: A Cultural Analysis of Chicana Literature* (Tucson: University of Arizona Press, 1995). For a critique of this revisioning, see Rosaura Sánchez, "Reconstructing Chicana Gender Identity," *American Literary History* 9 (summer 1997): 350–64.

73 Valentine, "The Geography of Women's Fear," 389.

74 Madriz, *Nothing Bad Happens,* 19.

75 Further complicating this story is the revelation, near its close, that Boy Baby might be a serial killer: "The next thing we hear, he's in the newspaper clippings his sister sends. A picture of him looking very much like stone, police hooked on either arm . . . *on the road to* Las Grutas de Xtacumbilxuna, *the Caves of the Hidden Girl . . . eleven female bodies . . . the last seven years . . .*" (34). This image contrasts with the portrait Boy Baby had built of himself as Chaq Uxmal Paloquín, a Mayan prince who will lead an uprising and "bring back the grandeur of my people from those who have broken the arrows, from those who have pushed the ancient stones off their pedestals" (29). Not surprisingly, Boy Baby has used this narrative to seduce the young narrator, and in granting her the status of his queen, "Ixtel," he has

ceremoniously erased the great age difference between them. More significant, however, is the suggestion here of a link between a serial killer and colonialism, between a nearly prosaic sense of a history of oppression and an individual figure who uses that history not to lead an uprising but to murder young girls. The story, in some sense, suggests in the geography lesson that "Chaq" imparts—"making a map with the heel of his boot, this is where I come from, the Yucatán, the ancient cities"—that serial killing is a latter-day version of imperialism, colonization individuated (27). Yet another way to approach this complicated plot detail is to read it as a critique of a kind of vulgar cultural nationalism, one that proclaims a readiness to revolt against oppressors while relying on a cinematic visual and narrative code that romanticizes and commodifies earlier resistance efforts and depends on the exploitation of women in its creation of a heroic masculinist warrior stance.

76 Saldívar-Hull, *Feminism on the Border,* 117.

77 Dolores Hayden, *The Power of Place: Urban Landscapes as Public History* (Cambridge, Mass.: MIT Press, 1995), 22.

78 See Masiello, "Melodrama, Sex, and Nation," 277.

79 See Sandra Cisneros, *My Wicked, Wicked Ways* (Berkeley, Calif.: Third Woman Press, 1987), and *Loose Woman* (New York: Alfred Knopf, 1994).

80 Yolanda Broyles-González, *El Teatro Campesino: Theater in the Chicano Movement* (Austin: University of Texas Press, 1994), xvi.

81 Evangelina Vigil-Piñón, "Tavern Taboo," in *Infinite Divisions: An Anthology of Chicana Literature,* ed. Tey Diana Rebolledo and Eliana S. Rivero (Tucson: University of Arizona Press, 1993), 188.

5 *"Against the Nostalgia for the Whole and the One"*

1 Emma Pérez, *The Decolonial Imaginary: Writing Chicanas into History* (Bloomington: Indiana University Press, 1999), 108.

2 Louis Althusser, *Lenin and Philosophy,* trans. Ben Brewster (London: Monthly Review Press, 1971). For a wonderful discussion of memory and interpellation see José Rabasa, *Writing Violence on the Northern Frontier: The Historiography of Sixteenth-Century New Mexico and Florida and the Legacy of Conquest* (Durham, N.C.: Duke University Press, 2000). See also Jonathan Boyarin, "Space, Time, and the Politics of Memory," in *Remapping Memory: The Politics of TimeSpace,* ed. Jonathan Boyarin (Minneapolis: University of Minnesota Press, 1994), 1–38.

3 Rabasa, *Writing Violence,* 7.

4 Norma Alarcón, "The Work of Armando Rascón: T(r)opographies for a

Critical Imaginary," in *Occupied Aztlán* (San Francisco: Adaline Kent Award Exhibition, San Francisco Art Institute, 1994), 12.

5 Cherríe Moraga, "Passage," in *Loving in the War Years: Lo que nunca pasó por sus labios* (Boston: South End Press, 1983).

6 Alurista, *Florícanto en Aztlán* (Los Angeles: Chicano Studies Center, 1971).

7 Luis Leal, "In Search of Aztlán," trans. Gladys Leal, in *Aztlán: Essays on the Chicano Homeland,* ed. Rudolfo Anaya and Francisco Lomelí (Albuquerque: University of New Mexico Press, 1989), 8.

8 Rafael Pérez-Torres, "Refiguring Aztlán," *Aztlán* 22, no. 2 (1997): 28, 37.

9 Miguel Méndez, *Pilgrims in Aztlán,* trans. David William Foster. (Tempe, Ariz.: Bilingual Press/Editorial Bilingue, 1992). Rudolfo Anaya, *Heart of Aztlán* (Albuquerque: University of New Mexico Press, 1976).

10 Rosa Linda Fregoso and Angie Chabram, "Chicana/o Cultural Representations: Reframing Alternative Critical Discourses," *Cultural Studies* 4 (1990): 204.

11 Anaya, *Heart of Aztlán,* 7.

12 "El Plan Espiritual de Aztlán," reprinted in *Aztlán: Essays on the Chicano Homeland,* ed. Rudolfo Anaya and Francisco Lomelí (Albuquerque: University of New Mexico Press, 1989), 1–5. Anaya, *Heart of Aztlán,* 18.

13 Rudolfo Anaya, "Aztlán: A Homeland without Boundaries," in *Aztlán: Essays on the Chicano Homeland,* ed. Rudolfo Anaya and Francisco Lomelí (Albuquerque: University of New Mexico Press, 1989), 230, 236.

14 Anaya, *Heart of Aztlán,* 130–31.

15 "El Plan," 1.

16 See, for example, Pérez-Torres, "Refiguring Aztlán"; Emma Pérez, *The Decolonial Imaginary,* 73–79; and Daniel Cooper Alarcón, *The Aztec Palimpsest: Mexico in the Modern Imagination* (Tucson: University of Arizona Press, 1997).

17 Genaro Padilla, "Myth and Comparative Cultural Nationalism: The Ideological Uses of Aztlán," in *Aztlán: Essays on the Chicano Homeland,* ed. Rudolfo Anaya and Francisco Lomelí (Albuquerque: University of New Mexico Press, 1989), 127–28.

18 Pérez, *The Decolonial Imaginary,* 78.

19 Edward Said, "Yeats and Decolonization," in *Remaking History,* ed. Barbara Kruger and Phil Mariani (Seattle: Bay Press, 1989), 10–11.

20 Ana María Alonso, *Thread of Blood: Colonialism, Revolution, and Gender on Mexico's Northern Frontier* (Tucson: University of Arizona Press, 1995), 59.

21 Ibid., 58–61.

22 "El Plan," 1.

23 Fregoso and Chabram, "Chicana/o Cultural Representations," 204.

24 Richard Thompson Ford, "The Boundaries of Race: Political Geography in Legal Analysis," *Harvard Law Review* 107 (June 1994): 1847.

25 Cherríe Moraga, *The Last Generation* (Boston: South End Press, 1993), 150.

26 Raymond Williams, *Marxism and Literature* (Oxford: Oxford University Press, 1977), 128. Alicia Arrizón offers a different analysis by drawing on Benedict Anderson's concept of "imagined communities" (*Latina Performance: Traversing the Stage* [Bloomington: Indiana University Press, 1999], 9–10).

27 Aihwa Ong, "The Gender and Labor Politics of Postmodernity," in *The Politics of Culture in the Shadow of Capital,* ed. Lisa Lowe and David Lloyd (Durham, N.C.: Duke University Press, 1997), 87.

28 Norma Alarcón, "Anzaldúa's *Frontera:* Inscribing Gynetics," in *Displacement, Diaspora, and Geographies of Identity,* ed. Smadar Lavie and Ted Swedenburg (Durham, N.C.: Duke University Press, 1996), 46.

29 See Steven Feld and Keith Basso, eds., *Senses of Place* (Seattle: University of Washington Press, 1996).

30 Cherríe Moraga, *Giving Up the Ghost: Teatro in Two Acts* (Los Angeles: West End Press, 1986), 3.

31 Barbara Christian, "The Race for Theory," in *The Nature and Context of Minority Discourse,* ed. Abdul JanMohamed and David Lloyd (New York: Oxford University Press, 1990), 37–49. See also Sonia Saldívar-Hull's analysis of Chicana feminist theorizing in her *Feminism on the Border: Chicana Gender Politics and Literature* (Berkeley: University of California Press, 2000).

32 For an extended discussion of this exhibit see Alicia Gaspar de Alba, *Chicano Art Inside/Outside the Master's House* (Austin: University of Texas Press, 1998).

33 Yvonne Yarbro-Bejarano, *The Wounded Heart: Writing on Cherríe Moraga* (Austin: University of Texas Press, 2001), 111.

34 Moraga more fully explores her relationship with her father, more thoroughly represents him, in *The Last Generation.* In some sense, what she suggests is that the problem with "whiteness" is that it has no memory.

35 Norma Alarcón, "Making 'Familia' from Scratch: Split Subjectivities in the Work of Helena Maria Viramontes and Cherríe Moraga," in *Chicana Creativity and Criticism: Charting New Frontiers in American Literature,* ed. María Herrera-Sobek and Helena Viramontes (Houston: Arte Público Press, 1988), 156.

36 Ibid., 157.

37 Ibid.

38 Paul Taylor and Clark Kerr, "Documentary History of the Strike of the Cotton Pickers in California, 1933," in Senate Subcommittee of the Committee on Education and Labor (the La Follette Committee), *Violations of Free Speech and the Rights of Labor: Hearings on S. Res. 266,* 75 parts (Washington, D.C.: Government Printing Office, 1936–1940), part 54, exhibit 8764, 19975.

39 Rabasa, *Writing Violence,* 146.

40 Ibid., 139.

41 Ibid., 140.

42 Ibid., 144.

43 Ibid.

44 Ibid.

45 Don Mitchell, *The Lie of the Land: Migrant Workers and the California Landscape* (Minneapolis: University of Minnesota Press, 1996), 26.

46 Ibid., 34.

47 Ibid., 82.

48 Chela Sandoval, "U.S. Third World Feminism: The Theory and Method of Oppositional Consciousness in the Postmodern World," *Genders* 10 (spring 1991): 12.

49 Cherríe Moraga, *Waiting in the Wings: Portrait of a Queer Motherhood* (Ithaca, N.Y.: Firebrand Books, 1997), 120.

6 *"War Again, or Somesuch"*

1 Alfred Chandler, *Scale and Scope: The Dynamics of Industrial Capitalism* (Cambridge, Mass.: Harvard University Press, 1990).

2 Alberto Alvaro Ríos, "The Child," in *The Iguana Killer: Twelve Stories of the Heart* (Lewiston, Idaho: Confluence Press, 1984). Mary Helen Ponce, "The Marijuana Party" in *Mirrors Beneath the Earth: Short Fiction by Chicano Writers,* ed. Ray González (Willimantic, Conn.: Curbstone Press, 1992), 140–56.

3 While the "war on drugs" officially dates to Ronald Reagan's declaration of war in 1982, I would argue that the rhetoric of crisis and enemy siege so typical of wars can be traced to the earliest public policy pronouncements against narcotics. For Ronald Reagan's official declaration see *Public Papers of the Presidents of the United States: Ronald Reagan, January 1 to July 31, 1982,* vol. 1 (Washington, D.C.: Government Printing Office, 1983), 813. See also Dan Baum, *Smoke and Mirrors: The War on Drugs and the Politics of Failure* (New York: Little, Brown, 1996), 162–76.

4 For helpful discussions of scale see Neil Smith, "Contours of a Spatialized Politics: Homeless Vehicles and the Production of Geographical Scale," *Social Text* 33 (1992): 54–81; Neil Brenner, "Between Fixity and Motion: Accumulation, Territorial Organization, and the Historical Geography of Spatial Scales," *Environment and Planning D: Society and Space* 16, no. 4 (1998): 459–81; Neil Brenner, "Global, Fragmented, Hierarchical: Henri Lefebvre's Geographies of Globalization," *Public Culture* 10, no. 1 (1997): 135–67; Neil Brenner, "State Territorial Restructuring and the Production of Spatial Scale: Urban and Regional Planning in the Federal Republic of Ger-

many, 1960–90," *Political Geography* 16, no. 4 (1997): 273–306; Don Mitchell, "The Scales of Justice: Localist Ideology, Large-Scale Production, and Agricultural Labor's Geography of Resistance in 1930s California," in *Organizing the Landscape: Geographical Perspectives on Labor Unionism,* ed. Andrew Herod (Minneapolis: University of Minnesota Press, 1998), 159–94.

5 Smith, "Contours," 66.

6 Mitchell, "Scales of Justice," 169.

7 David Harvey, *The Condition of Postmodernity* (London: Blackwell, 1990), 232.

8 Brenner, "Between Fixity and Motion," 462.

9 Ibid.

10 Richard Thompson Ford, "The Boundaries of Race: Political Geography in Legal Analysis," *Harvard Law Review* 107 (June 1994): 1849–53.

11 Smith develops the term "jumping scale" in "Contours of a Spatialized Politics." For a helpful discussion of a labor struggle becoming successful through jumping scale, see Jane Wills, "Space, Place, and Tradition in Working-Class Organization," in *Organizing the Landscape: Geographical Perspectives on Labor Unionism,* ed. Andrew Herod, (Minneapolis: University of Minnesota Press, 1998), 129–58.

12 For detailed discussion of the United Farm Workers' struggle see Richard Griswold del Castillo and Richard García, *César Chávez: A Triumph of Spirit* (Norman: University of Oklahoma Press, 1995).

13 I am suggesting two points here. First I am arguing that we understand the war on drugs in its totality–as an economy that includes both its formal manifestations (interdiction, education, treatment, imprisonment and so forth) and informal manifestations (the business of growing, harvesting, processing, distributing and selling illegal narcotics and drugs). Second, I am suggesting that this economy be understood in relationship to broader economic changes from the end of a post-WWII economy to the transitional economy of the seventies to the development of an economy based on flexible accumulation and economies of scale.

14 José David Saldívar, *Border Matters: Remapping American Cultural Studies* (Berkeley: University of California Press, 1997), 69.

15 Susan Bordo, *Unbearable Weight: Feminism, Western Culture, and the Body* (Berkeley: University of California Press, 1993), 16.

16 Another example of such body uses: morticians crossing borders for illegal purposes, using the pretense of transporting bodies to be embalmed. In my hometown, for example, the state police filed a case against a local mortuary owner who had been driving bodies back and forth across the border to camouflage drugs.

17 Smith, for example, uses the body as the starting point for theorizing scale.

18 In an informal conversation, Ríos explained that he based the story on an actual incident (Spring 1996). Having grown up on the border, I believed in the "realness" of "The Child" when I first read it. I found, however, that most readers—particularly middle-class Anglo audiences with little experience of the drug economy beyond their own purchase of narcotics—refused to believe that the story could have been based on an actual incident; instead, they dismissed it as an urban legend.

19 For a critique of this narrative see Luis Astorga, *Mitología del "narcotraficante" en México* (México, D.F.: Universidad Nacional Autónoma de México, 1995).

20 For a helpful discussion of the relationship between appropriate bodies and appropriate spaces see Tim Cresswell, *In Place/Out of Place: Geography, Ideology, and Transgression* (Minneapolis: University of Minnesota Press, 1996).

21 Elaine Scarry, *The Body in Pain: The Making and Unmaking of the World* (New York: Oxford University Press, 1985).

22 See for example Timothy Dunn, *The Militarization of the U.S.-Mexico Border* (Austin, Tex.: Center for Mexican American Studies, 1996).

23 For a very helpful discussion of the relationship between U.S. perceptions of the Mexican Revolution and the development of anti-marijuana/anti-Mexican rhetoric see Curtis Marez, *Drug Wars* (Minneapolis: University of Minnesota Press, forthcoming).

24 Rosa del Olmo, "The Geopolitics of Narcotrafficking in Latin America," *Social Justice* 20, nos. 3–4 (fall/winter 1993): 1–23.

25 For discussions of police corruption see William Chambliss, "Another Lost War: The Costs and Consequences of Drug Prohibition," *Social Justice* 22, no. 2 (1995): 101–24; David Carter, "Drug-Related Corruption of Police Officers: A Contemporary Typology," *Journal of Criminal Justice* 18, no. 2 (1990): 85–98; Sebastian Rotella, *Twilight on the Line: Underworlds and Politics at the U.S.-Mexico Border* (New York: Norton, 1998). A sampling of newspaper articles also suggest the ongoing U.S. struggle with narcotics-related police corruption: Henri Brickley, "Drug Cash Often Too Enticing to Border Police," *Arizona Republic,* 10 September 2000, sec. B, p. 10; James McCarty, "Previous Corruption Sweeps Can't Compare with this One," *Cleveland Plain Dealer,* 22 January 1998, sec. A, p. 12; Robert Jackson, "Border Agents Called Vulnerable to Corruption," *Los Angeles Times,* 15 May 1997, p. 19; Dan Gardner, "Asking Police to Fight a War that Can't Be Won: Trying to Enforce Drug Laws Can Sometimes Bring Out the Worst in Even the Best Officers," *Ottawa Citizen,* 14 September 2000.

26 For a discussion of economic changes see Luis Astorga, *El siglo de las drogas* (México, D.F.: Grupo Editorial Planeta de México, 1996). See also Molly Moore, "The Drug Fiefdom of Northern Mexico," *Washington Post,* 28 April 1996, sec. A, p. 1.

27   For a discussion of narco-corridos see Juan Carlos Ramírez-Pimienta, "Corrido de Narcotráfico en los Años Ochenta y Noventa: Un Juicio Moral Suspendido," *Bilingual Review* 23, no. 2 (May 1998): 145–56; María Herrera-Sobek, "The Theme of Smuggling in the Mexican Corrido," *Revista Chicano-Riqueño* 7, no. 4 (1979): 49–61; see also Luis Astorga, "Corridos: Etica, Estetica y Mitologia," in *Mitologia del "Narcotraficante" en Mexico* (México, D.F.: Universidad Nacional Autónoma de México, 1995).

28   Brenner, "State Territorial Restructuring," 299.

29   Popular culture as well as government documents have typically told the story of a young virgin girl's being seduced into addiction at the hands of a man of color. For a brief discussion see Michael Starks, *Cocaine Fiends and Reefer Madness: An Illustrated History of Drugs in the Movies* (New York: Cornwall Books, 1982).

30   Ruth Wilson Gilmore, "Terror Austerity Race Gender Excess Theater," in *Reading Rodney King/Reading Urban Uprising,* ed. Robert Gooding-Williams (New York: Routledge, 1993), 23–37.

31   Helena Viramontes's story "Neighbors" also explores the complexity of the relationships between the police and Latino neighborhoods (*The Moths and Other Stories* [Houston: Arte Público, 1985], 101–18). For a spatial reading of "Neighbors" see Raúl Villa, *Barrio-Logos: Space and Place in Urban Chicano Literature and Culture* (Austin: University of Texas Press, 2000), 115–34.

32   Jimmie Reeves and Richard Campbell, *Cracked Coverage: Television News, The Anti-Cocaine Crusade, and the Reagan Legacy* (Durham, N.C.: Duke University Press, 1994).

33   For discussions of the rhetoric of the narcotics economy see Craig Reinarman and Harry Levine, "The Crack Attack: Politics and Media in the Crack Scare," in *Crack in America: Demon Drugs and Social Justice,* ed. Craig Reinarman and Harry Levine (Berkeley: University of California Press, 1997), 18–52; William Elwood, *Rhetoric in the War on Drugs* (Westport, Conn.: Praeger, 1994); Richard Lawrence Miller, *Drug Warriors and Their Prey: From Police Power to Police State* (Westport, Conn.: Praeger, 1996); William Weir, *In the Shadow of the Dope Fiend* (North Haven, Conn.: Shoe String Press, 1995).

34   See "Campaign Battles Marihuana Weed," *New York Times,* 3 January 1937, p. 6; "State Clubwomen Meet," *New York Times,* 5 February 1937, p. 18; "War on Marihuana Urged on Parents," *New York Times,* 4 May 1937, p. 26.

35   Rosa Linda Fregoso, "Re-Imagining Chicana Urban Identities in the Public Sphere, Cool Chuca Style," in *Between Woman and Nation: Nationalisms, Transnational Feminisms, and the State,* ed. Caren Kaplan, Norma Alarcón, and Minoo Moallem (Durham, N.C.: Duke University Press, 1999), 78.

36   Richard Nixon, "Drug Abuse Prevention and Control: President's Message

to the Congress, 17 June 1971," *Public Papers of the President of the United States* (27 June 1971): 740.

37 See for example, "Poisoned Cigarettes," *New York Times,* 13 May 1914, p. 10; "Marihuana is Newest Drug," *New York Times,* 11 January 1923, p. 24.

38 "Mexico Bans Marihuana," *New York Times,* 29 December 1925, p. 7.

39 "Mexican Family Goes Insane," *New York Times,* 6 July 1927, p. 6.

40 "Use of Marijuana Spreading in West," *New York Times,* 16 September 1934, sec. 4, p. 6; C. M. Goethe, "Letter to Editor," *New York Times,* 15 September 1935, sec. 9, p. 4. See also Wayne Gard, "Youth Gone Loco," *Christian Century* (29 June 1936): 812–13; Harry Anslinger, "Marijuana: Assassin of Youth," *American Magazine* (July 1937): 18–19.

41 See Catherine Ramírez, "The Pachuca in Chicana/o Art, Literature, and History: Reexamining Nation, Cultural Nationalism, and Resistance," Ph.D. diss., University of California, 2000.

42 "Heroin Addicts Mount: U.S., Canada, and Britain Report 'Graduation' from Marijuana," *New York Times,* 3 December 1950, p. 4.

43 While exemplary work has been done on the racialization of narcotics policy, little of that work focuses on gender. For discussions of the history of narcotics policy in the United States see David Musto, *The American Disease,* 3d ed. (London: Oxford University Press, 1999); Clarence Lusane, *Pipe Dream Blues: Racism and the War on Drugs* (Boston: South End Press, 1991).

44 For discussions of the zoning ordinances aimed at curtailing Chinese immigrants' economic development see E. C. Sandmeyer, *The Anti-Chinese Movement in California* (Urbana: University of Illinois Press, 1939); Susan Craddock, *City of Plagues: Disease, Poverty, and Deviance in San Francisco* (Minneapolis: University of Minnesota Press, 2000); Raphael Fischler, "The Metropolitan Dimension of Early Zoning: Revisiting the 1916 New York City Ordinance," *Journal of the American Planning Association* 64, no. 2 (1998): 170–88.

45 Quoted in Raphael Fischler, "Health, Safety, and the General Welfare: Markets, Politics, and Social Science in Early Land-use Regulation and Community Design," *Journal of Urban History* 24, no. 6 (1998): 675–719. See also W. L. Pollard, "Outline of the Law of Zoning in the United States," *Annals of the American Academy of Political and Social Science* 155, part 2 (May 1931).

46 Fischler, "Health, Safety, and General Welfare," 709–10.

47 Edward Soja, *Postmetropolis: Critical Studies of Cities and Regions* (Oxford: Blackwell, 2000), 200.

48 Richard Thompson Ford, "The Boundaries of Race: Political Geography in Legal Analysis," *Harvard Law Review* 107 (June 1994): 1843–1921.

49 Ibid., 1871.

50 Fischler, "Health, Safety, and General Welfare," 679.

51 For example, the *Los Angeles Times* reported in 1997 that the City of Anaheim had designated all of its parks "drug-free zones." Such designation stiffened "penalties for anyone arrested and convicted of selling drugs at parks" (Orange County Edition, 19 March 1997, sec. B, p. 3). For an analysis of aspects of such laws' constitutionality see Seth Safra, "Note: The Amended Gun-Free School Zones Act: Doubt as to Its Constitutionality Remains," *Duke Law Journal* 50 (November 2000): 637; Shara Beth Mervis, "Note: Constitutional Law: Maryland's Drug-free School Zone Statute . . . Satisfies Due Process Requirements," *University of Baltimore Law Review* (spring 1995): 385–407.

52 Rosa del Olmo, "The Hidden Face of Drugs," *Social Justice* 18, no. 4 (1991): 34.

53 Soja, *Postmetropolis,* 200.

54 Deborah McDowell, *"The Changing Same": Black Women's Literature, Criticism, and Theory* (Bloomington: Indiana University Press, 1995).

Conclusion

1 See, for example, Dan Chapman, "The Changing Face of Metro Atlanta: A Decade of Change," *Atlanta Constitution,* 23 March 2001, sec. H, p. 1; Mark Sherman, "Watch for Hispanics to Expand Influence in Elected Positions," *Atlanta Constitution,* 18 March 2001, sec. B, p. 8; Cynthia Tucker, "Latino Growth a Wake-up Call for Black Folks," *Atlanta Constitution,* 18 March 2001, sec. B, p. 10; Robert Smith, "Cleveland's Latinos Find Success, Challenges," *Cleveland Plain Dealer,* 27 April 2001, sec. A, p. 1; Patrick McDonnel, "Mexicans Change Face of U.S. Demographics: Census: Study Shows Latinos on Rise, Settling in Many Parts of the Country," *Los Angeles Times,* 10 May 2001, sec. A, p. 1; Georgia Pabst, "Latino Population Moving South, West; Growing Community Stretches Way beyond City's Near South Side," *Milwaukee Journal Sentinel,* 15 April 2001, sec. B, p. 1; Mark Skertic, "Diversity is Gaining in 'White' Suburbs," *Chicago Sun-Times,* 8 April 2001, p. 10; Mike Swift and Jack Dolan, "Separated in the Suburbs: 2000 Census: Diversity and Segregation," *Hartford Courant,* 25 March 2001, sec. A, p. 1; Fran Spielman, "Hispanics Seek More Wards," *Chicago Sun-Times,* 16 March 2001, p. 8; Karen Branch-Brioso, "Hispanics See Their Numbers Swell in the St. Louis Area," *St Louis Post-Dispatch,* 7 March 2001, sec. A, p. 1; Cindy Rodriguez, "Latinos Surge in Census Count, Officials Surprised by 2000 Figures," *Boston Globe,* 8 March 2001, sec. A, p. 1; Tany Schevitz et al., "New Demographics Changing Everything," *San Francisco Chronicle,* 31 August 2000, sec. A, p. 1; Janny Scott, "Borough's Rise Driven Largely by Immigration,"

New York Times, 16 March 2001, sec. A, p. 1; Susan Sachs, "Hispanic New York Shifted in 1990's," *New York Times,* 22 May 2001, sec. B, p. 8; Margaret Ramirez, "Census Digs into City's Diversity," *New York Newsday,* 22 May 2001, sec. A, p. 7.

2   California anti-immigration activists who specialize in anti-Mexican immigration in particular have begun sending emissaries, indeed missionaries, to the East Coast to help stir up anti-immigrant fever in white working- and middle-class enclaves. See Al Baker and Susan Sachs, "Supporters of Immigrant Laborers Hold Pre-emptive Rally on L.I.," *New York Times,* 4 August 2001, sec. B, p. 1.

3   Raúl Villa uses "Mexopolis" to signify on Edward Soja's influential notion of exopolis (a sort of centerless city). Here Villa similarly argues for the need of spatial theorists to attend to Chicano insights. See his *Barrio-Logos: Space and Place in Urban Chicano Literature and Culture* (Austin: University of Texas Press, 2000), 131. See Edward Soja, *Thirdspace* (Oxford: Blackwell, 1997) and *Postmetropolis: Critical Studies of Cities and Regions* (Oxford: Blackwell, 2000).

4   Mike Davis, *Magical Urbanism: Latinos Reinvent the U.S. City* (London: Verso, 2000).

5   Villaregosa's loss was significant in part because he would have been the first Chicano since the late nineteenth century to hold the mayoral position in Los Angeles, where Latinos predominate. See Ruben Martinez, "L.A. Mayoral Campaign about Class, Not Race," *Baltimore Sun,* 10 June 2001, sec. C, p. 4; Ellis Close, "A Brownout in Los Angeles," *Newsweek* (18 June 2001): 32; Salim Muwakkil, "Changing the Guard," *In These Times,* 23 July 2001, p. 3.

6   Reies Lopez Tijerina, *They Called Me "King Tiger": My Struggle for the Land and Our Rights,* trans. and ed. José Angel Gutierrez (Houston, Tex.: Arte Público Press, 2000); Patricia Blawis, *Tijerina and the Land Grants: Mexican Americans in Struggle for Their Heritage* (New York: International Publishers, 1971).

7   Such a choice for the area was more than ironic — it was vituperative, since Carson had been so rabidly racist in his attacks on Mexicans in the Southwest.

8   Gina Valdés, *Puentes y fronteras: Bridges and Borders,* trans. Katherine King and Gina Valdés (Tempe, Ariz.: Bilingual Press, 1996), 4.

Bibliography

Acuña, Rodolfo. *Occupied America.* 3d ed. New York: Harper and Row, 1989.

Aiken, Susan, Ann Brigham, Sallie Marston, and Penny Waterstone, eds. *Making Worlds: Gender, Metaphor, Materiality.* Tucson: University of Arizona Press, 1998.

Alarcón, Daniel Cooper. *The Aztec Palimpsest: Mexico in the Modern Imagination.* Tucson: University of Arizona Press, 1997.

Alarcón, Norma. "Making 'Familia' from Scratch: Split Subjectivities in the Work of Helena Maria Viramontes and Cherríe Moraga." In *Chicana Creativity and Criticism: Charting New Frontiers in American Literature,* edited by María Herrera-Sobek and Helena Viramontes, 147–59. Houston: Arte Público Press, 1988.

———. "Traddutora, Traditora: A Paradigmatic Figure of Chicana Feminism." *Cultural Critique* 13 (fall 1989): 57–87.

———. "Chicana Feminism: In the Tracks of 'The' Native Woman." *Cultural Studies* 4, no. 3 (1990): 248–56.

———. "The Work of Armando Rascón: T(r)opographies for a Critical Imaginary." In *Occupied Aztlán,* 11–15. San Francisco: Adaline Kent Award Exhibition, San Francisco Art Institute, 1994.

———. "Tropology of Hunger: The 'Miseducation' of Richard Rodriguez." In *The Ethnic Canon: Histories, Institutions, and Interventions,* edited by David Palumbo-Liu. Minneapolis: University of Minnesota Press, 1995.

———. "Anzaldúa's *Frontera:* Inscribing Gynetics." In *Displacement, Diaspora, and Geographies of Identity,* edited by Smadar Lavie and Ted Swedenburg, 41–54. Durham, N.C.: Duke University Press, 1996.

Alarcón, Norma et al., eds. *Chicana Critical Issues.* Berkeley, Calif.: Third Woman Press, 1993.

Althusser, Louis. *Lenin and Philosophy.* Translated by Ben Brewster. London: Monthly Review Press, 1971.

Alonso, Ana María. *Thread of Blood: Colonialism, Revolution, and Gender on Mexico's Northern Frontier.* Tucson: University of Arizona Press, 1995.

Alurista. *Floricanto en Aztlán.* Los Angeles: Chicano Studies Center, 1971.

Ames, Charles R. "Along the Mexican Border—Then and Now." *Journal of Arizona History* 18, no. 4 (1977): 431–46.

Anaya, Rudolfo. *Heart of Aztlán*. Albuquerque: University of New Mexico Press, 1976.

———. "Aztlán: A Homeland without Boundaries." In *Aztlán,* edited by Rudolfo Anaya and Francisco Lomelí, 230–41. Albuquerque: University of New Mexico Press, 1989.

Anaya, Rudolfo, and Francisco Lomelí, ed. *Aztlán: Essays on the Chicano Homeland*. Albuquerque: University of New Mexico Press, 1989.

Anslinger, Harry. "Marijuana: Assassin of Youth." *American Magazine* (July 1937): 18–19.

Anzaldúa, Gloria. *Borderlands/La frontera: The New Mestiza*. San Francisco: Aunt Lute Press, 1987.

———, ed. *Making Face Making Soul/Haciendo caras*. San Francisco: Aunt Lute Press, 1990.

Arrizón, Alicia. *Latina Performance: Traversing the Stage*. Bloomington: Indiana University Press, 1999.

Astorga, Luis. *Mitología del "narcotraficante" en México*. México, D.F.: Universidad Nacional Autónoma de México, 1995.

———. *El siglo de las drogas*. México, D.F.: Grupo Editorial Planeta de México, 1996.

Avila, Erica. "The Folklore of the Freeway: Space, Culture, and Identity in Postwar Los Angeles." *Aztlán* 23, no. 1 (1998): 14–31.

Balderrama, Francisco, and Raymond Rodríguez, *Decade of Betrayal: Mexican Repatriation in the 1930s*. Albuquerque: University of New Mexico Press, 1995.

Bancroft, Hubert Howe. *The History of Arizona and New Mexico, 1530–1888*. 1889. Reprint, Albuquerque: Horn and Wallace, 1962.

Barnes, Trevor J., and James S. Duncan, eds. *Writing Worlds: Discourse, Text, and Metaphor in the Representation of Landscape*. London: Routledge, 1992.

Barrera, Angela. "To Heal Humanity: Teresa Urrea's Lifelong Threat and Posthumous Legacy." Master's thesis, Indiana University, 1999.

Bartlett, John Russell. *Personal Narrative of Explorations and Incidents in Texas, New Mexico, California, Sonora, and Chihuahua, Connected with the United States and Mexican Boundary Commission During the Years 1850, '51, '52, and '53*. New York: D. Appleton, 1854.

Baum, Dan. *Smoke and Mirrors: The War on Drugs and the Politics of Failure*. New York: Little, Brown, 1996.

Bell, William. *New Tracks in North America: A Journal of Travel and Adventure Whilst Engaged in the Survey for a Southern Railroad to the Pacific Ocean, 1867–68*. Vol. 1. London: Chapman and Hall, 1869.

Blawis, Patricia. *Tijerina and the Land Grants: Mexican Americans in Struggle for Their Heritage*. New York: International Publishers, 1971.

Blunt, Alison, and Gillian Rose, ed. *Writing Women and Space: Colonial and Postcolonial Geographies.* New York: Guilford Press, 1994.

Borah, Woodrow. "Queen of Mexico and Empress of the Americas: La Guadalupana of Tepeyac." *Mexican Studies/Estudios Mexicanos* 12 (summer 1996): 327–39.

Bordo, Susan. *Unbearable Weight: Feminism, Western Culture, and the Body.* Berkeley: University of California Press, 1993.

Bourke, John Gregory. *On the Border with Crook.* New York: Charles Scribner's Sons, 1891.

Boyarin, Jonathan. "Space, Time, and the Politics of Memory." In *Remapping Memory: The Politics of TimeSpace,* edited by Jonathan Boyarin, 1–38. Minneapolis: University of Minnesota Press, 1994.

———, ed. *Remapping Memory: The Politics of TimeSpace.* Minneapolis: University of Minnesota Press, 1994.

Brady, Mary Pat. "The Fungibility of Borders." *Nepantla: Views from South* 1, no. 1 (spring 2000): 171–90.

———. " 'Full of Empty': Creating the Southwest as Terra Incognito." In *Nineteenth-Century Geographies,* edited by Helena Michie and Ronald Thomas. New Brunswick, N.J.: Rutgers University Press, forthcoming.

Brear, Holly. *Inherit the Alamo: Myth and Ritual at an American Shrine.* Austin: University of Texas Press, 1995.

Breckenridge, Gerald. *The Radio Boys on the Mexican Border.* New York: A. L. Burt, 1922.

Brenner, Neil. "Global, Fragmented, Hierarchical: Henri Lefebvre's Geographies of Globalization." *Public Culture* 10, no. 1 (1997): 135–67.

———. "State Territorial Restructuring and the Production of Spatial Scale: Urban and Regional Planning in the Federal Republic of Germany, 1960–90." *Political Geography* 16, no. 4 (1997): 273–306.

———. "Between Fixity and Motion: Accumulation, Territorial Organization, and the Historical Geography of Spatial Scales." *Environment and Planning D: Society and Space* 16, no. 4 (1998): 459–81.

———. "Globalization as Reterritorialization: The Re-Scaling of Urban Governance in the European Union." *Urban Studies* 36, no. 3 (1999): 431–51.

Brown, Bill. "Science Fiction, the World's Fair, and the Prosthetics of Empire, 1910–1915." In *Cultures of U.S. Imperialism,* edited by Amy Kaplan and Donald E. Pease, 129–63. Durham, N.C.: Duke University Press, 1993.

Browne, J. Ross. *Adventures in the Apache Country: A Tour Through Arizona and Sonora, with Notes on the Silver Regions of Nevada.* New York: Harper and Brothers, 1869.

Broyles-González, Yolanda. *El Teatro Campesino: Theater in the Chicano Movement.* Austin: University of Texas Press, 1994.

Bruce-Novoa, Juan. *RetroSpace: Collected Essays on Chicana Literature, Theory, and History.* Houston: Arte Público Press, 1990.

Butler, Judith. "Imitation and Gender Insubordination." In *Inside/Out: Lesbian Theories, Gay Theories,* edited by Diana Fuss, 13–31. New York: Routledge Press, 1991.

Camín, Hector Aguilar. *La frontera nómada: Sonora y la Revolución Mexicana.* México: Siglo Veintiuno Editores, 1977.

Cantú, Norma Elia. *Canícula: Snapshots of a Girlhood en la Frontera.* Albuquerque: University of New Mexico Press, 1995.

Carby, Hazel. "On the Threshold of Woman's Era": Lynching, Empire, and Sexuality in Black Feminist Theory." In *"Race," Writing, and Difference,* edited by Henry Louis Gates Jr., 301–16. Chicago: University of Chicago Press, 1986.

Carraway, G. Chezia. "Violence against Women of Color." *Stanford Law Review* 43 (July 1991): 1303–50.

Carter, David. "Drug-related Corruption of Police Officers: A Contemporary Typology." *Journal of Criminal Justice* 18, no. 2 (1990): 85–98.

Castillo, Ana, ed. *Goddess of the Americas/La diosa de las Américas: Writings on the Virgin of Guadalupe.* New York: Riverhead Books, 1996.

Chabram-Dernersesian, Angie. "I Throw Punches for My Race, but I Don't Want to Be a Man: Writing Us—Chica-nos (Girl, Us)/Chicanas—into the Movement Script." In *Cultural Studies,* edited by Lawrence Grossberg, Cary Nelson, and Paula Treichler, 81–95. New York: Routledge, 1992.

Chambers, Ross. "Messing Around: Gayness and Loiterature in Alan Hollinghurst's *The Swimming-Pool Library.*" In *Textuality and Sexuality: Reading Theories and Practices,* edited by Judith Still and Michael Worten, 205–20. Manchester, Eng.: Manchester University Press, 1993.

———. "Mediations and the Escalator Principle." *Modern Fiction Studies* 40 (1994): 765–806.

———. "Pointless Stories, Storyless Points: Roland Barthes between 'Soirées de Paris' and 'Incidents.'" *L'Esprit Créateur* 34 (summer 1994): 12–30.

Chambliss, William. "Another Lost War: The Costs and Consequences of Drug Prohibition." *Social Justice* 22, no. 2 (1995): 101–24.

Chandler, Alfred. *Scale and Scope: The Dynamics of Industrial Capitalism.* Cambridge, Mass.: Harvard University Press, 1990.

Cho, Milyoung. "Waking Up from a Domestic Nightmare." *Third Force* 2 (May/June 1994): 25–29.

Christian, Barbara. "The Race for Theory." In *The Nature and Context of Minority Discourse,* edited by Abdul JanMohamed and David Lloyd, 37–49. Berkeley: University of California Press, 1990.

Cisneros, Sandra. "Ghosts and Voices: Writing from Obsession." *The Americas Review* 15 (1987): 69–72.

———. *My Wicked, Wicked Ways.* Berkeley, Calif.: Third Woman Press, 1987.

———. *Woman Hollering Creek and Other Stories.* New York: Random House, 1991.

———. *Loose Woman.* New York: Alfred Knopf, 1994.

Cleland, Robert Glass. *A History of Phelps Dodge, 1834–1950.* New York: Alfred Knopf, 1952.

Clifford, James. *Routes: Travel and Translation in the Late Twentieth Century.* Boston: Harvard University Press, 1997.

Close, Ellis. "A Brownout in Los Angeles." *Newsweek* (18 June 2001): 32.

Coffey, Frederic A. "Some General Aspects of the Gadsden Treaty." *New Mexico Historical Review* 8, no. 3 (July 1933): 145–64.

Comer, Krista. *Landscapes of the New West: Gender and Geography in Contemporary Women's Writing.* Chapel Hill: University of North Carolina Press, 1999.

Comision Pesquisidora de la frontera del Norte. *Reports of the Committee of Investigation: Sent in 1873 by the Mexican Government to the Frontier of Texas.* New York: Baker and Goodwon, 1875.

Congressional Globe. 37th Cong., 2d sess., 8 May 1862: 2023–29.

———. 37th Cong., 3rd Sess., 19 February 1863: 1101–2.

———. 37th Cong., 3rd Sess., 20 February 1863: 1125–28.

———. 38th Cong., 2d sess., 3 February 1865.

Coronil, Fernando. "Transcultural and the Politics of Theory: Countering the Center, Cuban Counterpoint." Introduction to Fernando Ortiz, *Cuban Counterpoint: Tobacco and Sugar.* Translated by Harriet De Onís, ix–lvi. Durham, N.C.: Duke University Press, 1995.

Corpi, Lucha. *Cactus Blood.* Houston: Arte Público Press, 1995.

Cozzens, Samuel Woodworth. *The Marvellous Country; Or, Three Years in Arizona and New Mexico, the Apaches' Home Comprising Description of this Wonderful Country, Its Immense Mineral Wealth, Its Magnificent Mountain Scenery, the Ruins of Ancient Towns and Cities found therein, with a Complete History of the Apache Tribe, and a Description of the Author's Guide, Cochise, the Great Apache War Chief. The Whole Interspersed with Strange Events and Adventures.* 1874. Reprint, Minneapolis: Ross and Haines, 1967.

Craddock, Susan. *City of Plagues: Disease, Poverty, and Deviance in San Francisco.* Minneapolis: University of Minnesota Press, 2000.

Cremory, John C. *Life among the Apaches.* San Francisco: A. Roman and Company, 1868.

Crenshaw, Kimberle. "Mapping the Margins: Intersectionality, Identity Politics, and Violence against Women of Color." *Stanford Law Review* 43 (July 1991): 1241–99.

Cresswell, Tim. *In Place/Out of Place: Geography, Ideology, and Transgression.* Minneapolis: University of Minnesota Press, 1996.

Davalos, Karen Mary. *Exhibiting Mestizaje: Mexican (American) Museums in the Diaspora.* Albuquerque: University of New Mexico Press, 2001.

de Certeau, Michel. *The Practice of Everyday Life.* Translated by Steven Rendall. Berkeley: University of California Press, 1984.

Deering, Fremont B. *The Border Boys across the Frontier.* New York: A. L. Burt, 1911.

de Hughes, Atanacia Santa Cruz. "The Mexican Troops' Departure from Tucson as recalled by Doña Atanacia Santa Cruz de Hughes as told to Donald W. Page." 12 May 1929. Bancroft Collection. Bancroft Library, University of California, Berkeley, MSS P-D 101.

———. "As Told by the Pioneers." *Arizona Historical Review* 6, no.2 (April 1935): 66–74.

DeJean, Joan. "No Man's Land: The Novel's First Geography." *Yale French Studies* 73 (1987): 179.

de la Peña, Terri. *Margins.* Seattle: Seal Press, 1992.

De Leon, Arnoldo, and Kenneth Stewart, "A Tale of Three Cities: A Comparative Analysis of the Socio-Economic Conditions of Mexican-Americans in Los Angeles, Tucson, and San Antonio, 1850–1900." *Journal of the West* 24, no. 2 (1985): 64–74.

Dimendberg, Edward. "Henri Lefebvre on Abstract Space." In *The Production of Public Space,* edited by Andrew Light and Jonathan Smith, 17–48. Lanham, Md.: Rowman and Littlefield, 1998.

Dixon, Melvin. *Ride Out the Wilderness: Geography and Identity in Afro-American Literature.* Urbana: University of Illinois Press, 1987.

Dunn, Timothy. *The Militarization of the U.S.-Mexico Border.* Austin, Tex.: Center for Mexican American Studies, 1996.

Durand, Jorge, and Douglas Massey. *Miracles on the Border: Retablos of the Mexican Migrants to the United States.* Tucson: University of Arizona Press, 1995.

Dussel, Enrique. *The Invention of the Americas: Eclipse of "the Other" and the Myth of Modernity.* Translated by Michael Barber. New York: Continuum, 1995.

"El Plan Espiritual de Aztlán." In *Aztlán: Essays on the Chicano Homeland,* edited by Rudolfo Anaya and Francisco Lomelí, 1–5. Albuquerque: University of New Mexico Press, 1989.

Elwood, William. *Rhetoric in the War on Drugs: the Triumphs and Tragedies of Public Relations.* Westport, Conn.: Praeger, 1994.

Emory, William H. *Notes of a Military Reconnaissance, from Fort Leavenworth, in Missouri to San Diego, in California.* New York: H. Long and Brothers, 1848.

———. *Report on the United States and Mexican Boundary Survey Made under* the Direction of the Secretary of the Interior. 2 vols. Washington, D.C.: A. O. P. Nicholson, 1857–1859.

Fabian, Johannes. *Time and the Other: How Anthropology Makes Its Object.* New York: Columbia University Press, 1983.

Farish, Thomas. *History of Arizona.* Phoenix, Ariz.: Filmer Bros. Electrotype Co., 1915.

Feld, Steven, and Keith Basso, eds. *Senses of Place.* Seattle: University of Washington Press, 1996.

Ferguson, Russell, et al., eds. *Out There: Marginalization and Contemporary Cultures.* New York: New Museum of Contemporary Art, 1990.

Fischler, Raphael. "Health, Safety, and the General Welfare: Markets, Politics, and Social Science in Early Land-use Regulation and Community Design." *Journal of Urban History* 24, no. 6 (1998): 675–710.

———. "The Metropolitan Dimension of Early Zoning: Revisiting the 1916 New York City Ordinance." *Journal of the American Planning Association* 64, no. 2 (1998): 170–89.

Fisher, Philip. *Hard Facts: Setting and Form in the American Novel.* New York: Oxford University Press, 1985.

Fisk, Turbesé Lummis, ed. *General Crook and the Apache Wars.* Flagstaff: Northland Press, 1966.

Flores, Richard. "Private Visions, Public Culture: The Making of the Alamo." *Cultural Anthropology* 10 (February 1995): 99–115.

Flores, William, and Rina Benmayor, eds. *Latino Cultural Citizenship: Claiming Identity, Space, and Rights.* Boston: Beacon Press, 1997.

Foley, Neil. *The White Scourge: Mexicans, Blacks, and Poor Whites in Texas Cotton Culture.* Berkeley: University of California Press, 1997.

Fontes, Montserrat. *Dreams of the Centaur.* New York: Norton, 1996.

Ford, Richard Thompson. "The Boundaries of Race: Political Geography in Legal Analysis." *Harvard Law Review* 107 (June 1994): 1843–1921.

Foucault, Michel. "Of Other Spaces." Translated by Jay Miskowiec. *Diacritics* 16 (1986): 22–27.

———. *The History of Sexuality.* Vol. 1. Translated by Robert Hurley. New York: Pantheon, 1990.

Frank, Joseph. *The Idea of Spatial Form.* New Brunswick, N.J.: Rutgers University Press, 1991.

Fregoso, Rosa Linda. "Re-Imagining Chicana Urban Identities in the Public Sphere, *Cool Chuca* Style." In *Between Woman and Nation: Nationalisms, Transnational Feminisms, and the State,* edited by Caren Kaplan, Norma Alarcón, and Minoo Moallem, 72–91. Durham, N.C.: Duke University Press, 1999.

Fregoso, Rosa Linda, and Angie Chabram. "Chicana/o Cultural Representations: Reframing Alternative Critical Discourses." *Cultural Studies* 4 (1990): 203–12.

Gates, Henry Louis, Jr., ed. *"Race," Writing, and Difference.* Chicago: University of Chicago Press, 1986.

García, Mario. "La Frontera: The Border as Symbol and Reality in Mexican-American Thought." *Mexican Studies/Estudios Mexicanos* 1, no. 2 (summer 1985): 195–225.

Gard, Wayne. "Youth Gone Loco." *Christian Century* (29 June 1936): 812–13.

Gaspar de Alba, Alicia. *"Tortillerismo:* Work by Chicana Lesbians." *Signs* 18, no. 4 (1993): 956–63.

———. *Chicano Art Inside/Outside the Master's House.* Austin: University of Texas Press, 1998.

Gassier, Alfred. "Juarez o la guerra de México." *El Fronterizo,* 9 Jan. 1881.

Gilmore, Ruth Wilson. "Terror Austerity Race Gender Excess Theater." In *Reading Rodney King/Reading Urban Uprising,* edited by Robert Gooding-Williams, 23–37. New York: Routledge, 1993.

———. "From Military Keynesianism to Post-Keynesian Militarism: Finance Capital, Land, Labor, and Opposition in the Rising California Prison State." Ph.D. diss., Rutgers University, 1998.

———. "Globalization and U.S. Prison Growth: From Military Keynesianism to Post-Keynesian Militarism." *Race and Class* 40, no. 3 (1998/99): 171–88.

Goldsmith, Raquel Rubío. "Shipwrecked in the Desert: A Short History of the Mexican Sisters of the House of the Providence in Douglas, Arizona, 1927–1949." In *Women on the U.S.-Mexican Border,* edited by Vicki Ruíz and Susan Tiano, 177–96. Boston: Allen and Unwin, 1987.

———. "Civilization, Barbarism, and Norteña Gardens." In *Making Worlds: Gender, Metaphor, Materiality,* edited by Susan Aiken, Ann Brigham, Sallie Marston, Penny Waterstone, 274–287. Tucson: University of Arizona Press, 1998.

González, Ray, ed. *Mirrors Beneath the Earth: Short Fiction by Chicano Writers.* Willimantic, Conn.: Curbstone Press, 1992.

Gooding-Williams, Robert, ed. *Reading Rodney King/Reading Urban Uprising.* New York: Routledge, 1993.

Griswold del Castillo, Richard. "Tucsonenses and Angelenos: A Socio-Economic Study of Two Mexican-American Barrios, 1860–1880." *Journal of the West* 18, no. 1 (1979): 58–66.

Griswold del Castillo, Richard, and Richard García. *César Chávez: A Triumph of Spirit.* Norman: University of Oklahoma Press, 1995.

Grossberg, Lawrence, Cary Nelson, and Paula Treichler, eds. *Cultural Studies.* New York: Routledge, 1992.

Guitiérrez, David. *Walls and Mirrors: Mexican Americans, Mexican Immigrants, and the Politics of Ethnicity.* Berkeley: University of California Press, 1995.

Guitiérrez, Ramón. "Aztlán, Montezuma, and New Mexico: The Political Uses of American Indian Mythology." In *Aztlán: Essays on the Chicano Homeland,* edited by Rudolfo Anaya and Francisco Lomelí, 172–90. Albuquerque: University of New Mexico Press, 1989.

Gutiérrez-Jones, Carl. "Desiring B/orders." *diacritics* 25, no. 1 (1995): 99–112.

———. *Rethinking the Borderlands: Between Chicano Culture and Legal Discourse.* Berkeley: University of California Press, 1995.

Hall, Stuart. "Subjects in History: Making Diasporic Identities." In *The House that Race Built,* edited by Wahneema Lubiano, 289–99. New York: Vintage, 1998.

Harley, Brian. "Deconstructing the Map." In *Writing Worlds: Discourse, Text, and Metaphor in the Representation of Landscape,* edited by Trevor J. Barnes and James S. Duncan, 231–47. London: Routledge, 1992.

Harper, Phillip Brian. *Framing the Margins.* New York: Oxford University Press, 1994.

Harris, Cheryl I. "Whiteness as Property." *Harvard Law Review* 106 (1993): 1709–91.

Harvey, David. *The Condition of Postmodernity.* Cambridge, Mass.: Blackwell, 1990.

———. *Justice, Nature, and the Geography of Difference.* Cambridge, Mass.: Blackwell, 1996.

Haven, Solomon G. "Remarks of Mr. S. G. Haven of New York on the bill to enable the President to fulfill the third article of the treaty between the United States and the Mexican Republic known as the ten million Mexican treaty bill. Delivered in the House of Representatives. June 27, 1854." Washington, D.C.: John T. and Lem. Towers, 1854.

Hayden, Dolores. *The Power of Place: Urban Landscapes as Public History.* Cambridge, Mass.: MIT Press, 1995.

Henderson, George. *California and the Fictions of Capital.* New York: Oxford University Press, 1999.

Hernández Sáenz, Luz María. "Smuggling for the Revolution: Illegal Traffic of Arms on the Arizona-Sonora Border, 1912–1914." *Arizona and the West* 28 (winter 1986): 357–77.

Herod, Andrew, ed. *Organizing the Landscape: Geographical Perspectives on Labor Unionism.* Minneapolis: University of Minnesota Press, 1998.

Herrera, Hayden. *Frida Kahlo: The Paintings.* New York: Harper Collins, 1991.

Herrera-Sobek, María. "The Theme of Smuggling in the Mexican Corrido." *Revista Chicano-Riqueño* 7, no. 4 (1979): 49–61.

———. *The Mexican Corrido: A Feminist Analysis.* Bloomington: Indiana University Press, 1990.

———. "Toward the Promised Land: La Frontera as Myth and Reality in Ballad and Song." *Aztlan* 21, nos. 1 and 2 (1992–1996): 227–56.

Herrera-Sobek, María, and Helena Viramontes, eds. *Chicana (W)rites: On Word and Film.* Berkeley, Calif.: Third Woman Press, 1995.

———. *Chicana Creativity and Criticism: Charting New Frontiers in American Literature.* Houston: Arte Público Press, 1988.

Hinojosa, Tish. *Frontejas.* Cambridge, Mass.: Rounder Records, 1995. CD 3132.

Hodge, Hiram. *Arizona as It Is: Or, the Coming Country.* New York: Hurd and Houghton, 1877.

Hu-DeHart, Evelyn. *Yaqui Resistance and Survival: The Struggle for Land and Autonomy, 1821–1910.* Madison: University of Wisconsin Press, 1984.

Huginnie, A. Yvette. "Strikitos: Race, Class, and Work in the Arizona Copper Industry, 1870–1920." Ph.D. diss., Yale University, 1991.

———. "A New Hero Comes to Town: The Anglo Mining Engineer and 'Mexican Labor' as Contested Terrain in Southeastern Arizona, 1880–1920." *New Mexico Historical Review* 69 (October 1994): 323–44.

Inda, Jonathan Xavier. "Migrants, Borders, Nations." Ph.D. diss., University of California, 1996.

Ingram, Gordon Brent, Anne-Marie Bouthillette, and Yolanda Retter, eds. *Queers in Space: Communities/Public Places/Sites of Resistance.* Seattle: Bay Press, 1997.

Islas, Arturo. *Migrant Souls.* New York: Avon Books, 1990.

———. "On the Bridge, At the Border: Migrants and Immigrants." Ernesto Galarza Commemorative Lecture. Stanford, Calif.: Stanford Center for Chicano Research, 1990.

JanMohamed, Abdul, and David Lloyd, eds. *The Nature and Context of Minority Discourse.* New York: Oxford University Press, 1990.

Jeffrey, Robert, "The History of Douglas Arizona." Master's thesis, University of Arizona, 1951.

Johnson, Barbara. *The Feminist Difference: Literature, Psychoanalysis, Race, and Gender.* Cambridge, Mass.: Harvard University Press, 1998.

Kaiser, Frederick. "The U.S. Customs Service: History, Reorganization, and Congressional Jurisdiction." Congressional Research Service Report No. 78-128 (Gov), 6 June 1978.

Kaplan, Amy. "Romancing the Empire: The Embodiment of American Masculinity in the Popular Historical Novel of the 1890s." *American Literary History* 2, no. 4 (1990): 659–90.

Kaplan, Amy, and Donald E. Pease, eds. *Cultures of U.S. Imperialism.* Durham, N.C.: Duke University Press, 1993.

Kaplan, Caren. *Questions of Travel: Postmodern Discourses of Displacement.* Durham, N.C.: Duke University Press, 1996.

Kaplan, Caren, Norma Alarcón, and Minoo Moallem, eds. *Between Woman and Nation: Nationalisms, Transnational Feminisms, and the State.* Durham, N.C.: Duke University Press, 1999.

Katz, Cindi. "Growing Girls/Closing Circles." In *Full Circles: Geographies of Women over the Life Course,* edited by Cindi Katz and Janice Monk, 88–106. New York: Routledge, 1993.

Katz, Cindi, and Janice Monk, eds. *Full Circles: Geographies of Women over the Life Course.* New York: Routledge, 1993.

Keith, Eugene Chamberlin. "Mexican Colonization versus American Interests in Lower California." *Pacific Historical Review* 20, no. 1 (1951): 43–55.

Keith, Michael, and Steven Pile, eds. *Place and the Politics of Identity.* London: Routledge, 1993.

Klahn, Norma. "Writing the Border: The Languages and Limits of Representation." *Journal of Latin American Cultural Studies* 3, no. 1–2 (1994): 19–34.

Knopp, Lawrence. "Sexuality and the Spatial Dynamics of Capitalism." *Environment and Planning D: Society and Space* 10, no. 6 (1992): 651–69.

Kristeva, Julia. *Powers of Horror: An Essay on Abjection.* Translated by Leon Roudiez. New York: Columbia University Press, 1982.

Kruger, Barbara, and Phil Mariani, eds. *Remaking History.* Seattle: Bay Press, 1989.

Lafaye, Jacques. *Quetzalcóatl and Guadalupe: The Formation of Mexican National Consciousness, 1531–1813.* Translated by Benjamin Keen. Chicago: University of Chicago Press, 1975.

Lavie, Smadar, and Ted Swedenburg, eds. *Displacement, Diaspora, and Geographies of Identity.* Durham, N.C.: Duke University Press, 1996.

Laviera, Tato. *AmeRícan.* Houston: Arte Público, 1985.

Leal, Luis. "In Search of Aztlán." Translated by Gladys Leal. In *Aztlán: Essays on the Chicano Homeland,* edited by Rudolfo Anaya and Francisco Lomelí, 6–13. Albuquerque: University of New Mexico Press, 1989.

Lefebvre, Henri. *The Production of Space.* Translated by Donald Nicholson-Smith. Oxford: Blackwell, 1991.

Light, Andrew, and Jonathan Smith, eds. *The Production of Public Space.* Lanham, Md.: Rowman and Littlefield, 1998.

Lionnet, François. "Geographies of Pain: Captive Bodies and Violent Acts in the Fictions of Myriam Warner-Vieyra, Gayle Jones, and Bessie Head." *Callaloo* 16, no. 1 (1993): 132–52.

López, Miguel. *Chicano Timespace: The Poetry and Politics of Ricardo Sánchez.* College Station: Texas A&M Press, 2001.

Lowe, Lisa. *Immigrant Acts: On Asian American Cultural Politics.* Durham, N.C.: Duke University Press, 1996.

Lowe, Lisa, and David Lloyd, eds. *The Politics of Culture in the Shadow of Capital.* Durham, N.C.: Duke University Press, 1997.

Lubiano, Wahneema, ed. *The House that Race Built: Black Americans, U.S. Terrain.* New York: Pantheon, 1997.

Lucero, Carmen. "As Told by the Pioneers." *Arizona Historical Review* 6, no. 2 (1935): 66–74.

Lusane, Clarence. *Pipe Dream Blues: Racism and the War on Drugs.* Boston: South End Press, 1991.

Madriz, Esther. *Nothing Bad Happens to Good Girls: Fear of Crime in Women's Lives.* Berkeley: University of California Press, 1997.

Marez, Curtis. *Drug Wars.* Minneapolis: University of Minnesota Press, forthcoming.

Marston, Sallie. "Who Are 'The People'?: Gender, Citizenship, and the Making of the American Nation." *Environment and Planning D: Society and Space* 8, no. 4 (1991): 449–58.

Martin, Patricia Preciado. *Songs My Mother Sang to Me.* Tucson: University of Arizona Press, 1992.

——. "The Journey." In *Infinite Divisions: An Anthology of Chicana Literature,* edited by Tey Diana Rebolledo and Eliana S. Rivero, 167–71. Tucson: University of Arizona Press, 1993.

Mártinez, Oscar J. *Troublesome Border.* Tucson: University of Arizona Press, 1988.

Masiello, Francine. "Melodrama, Sex, and Nation in Latin America's *Fin de Siglo.*" *Modern Language Quarterly* 57, no. 2 (June 1996): 269–284.

Massey, Doreen. *Space, Place, and Gender.* Minneapolis: University of Minnesota Press, 1994.

Mattison, Ray. "The Tangled Web: The Controversy over the Tumacacori and Baca Land Grants." *Journal of Arizona History* 8 (1967): 70–91.

Mauer, Marc. *Race to Incarcerate.* New York: New Press, 1999.

McDowell, Deborah. *"The Changing Same": Black Women's Literature, Criticism, and Theory.* Bloomington: Indiana University Press, 1995.

McDowell, Linda. *Gender, Identity, and Place: Understanding Feminist Geographies.* Minneapolis: University of Minnesota Press, 1999.

Meek, Sterner St. Paul. *Pagan: A Border Patrol Horse.* New York: Alfred Knopf, 1951.

Meijer, Irene Costera, and Baukje Prins. "How Bodies Come to Matter: An Interview with Judith Butler." *Signs: Journal of Women in Culture and Society* 23, no. 2 (1998): 275–86.

Meléndez, A. Gabriel. *So All Is Not Lost: The Poetics of Print in Nuevo-*

mexicano Communities, 1834–1958. Albuquerque: University of New Mexico Press, 1997.

Mellinger, Philip. *Race and Labor in Western Copper.* Tucson: University of Arizona Press, 1995.

Memorandum Prepared for the Committee on Claims with Reference to S. 15. 76th Cong., 1st sess., 1939.

Méndez, Miguel. *Pilgrims in Aztlán.* Translated by David William Foster. Tempe, Ariz.: Bilingual Press/Editorial Bilingue, 1992.

Mervis, Sara Beth. "Note: Constitutional Law: Maryland's Drug-free School Zone Statute . . . Satisfies Due Process Requirements." *University of Baltimore Law Review* (spring 1995): 385–407.

Michaelsen, Scott, and David Johnson, eds. *Border Theory: The Limits of Cultural Politics.* Minneapolis: University of Minnesota Press, 1997.

Michie, Helena, and Ronald Thomas, eds. *Nineteenth-Century Geographies.* New Brunswick, N.J.: Rutgers University Press, forthcoming.

Mignolo, Walter. *The Darker Side of the Renaissance.* Ann Arbor: University of Michigan Press, 1995.

Miguelez, Armando. *Antologica historica del cuento literario chicano (1877–1950).* Ph.D. diss., Arizona State University, 1981.

Miller, J. Hillis. *Topographies.* Stanford, Calif.: Stanford University Press, 1995.

Miller, Richard Lawrence. *Drug Warriors and Their Prey: From Police Power to Police State.* Westport, Conn.: Praeger, 1996.

Mitchell, Don. *The Lie of the Land: Migrant Workers and the California Landscape.* Minneapolis: University of Minnesota Press, 1996.

———. "The Scales of Justice: Localist Ideology, Large-Scale Production, and Agricultural Labor's Geography of Resistance in 1930s California." In *Organizing the Landscape: Geographical Perspectives on Labor Unionism,* edited by Andrew Herod, 159–94. Minneapolis: University of Minnesota Press, 1998.

Montejano, David. *Anglos and Mexicans in the Making of Texas: 1836–1986.* Austin: University of Texas Press, 1987.

Moraga, Cherríe. *Loving in the War Years: Lo que nunca pasó por sus labios.* Boston: South End Press, 1983.

———. *Giving Up the Ghost: Teatro in Two Acts.* Los Angeles: West End Press, 1986.

———. *The Last Generation.* Boston: South End Press, 1993.

———. *Heroes and Saints and Other Plays.* Albuquerque, N.M.: West End Press, 1994.

———. *Waiting in the Wings: Portrait of a Queer Motherhood.* Ithaca, N.Y.: Firebrand Books, 1997.

Morrison, Toni. "The Site of Memory." In *Out There: Marginalization and Con-*

temporary Culture, edited by Russell Ferguson et al., 299–305. New York: New Museum of Contemporary Art, 1990.

Mowry, Sylvester. *Memoir of the Proposed Territory of Arizona.* Washington, D.C.: Henry Polkinhorn Printer, 1857.

Mullen, Harryette. "'A Silence between Us Like a Language': The Untranslatability of Experience in Sandra Cisneros's *Woman Hollering Creek." MELUS* 21 (summer 1996): 3–20.

Muñoz, José. *Disidentifications: Queers of Color and the Performance of Politics.* Minneapolis: University of Minnesota Press, 1998.

Musto, David. *The American Disease.* 3d ed. London: Oxford University Press, 1999.

Nevins, Joseph. *Operation Gatekeeper: The Rise of the "Illegal Alien" and the Making of the U.S.-Mexico Boundary.* New York: Routledge University Press, 2002.

Nixon, Richard. "Drug Abuse Prevention and Control: President's Message to the Congress, 17 June 1971." *Public Papers of the Presidents of the United States, 1971* (21 June 1971): 739–49.

Offman, Craig. "The 10 Most Corrupt Cities in America." *George* (March 1998): 90–102.

Olmo, Rosa del. "The Hidden Face of Drugs." *Social Justice* 18, no. 4 (1991): 10–48.

———. "The Geopolitics of Narcotrafficking in Latin America." *Social Justice* 20, nos. 3–4 (fall/winter 1993): 1–23.

Ong, Aihwa. "The Gender and Labor Politics of Postmodernity." In *The Politics of Culture in the Shadow of Capital,* edited by Lisa Lowe and David Lloyd, 60–97. Durham, N.C.: Duke University Press, 1997.

Ortiz, Fernando. *Cuban Counterpoint: Tobacco and Sugar.* Translated by Harriet De Onís. Durham, N.C.: Duke University Press, 1995.

Ortiz, Yvette Flores. "La Mujer y La Violencia: A Culturally Based Model for the Understanding and Treatment of Domestic Violence in Chicana/Latina Communities." In *Chicana Critical Issues,* edited by Norma Alarcón et al., 169–82. Berkeley, Calif.: Third Woman Press, 1993.

Ó Tuathail, Gearóid. *Critical Geopolitics: The Politics of Writing Global Space.* Minnesota: University of Minnesota Press, 1996.

Padgett, Martin. "Travel, Exoticism, and Writing the Region: Charles Fletcher Lummis and the 'Creation' of the Southwest." *Journal of the Southwest* 37, no. 3 (autumn 1995): 421–49.

Padilla, Genaro. "Myth and Comparative Cultural Nationalism: The Ideological Uses of Aztlán." In *Aztlán: Essays on the Chicano Homeland,* edited by Rudolfo Anaya and Francisco Lomelí, 111–34. Albuquerque: University of New Mexico Press, 1989.

Pain, Rachel. "Space, Sexual Violence, and Social Control: Integrating Geo-graphical and Feminist Analyses of Women's Fear of Crime." *Progress in Human Geography* 15 (December 1991): 415–31.

Parenti, Christian. *Lockdown America: Police and Prisons in the Age of Crisis.* London: Verso, 2000.

Park, Joseph. "The History of Mexican Labor in Arizona during the Territo-rial Period." Master's thesis, University of Arizona, 1961.

Pérez, Emma. "Sexuality and Discourse: Notes from a Chicana Survivor." In *Chicana Lesbians: The Girls Our Mothers Warned Us About,* edited by Carla Trujillo, 159–84. Berkeley: Third Woman Press: 1991.

———. *The Decolonial Imaginary: Writing Chicanas into History.* Bloomington: Indiana University Press, 1999.

Pérez-Torres, Rafael. *Movements in Chicano Poetry: Against Myths, Against Mar-gins.* New York: Cambridge University Press, 1995.

———. "Refiguring Aztlán." *Aztlán* 22, no. 2 (1997): 15–41.

Pollard, W. L. "Outline of the Law of Zoning in the United States." *Annals of the American Academy of Political and Social Science* 155, part 2 (May 1931): 15–33.

Ponce, Mary Helen. "The Marijuana Party." In *Mirrors Beneath the Earth: Short Fiction by Chicano Writers,* edited by Ray González, 140–56. Willimantic, Conn.: Curbstone Press, 1992.

Poovey, Mary. *Making a Social Body: British Cultural Formation, 1830–1864.* Chicago: University of Chicago Press, 1995.

Pratt, Mary Louise. *Imperial Eyes: Travel Writing and Transculturation.* London: Routledge, 1992.

Pulido, Laura. *Environmentalism and Economic Justice: Two Chicano Struggles in the Southwest.* Tucson: University of Arizona Press, 1996.

Pumpelly, Raphael. *Across America and Asia: Notes of a Five Years' Journey around the World and of Residence in Arizona, Japan, and China.* New York: Leypoldt and Holt, 1870.

Rabasa, José. *Writing Violence on the Northern Frontier: The Historiography of Sixteenth-Century New Mexico and Florida and the Legacy of Conquest.* Durham, N.C.: Duke University Press, 2000.

Ramírez, Catherine. "The Pachuca in Chicana/o Art, Literature, and History: Reexamining Nation, Cultural Nationalism, and Resistance." Ph.D. diss., University of California, 2000.

Ramírez-Pimienta, Juan Carlos. "Corrido de Narcotráfico en los Años Ochenta y Noventa: Un Juicio Moral Suspendido." *Bilingual Review* 23, no. 2 (May 1998): 145–56.

Reagan, Ronald. *Public Papers of the Presidents of the United States: Ronald Reagan,*

January 1 to July 2, 1982. Vol. 1. Washington, D.C.: Government Printing Office, 1983: 813.

Rebolledo, Tey Diana. *Women Singing in the Snow: A Cultural Analysis of Chicana Literature*. Tucson: University of Arizona Press, 1995.

Rebolledo, Tey Diana, and Eliana S. Rivero, eds. *Infinite Divisions: An Anthology of Chicana Literature*. Tucson: University of Arizona Press, 1993.

Reeves, Jimmie, and Richard Campbell. *Cracked Coverage: Television News, The Anti-Cocaine Crusade, and the Reagan Legacy*. Durham, N.C.: Duke University Press, 1994.

Reinarman, Craig, and Harry Levine. "The Crack Attack: Politics and Media in the Crack Scare." In *Crack in America: Demon Drugs and Social Justice,* edited by Craig Reinarman and Harry Levine, 18–52. Berkeley: University of California Press, 1997.

"Reminiscences of Carmen Lucero as Interpreted by Miss Maggie Brady to Mrs. George F. Kitt, 1928." Carmen Lucero Hayden Files. Arizona Historical Society, Tucson, Arizona.

"Report of the Governor of Arizona to the Secretary of the Interior." Washington: Government Printing Office, 1893.

Retter, Yolanda. "Lesbian Spaces in Los Angeles, 1970–90." In *Queers in Space: Communities/Public Places/Sites of Resistance,* edited by Gordon Brent Ingram, Anne-Marie Bouthillette, and Yolanda Retter, 325–37. Seattle: Bay Press, 1997.

Ríos, Alberto Alvaro. *The Iguana Killer: Twelve Stories of the Heart*. Lewiston, Idaho: Confluence Press, 1984.

Ríos, Katherine. "'And You Know What I Have to Say Isn't Always Pleasant': Translating the Unspoken Word in Cisneros' *Woman Hollering Creek*." In *Chicana (W)rites: On Word and Film,* edited by María Herrera-Sobek and Helena Viramontes, 201–23. Berkeley, Calif.: Third Woman Press, 1995.

Ritch, William. *Aztlán: The History, Resources, and Attractions of New Mexico*. Boston: D. Lothrop & Co., 1885.

Rolak, Bruno. "General Miles' Mirrors." *Journal of American History* 16, no. 2 (1975): 145–60.

Ronstadt, Federico José María. *Borderman: Memoirs of Federico José María Ronstadt,* edited by Edward F. Ronstadt. Albuquerque: University of New Mexico Press, 1993.

Rosaldo, Renato. "Imperialist Nostalgia." *Representations* 26 (spring 1989): 107–22.

———. "Forward." *Stanford Law Review* 48 (May 1996): 1037–45.

———. "Cultural Citizenship, Inequality, and Multiculturalism." In *Latino Cultural Citizenship: Claiming Identity, Space, and Rights,* edited by William Flores and Rina Benmayor, 27–38. Boston: Beacon Press, 1997.

Rose, Gillian. *Feminism and Geography: The Limits of Geographical Knowledge.* Minneapolis: University of Minnesota Press, 1993.

Ross, Kristin. *The Emergence of Social Space: Rimbaud and the Paris Commune.* Minneapolis: University of Minnesota Press, 1988.

———. *Fast Cars, Clean Bodies: Decolonization and the Reordering of French Culture.* Cambridge, Mass.: MIT Press, 1995.

Rotella, Carl. *October Cities: The Redevelopment of Urban Literature.* Berkeley: University of California Press, 1998.

Rotella, Sebastian. *Twilight on the Line: Underworlds and Politics at the U.S.-Mexico Border.* New York: Norton, 1998.

Rubio-Goldsmith, Raquel. "Shipwrecked in the Desert: A Short History of the Mexican Sisters of the House of the Providence in Douglas, Arizona, 1927–1949." In *Women on the U.S.-Mexican Border,* edited by Vicki Ruíz and Susan Tiano, 177–96. Boston: Allen and Unwin, 1987.

———. "Civilization, Barbarism, and Norteña Gardens." In *Making Worlds: Gender, Metaphor, Materiality,* edited by Susan Aiken, Ann Brigham, Sallie Marston, and Penny Waterstone, 274–87. Tucson: University of Arizona Press, 1998.

Ruiz, Ramón Eduardo. *The People of Sonora and Yankee Capitalists.* Tucson: University of Arizona Press, 1988.

Ruiz, Vicki, and Susan Tiano, eds. *Women on the U.S.-Mexican Border.* Boston: Allen and Unwin, 1987.

Ruiz de Burton, María Amparo. *Who Would Have Thought It?* Edited by Rosaura Sánchez and Beatrice Pita. 1872. Reprint, Houston: Arte Público Press, 1995.

———. *The Squatter and the Don.* Edited by Rosaura Sánchez and Beatrice Pita. 1885. Reprint, Houston: Arte Público Press, 1992.

Safra, Seth. "Note: The Amended Gun-Free School Zones Act: Doubt as to Its Constitutionality Remains." *Duke Law Journal* 50 (November 2000): 637–662.

Said, Edward. "Yeats and Decolonization." In *Remaking History,* edited by Barbara Kruger and Phil Mariani, 3–29. Seattle: Bay Press, 1989.

———. *Culture and Imperialism.* New York: Vintage, 1994.

Saldívar, José David. *Border Matters: Remapping American Cultural Studies.* Berkeley: University of California Press, 1997.

Saldívar, Manuel Murrieta. *Mi letra no es en inglés: La resistencia cultural sonorense en la poesía de "El Tucsonense" 1915–1957.* Hermosillo: Instituto Sonorense de Cultura y Gobierno del Estado de Sonora, 1991.

Saldívar-Hull, Sonia. *Feminism on the Border: Chicana Gender Politics and Literature.* Berkeley: University of California Press, 2000.

Sánchez, Rosaura. *Telling Identities: The California Testimonios.* Minneapolis: University of Minnestoa Press, 1995.

―――. "Reconstructing Chicana Gender Identity." *American Literary History* 9 (summer 1997): 350–64.

Sandmeyer, E. C. *The Anti-Chinese Movement in California.* Urbana: University of Illinois Press, 1939.

Sandoval, Chela. "Feminism and Racism: A Report on the 1981 National Women's Studies Association Conference." In *Making Face, Making Soul/Haciendo caras,* edited by Gloria Anzaldúa, 55–71. San Francisco: Aunt Lute Press, 1990.

―――. "U.S. Third World Feminism: The Theory and Method of Oppositional Consciousness in the Postmodern World." *Genders* 10 (spring 1991): 2–24.

―――. *Methodology of the Oppressed.* Minneapolis: University of Minnesota Press, 2000.

Santaballa, Sylvia. "Nican Motecpana: Nahuatl Miracles of the Virgin of Guadalupe." *Latin American Indian Literature Journal* 11, no. 1 (spring 1995): 34–54.

Saragoza, Alex. "The Border in American and Mexican Cinema." *Aztlán* 21, nos. 1 and 2 (1992–1996):155–90.

Scarry, Elaine. *The Body in Pain: The Making and Unmaking of the World.* New York: Oxford University Press, 1985.

Schmidt, Louis Bernard. "Manifest Opportunity and the Gadsden Purchase." *Arizona and the West* 3, no. 3 (autumn 1961): 245–64.

Schoelwer, Susan Prendergast, ed. *Alamo Images: Changing Perceptions of a Texas Experience.* Dallas: Southern Methodist University Press, 1985.

Sedgwick, Eve Kosofsky. *Epistemology of the Closet.* Berkeley: University of California Press, 1990.

Seed, Patricia. *Ceremonies of Possession in Europe's Conquest of the New World, 1492–1640.* Cambridge: Cambridge University Press, 1995.

Seltzer, Mark. "Serial Killers (II): The Pathological Public Sphere." *Critical Inquiry* 22, no. 1 (fall 1995): 122–49.

Servín, Manuel P., and Robert Spude. "Historical Conditions of Early Mexican Labor in the United States: Arizona—A Neglected Story." *Journal of Mexican American History* 5 (1975): 43–56.

Sheridan, Thomas. *Los Tucsonenses: The Mexican Community in Tucson, 1854–1941.* Tucson: University of Arizona, 1986.

―――. *Arizona: A History.* Tucson: University of Arizona Press, 1995.

Smith, Neil. "Contours of a Spatialized Politics: Homeless Vehicles and the Production of Geographical Scale." *Social Text* 33 (1992): 54–81.

―――. "Antinomies of Space and Nature in Henri Lefebvre's *The Produc-*

tion of Space." In *The Production of Public Space,* edited by Andrew Light and Jonathan Smith, 49–70. Lanham, Md.: Rowman and Littlefield, 1998.

Smith, Neil, and Cindi Katz. "Grounding Metaphor: Towards a Spatialized Politics." In *Place and the Politics of Identity,* edited by Michael Keith and Steve Pile, 67–83. London: Routledge, 1993.

Soja, Edward. *Postmodern Geographies.* London: Verso, 1989.

———. "The Socio-Spatial Dialectic." *Annals of the Association of American Geographers* 70 (June 1989): 210.

———. *Thirdspace: Journeys to Los Angeles and Other Real-and-Imagined Places.* Cambridge, Mass.: Blackwell, 1996.

———. *Postmetropolis: Critical Studies of Cities and Regions.* Oxford: Blackwell, 2000.

Soja, Edward, and Barbara Hooper. "The Spaces that Difference Makes." In *Place and the Politics of Identity,* edited by Michael Keith and Steven Pile, 183–205. London: Routledge, 1993.

Spain, Daphne. *Gendered Spaces.* Chapel Hill: University of North Carolina Press, 1992.

Starks, Michael. *Cocaine Fiends and Reefer Madness: An Illustrated History of Drugs in the Movies.* New York: Cornwall Books, 1982.

Stein, Marc. *City of Sisterly and Brotherly Loves: Lesbian and Gay Philadelphia, 1945–1972.* Chicago: University of Chicago Press, 2000.

Still, Judith, and Michael Worten, eds. *Textuality and Sexuality: Reading Theories and Practices.* Manchester, Eng.: Manchester University Press, 1993.

Taylor, Paul, and Clark Kerr. "Documentary History of the Strike of the Cotton Pickers in California, 1933." In Senate Subcommittee of the Committee on Education and Labor (the La Follette Committee), *Violations of Free Speech and the Rights of Labor: Hearings on S. Res. 266,* 75 parts (Washington, DC: Government Printing Office, 1936–1940), part 54, exhibit 8764, 19945–20036.

Tijerina, Reies López. *They Called Me "King Tiger": My Struggle for the Land and Our Rights.* Translated and edited by José Angel Gutierrez. Houston, Tex.: Arte Público Press, 2000.

Tinker Salas, Miguel. *In the Shadow of the Eagles: Sonora and the Transformation of the Border during the Porfiriato.* Berkeley: University of California Press, 1997.

Trover, Ellen, ed. *Chronology and Documentary Handbook of the State of Arizona.* Dobbs Ferry, N.Y.: Oceana Publications, 1972.

Trujillo, Carla. "Chicana Lesbians: Fear and Loathing in the Chicano Community." In *Chicana Critical Issues,* edited by Norma Alarcón et al., 117–26. Berkeley: Third Woman Press, 1993.

———, ed. *Chicana Lesbians: The Girls Our Mothers Warned Us About.* Berkeley: Third Woman Press, 1991.

Tuan, Yi-fu. *Topophilia: A Study of Environmental Perception, Attitudes, and Values.* Englewood Cliffs, N.J.: Prentice-Hall, 1974.

U.S. House Subcommittee of the Committee on the Judiciary. *To Establish a Border Patrol.* 69 Cong, 1 sess., 12 April 1926.

U.S. Senate Subcommittee of the Committee on Education and Labor (the La Follette Committee). *Violations of Free Speech and the Rights of Labor: Hearings on S. Res. 266,* 75 parts (Washington, DC: Government Printing Office, 1936–1940), part 54, exhibit 8764, 19945–20036.

Valdés, Gina. *There Are No Madmen Here.* San Diego: Maize Press, 1981.

———. *Puentes y fronteras: Bridges and Borders.* Translated by Katherine King and Gina Valdés. Tempe, Ariz.: Bilingual Press, 1996.

———. "Where You From?" *La Linea Quebrada* (1987): 23.

Valentine, Gill. "The Geography of Women's Fear." *Area* 21 (December 1989): 385–90.

Vidler, Anthony. "Bodies in Space/Subjects in the City: Psychopathologies of Modern Urbanism." *Differences* 5, no. 3 (1993): 31–51.

Vigil-Piñón, Evangelina. "Tavern Taboo." In *Infinite Divisions: An Anthology of Chicana Literature,* edited by Tey Diana Rebolledo and Eliana S. Rivero, 188. Tucson: University of Arizona Press, 1993.

Villa, Raúl. "Marvelous Re-creations: Utopian Spatial Critique in *The Road to Tamazunchale.*" *Aztlán* 23, no. 1 (1998): 77–93.

———. "Ghosts in the Growth Machine: Critical Spatial Consciousness in Los Angeles Chicano Writing." *Social Text* 17, no. 1 (1999): 111–31.

———. *Barrio-Logos: Space and Place in Urban Chicano Literature and Culture.* Austin: University of Texas Press, 2000.

Viramontes, Helena. *The Moths and Other Stories.* Houston: Arte Público, 1985.

———. *Under the Feet of Jesus.* New York: Dutton Press, 1995.

Wallace, Edward. *The Great Reconnaissance: Soldiers, Artists, and Scientists on the Frontier, 1841–1861.* Boston: Little, Brown, and Company, 1955.

Watson, Sophie, and Katherine Gibson, eds. *Postmodern Cities and Spaces.* Oxford: Blackwell, 1995.

Weber, David. *The Mexican Frontier, 1821–1846: The American Southwest under Mexico.* Albuquerque: University of New Mexico Press, 1982.

Weir, William. *In the Shadow of the Dope Fiend.* North Haven, Conn.: Archon Books, 1995.

Weisman, Leslie Kane. *Discrimination by Design: A Feminist Critique of the Man-Made Environment.* Urbana: University of Illinois, 1992.

Wells, Tim, and William Triplett. *Drug Wars: An Oral History from the Trenches.* New York: William Morrow, 1992.

Weston, Kath. "Get Thee to a Big City: Sexual Imaginary and the Great Gay Migration." *GLQ* 2 (1995): 253–77.

Williams, Raymond. *Marxism and Literature.* Oxford: Oxford University Press, 1977.

Wills, Jane. "Space, Place, and Tradition in Working-Class Organization." In *Organizing the Landscape: Geographical Perspectives on Labor Unionism,* edited by Andrew Herod, 129–58. Minneapolis: University of Minnesota Press, 1998.

Wilson, Elizabeth. "The Invisible Flaneur." In *Postmodern Cities and Spaces,* edited by Sophie Watson and Katherine Gibson, 59–79. Oxford: Blackwell, 1995.

Yarbro-Bejarano, Yvonne. "Gloria Anzaldúa's *Borderlands/La frontera:* Cultural Studies, 'Difference,' and the Non-Unitary Subject." *Cultural Critique* 17, no. 4 (fall 1994): 5–28.

———. "Sexuality and Chicana/o Studies: Toward a Theoretical Paradigm for the Twenty-First Century." *Cultural Studies* 13, no.2 (1999): 335–45.

———. *The Wounded Heart: Writing on Cherríe Moraga.* Austin: University of Texas Press, 2001.

Yudice, George. "Testimonio and Postmodernism." In *The Real Thing: Testimonial Discourse and Latin America,* edited by George Gugelberger, 42–57. Durham, N.C.: Duke University Press, 1996.

Zires, Margarita. "Los mitos de la Virgen de Guadalupe: Su proceso de construcción y reinterpretación en el Mexico pasado y contemporáneo." *Mexican Studies/Estudios Mexicanos* 10, no. 1 (summer 1994): 281–314.

Zorilla, Luis. *Historia de las relaciones entre México y los Estados Unidos de América 1800–1958.* Vol 1. Mexico City: Editorial Porrúa, 1965.

Index

Mary Pat Brady is an Assistant

Professor of English and Latino/a Studies

at Cornell University.